How does a veteran surviv   in a maximum-security
psychiatric hospital to earn a faculty appointment to a medical school, national
advocacy awards, and to lecture in an Ivy League university?

How can a Liberal Arts degree save your life ... and give you your destiny?

An American's Resurrection

"This book brings a new perspective and viewpoint to the discussion and treatment of patients with co-occurring disorders. It highlights and underscores the necessity to accurately diagnose and treat patients in order to obtain the best possible treatment outcomes that will not only be cost effective, but provide the efficacy of treatment that the patients, so afflicted, require and deserve."

Louis E. Baxter, Sr., M.D., FASAM
Immediate Past President, American Society of Addiction Medicine;
Executive Medical Director, Professional Assistance Program NJ, Inc.

"This book is Epic ... F-cking Epic!"

Seamus McGuinness
Disabled American Veteran, United States Air Force:
Operation Enduring Freedom/Operation Iraqi Freedom

"*An American's Resurrection* for me, at times, was a journey into my own childhood. Eric put words to explain the trauma that our family experienced at the hands of my father. I agree so strongly with Eric, that as a young person, and as you grow older, the shame cannot be explained away. Like Eric, I loved my father until the day he committed suicide. This action caused my first bout of mania.

As the treatment of trauma has lost its way over the past thirty years, I would strongly recommend *An American's Resurrection* be compulsory reading for anyone wishing to work in the mental health field."

Anthony C. Stratford
Senior Business Manager, Mind Australia
Visiting Scholar, Yale University School of Medicine (2012)
Honorary Fellow, Faculty of Medicine, Dentistry and Health Sciences,
the University of Melbourne

An American's Resurrection

My Pilgrimage from Child Abuse
and Mental Illness to Salvation

Eric C. Arauz

Arauz Inspirational Enterprises
East Brunswick, NJ

Arauz Inspirational Enterprises

Published by Arauz Inspirational Enterprises L.L.C., East Brunswick, N.J. 08816,
in cooperation with Blank Slate Communications,
Saint Louis, MO, 63110.
For more information:
www.mylifemylimits.com | www.blankslatecommunications.com

For information about special discounts or bulk purchases, please
contact Treehouse Publishing at treehouse@blankslatecommunications.com.

Manufactured in the United States of America

Interior Design by Kristina Blank Makansi
Set in Adobe Garamond Pro
Cover Design by Jane Colvin

Library of Congress Control Number: 2012919244

ISBN-13: 978-0-9883565-0-4

To my mother, Nadine, for fighting into the depths of Hell to save me; to my wife, Cheryl, for making me believe I could live back in the Light; and to my beloved daughter, Olivia Nadine, for giving me the courage to fight back into the Flames forever looking for survivors.

Table of Contents

An American's Resurrection

My Pilgrimage from Child Abuse
and Mental Illness to Salvation

Foreword

To those of you who are about to turn to page one of this riveting story of triumph over the demons of substance abuse, child abuse, psychosis, and post-traumatic stress disorder, I have the privilege of introducing you to the author, Eric Arauz.

If you have not had the opportunity to meet Eric, either through attending one of his many compelling public speaking or consulting events, I would like to introduce him to you in the same way he introduced himself to me. First, to put our meeting in context, let me tell you a little about me. I am an Associate Professor and the Specialty Director for the Psychiatric Nurse Practitioner Programs at the Yale University School of Nursing in New Haven, CT. I have been a nurse since 1971 and a psychiatric nurse since 1978. I have been active in the National Alliance on Mental Illness (NAMI) for over twenty years and received the NAMI Professional of the Year Award in 1996. Additionally, I am a past president of the American Psychiatric Nurses Association, and I have lectured all over the world. In my forty-year career, I've met with thousands of patients. Eric Arauz is all of those patients rolled into one incredible human being, and he has embraced the life mission of being a voice for the voiceless. He is the real-life Jimmy Stewart in *A Wonderful Life*, and I cannot imagine the world of mental health advocacy without Eric in it.

One morning in July of 2009, I received a self-promotional email from a person I did not know, stating that he was an award-winning mental health advocate and he would like to come and talk with my students about recovery from mental illness. I must honestly admit that while I frequently receive these kinds of emails, I often do not read them. But there was something about the passion expressed in the first sentence that made me read on. In the email, he provided a link to his website which I went to immediately. On the site, I found a video clip to which I listened with rapt attention. (Before you go any further, please go to www.ericarauz.com and click on any of the video links under Speeches and Lectures.) To fully understand his passion and dedication, you must see and hear him tell his story and see for yourself that it instills nothing but hope for all who hear it.

After I digested his message, I emailed him immediately and asked him to come to New Haven to speak to our students the end of January 2010. Before we finalized the event, however, I asked Eric to come from his home in New Jersey so we could meet and discuss in person his philosophy of treatment and the aspects of his story that would resonate with our 100 nursing students. I felt I needed to be in his presence for the conversation; it could not be a conversation limited to email.

Yale nursing students are focused, directed, intense, and have high expectations for every classroom experience. They are quick to write-off what they perceive as fluff. In January and February, 2010, I taught the seven-week psychiatric nursing rotation that occurred five months into an eleven-month accelerated RN program for students who already had a bachelor's degree and who were changing careers to nursing. After completing the accelerated pre-licensure program, each student would immediately enter a nurse practitioner program. I knew it would be a tough audience, but knowing that one out of every four families has a member with a psychiatric diagnosis, I knew many would relate to Eric in a personal manner. And that would be a good thing.

Eric and I spent three hours together. That conversation ranks in the top five conversations I have ever had in my professional career. He is a quick study of those he chooses to reach out to and meet. He quickly sensed my passion for improving the care and lives of individuals suffering with psychiatric illnesses as he had also searched out my websites www.psychiatricwellness.com and http://nursing.yale/faculty/moller.html. My research career has focused on a wellness approach to psychiatric rehabilitation that encompasses four domains of wellness: health (biological), attitudes and behaviors (psychological), environment and relationships (sociological) and spiritual. I learned in my early days of psychiatric nursing that to ignore the spiritual dimension of life in individuals who experience profound hopelessness and alienation, believe they are abandoned by God and man, or even believe that they are God, is a gross injustice and becomes only lip-service to the statement of providing holistic care. I found myself engaged in a discussion of spirituality that could only happen with someone who has descended to Dante's Inferno and risen on the wings of angels to salvation.

After that conversation I knew the Yale students would quickly grasp the implications of Eric's message for health care providers, the health care system, and most importantly for themselves as future nurse practitioners. Eric put a face on the anguish and alienation created by mental illness and made an impact on these future pediatric, adult, family, geriatric, women's health, acute care, oncology, and psychiatric nurse practitioners and nurse midwives. After meeting him and listening to Eric's story, I am confident that when these future health care providers have a patient with a mental illness, they will be more tender, less judgmental, and more tolerant.

Shortly after meeting Eric, I was inducted as the 2010-2011 President of the American Psychiatric Nurses Association (APNA). I knew immediately that I wanted Eric to be one of my keynoters at the 2010 APNA conference in Louisville, KY. When I mentioned this to my colleagues and previous presidents, I was cautioned that perhaps it might not be a good idea, that he needed to be properly vetted. I reassured them that I had personally vetted him and that it was most important that Eric be front and center of the program because the theme of my presidency was going to be advocacy. I invited him, and he graciously agreed, to be on the steering committee of the APNA Recovery to Practice grant from the Substance Abuse and Mental Health Services Administration (SAMHSA). In that role, he has provided invaluable insights and a narrative approach to the development of a training program to bring the concept of recovery to inpatient psychiatric nurses.

Eric was the opening keynote speaker at the conference in Louisville and, by the time he was finished, there was not a dry eye in the room. Words cannot adequately express the profound effect he had on the over 1,000 nurses in the audience. To this day, when we discuss his talk and quote his last statement, we are, once again, brought to tears. His message moves us and it will move you. After pouring out his heart and soul to us and sharing his greatest shame, he helped us to understand—*to feel*—the power a nurse has to promote healing at the soul level. By simply being with a patient in the throes of psychosis, by simply wiping a tortured brow with gentleness in her touch and in her eyes, a nurse can save a life. He closed with, "In about twenty years, if you have a patient on your ward named Olivia Arauz, give her everything you've got, let her know she can succeed and that she can make it, just like her father did."

In *An American's Resurrection: My Pilgrimage from Child Abuse and Mental Illness to Salvation*, Eric has created an incredible narrative of his life's journey. He offers a rare glimpse into the depths of a man's tripartitite agony of mind, body, and spirit broken by violence and restored by kindness. In his inimitable style, he describes how he survived attempted murder at the hands of his father, the brutal horrors of psychosis, including four-point restraints and the mind-numbing effects of medications and fulminating substance abuse, to create a life transformation into health, wellness, and a mission of healing. In his riveting style of story-telling, he shares with the reader a tutorial in existential philosophy embedded in spirituality, and coupled with his personal resolve to use the power of forgiveness to discover the meaning of his own human existence. He will leave you stronger and more confident about your own ability to reach out to someone with a mental illness and say, "You can do it, the person who is you is not gone, you will find yourself, you will be strong again. You will live."

I hope that this forward has presented an introduction to my colleague, and now friend, Eric Arauz, proud son of Einar Arauz and Bud Powers, that helps you connect with him at a gut level—at a human level—and encourages you to read his story. I want you to come to know this incredible man, to cry with him, to despair with him, to rejoice with him, and to learn from him. But, most importantly, I hope that, through the narrative of his life story, you gain a deeper understanding of the mental, physical and spiritual challenges and possibilities for healing open to those individuals with mental illness and their families.

Mary D. Moller
DNP, ARNP, APRN,
PMHCNS-BC, CPRP, FAAN
Associate Professor, Speciality Director
Psychiatric Mental Health Nursing
Yale University School of Nursing
New Haven, Connecticut

"It is unbelievable, but it is not unlivable," he said. "The universe has no limits, and the possibilities at play in the universe at large are indeed incommensurable. So don't fall prey to the axiom, 'I believe only what I see,' because it is the dumbest stand one can possibly take."

~ The sorcerer Don Juan speaking to Carlos Castaneda in
The Active Side Infinity by Carlos Castaneda

Book 1 Life

God had one son on earth without sin, but never one without suffering.

~ Saint Augustine of Hippo, Author of the First Spiritual Autobiography,
The Confessions

As a single withered tree, if set aflame, causes a whole forest to burn,
so does a rascal son destroy a whole family.

~ Chanakya, Pioneer Economist of India

Am I entitled to live? I am alive by a fluke, like the sole survivor of Treblinka,
who lived by a fluke, but did not really feel entitled to live.

~ Southerner Walker Percy, American author whose grandfather and father
died by suicide. From the work The Second Coming

Life | Chapter 1

Four-point restraints are only bothersome when your desire to move is greater than your desire to not move. When that point is reached, it is a living death.

The first time I woke up in four-point restraints, I was tied down to a mattress on the cold, foreign floor of a locked ward in a maximum-security psychiatric hospital. This was the only reality I was aware of—that mattress, that floor and the fact that the entire room was white. Floor to ceiling WHITE.

My white room could have been located anywhere on the planet. I was in New Jersey, but I didn't know it. I didn't know what city I was in, I didn't know what country I was in. I didn't know the name of the hospital. I didn't know it was a hospital. I didn't know that everything I had known about my life was gone. I was absolutely lost.

Coming out of your first manic episode in the maximum-security ward of a psychiatric hospital is like scratching to the surface of reality from inside a dream ... inside a dream ... inside a dream. You are never sure when you are awake. Or alive.

Sluggishly, my eyes stumbled across my new surroundings while an unknown man sat at a nearby desk methodically writing on something. He was wearing a white shirt, white pants, and white shoes. He heard me struggling and I watched as he began to turn his head to meet my glance. His eyes were soulful and yet detached. Silently, he watched me fight my restraints. The more I arched my back or wrenched my arms the less he seemed to even breathe.

A thought struck me while I was fighting my mattress prison: If he talks, if he speaks, it will confirm the reality of this nightmare, and I will be forced to do something to allow me to retreat back into the sanctuary of my sickened mind. I will have to bite through my tongue and pass out from the pain. I will fill my mouth with blood and swallow the jagged pieces of flesh if that means I can keep this a non-reality.

I begged my captor to stay silent, mute. Do not speak, sir. *Do not speak!* As long as the man in white stayed silent, I could tell myself that my mother would walk in any second, that my family waited just outside, that my buddies Robbie and Matt were trying to get me released. Like the delusional director of my own manic movie, I needed the man in white to stay in character to ensure a happy ending.

Cemented in place, he continued to observe me. The unknown observer watched my physical struggles diminish as my strength waned. We stared at each other. As my eyes got more and more used to the lighting, I could see the other two rooms behind him come into focus. The other patients were sleeping, or, to be more exact, the patient I could see looked like he was sleeping and the other I could not see sounded like he was sleeping.

The patient I could see was not on the floor. Not on the floor like me. What the hell is that? Why am I on the floor? Indignant, I was on the verge of asking for some demented concierge to demand an upgrade to a hell with a view when I saw the attendant's walkie talkie, his radio, next to his journal. He watched me closely for a couple of seconds and started to reach for the handheld device.

I needed silence. I needed the only voice I heard to be my own in my head, but I could not stop him. The delusion of my fantasy was on its death march as his lips made their way to the speaker. He depressed the send button on the side of the handheld and inhaled. My mind went black as a perverse panic swept over me. What would it feel like to completely break, to crash face first through a thousand floors into the abyss of my life? Could I handle it? Could I handle it?

I watched his lips move. "The patient is awake."

Well that wasn't so bad, nothing really changed. Still no proper names, the dreamscape remained unaltered. He said a few medical terms that were not in my current psychotic lexicon and I started to actually relax. My eyes scanned the room. The floor was a clean tile and not actually all white on closer inspection. The accommodations were spartan, like the room of a 13th century monk. My door was open. It was exaggeratedly wide and it looked impenetrable, like a door to a bank vault. Obviously, it locked from the outside and my keeper had an impressive ring of keys to various other cells. The enormous door had a small square window high up on its face.

For some reason, I noticed there were no brand names on anything in the room, no GE, Phillips, Sealy, or whatever. Label-less. I started to look for anything that marked anything in this place as being from another place. My keeper's clothes had no visible tags and his shoes were that anonymous brand fitted to the hospital environment. I was clearly awake and clearly here but I was getting sick of this pronoun landscape. Again the panic of questions started.

Where am I? What the hell is this place? Who the fuck put me in these restraints? I'm a United States Navy veteran, I served my country, *no one restrains me!*

I saw myself at the pyramids of Giza outside Cairo, Egypt, walking through the Vatican in Rome, running up ladders on my ship, the USS Briscoe DD-977, responding to a General Quarters alert in the Red Sea, and going to Flight Quarters as a "smash and crash" team member. From 1990-1994, I had served proudly and now I was ... where the hell was I?

It is an odd sensation to think only in general terms, to not even allow yourself to use your own name in self correspondence as the last ditch effort of a reeling psyche to avoid a cognitive suicide.

I was "I," my past was "he," and "we" did not allow a future.

As my thoughts raced and my personal memory allowed bits and pieces of me to enter my awareness, the fight for my identity was being lost by my essence and won by a rapacious and diseased ego. I was working my eyes up the front of the door to my room as my mind fought for a name for this patient.

Whose wrists are red and raw in these restraints? Whose hips are cramped and aching? Whose surgically repaired toes are these? What poor motherfucker was going to have to wake up to this?

I knew it was me, but who was me? *Who was me?* That question was much more terrifying than where was I?

As I searched the door, I saw something near the security window, below it actually. I couldn't tell what it was. I tried to turn my head a little more and lurch my torso a few inches to the left.

It looked at first like a straight line. My eyes were beginning to work as my external world came more into focus. The symbol had a definite turn at its top. It moved six inches straight up and at the top came down an inch at a 45 degree angle to the left.

As I was breaking the code of the door symbol, another door I couldn't see was being unlocked. I heard the heavy latch turn and foreign voices entered the main cell. I know that symbol, I thought. As my brain fought to decipher it, the foreign voices addressed the guard. He was familiar with them but not pleasant.

As their combined voices started to synch with my comprehension, the symbol came to me. I know what it is, I've got it ….

The guard pointed my way as the footsteps got closer.

It is a "1." I am in Room 1. One. A real number, a label in this relativistic landscape of everything and nothing. I am the resident in Room 1. I am … I am….

The men rounded the corner into my room, Room 1, and blocked all the light and whiteness previously ubiquitous.

"Patient Number 1, Patient Number 1, you are awake, we know you are awake and have been struggling. Just stay calm and we can help you. Patient Number 1, answer me. Answer me."

Now brutally aware this was not a dream, I demanded my death. Not figuratively. Actively and wholeheartedly, to the limited resources of my fractured mind, I sought my actual demise.

My thoughts screamed: Die, die, die Patient Number 1!

"Patient Number 1, I am going to step forward. What I am going to inject in you will calm you down, it's OK. It's OK. Patient Number 1, Patient Number 1, acknowledge me! Look at me Patient Number 1!"

Lazily, I swam deeper into my floor-based tomb. Once buried, I attempted to drift into that which was unknown but better than my known … die … die Patient Number 1, die….

"Eric … Eric Arauz … Patient Number 1 … Answer me. Answer me! Eric Arauz, I am going to do this with or without your consent. ERIC, LOOK AT ME!"

My breach into the psychic Bardo disturbed ad infinitum, I was jettisoned back behind my eyes … I am Patient Number 1! … I am Eric Arauz! … Eric Arauz! … Psychic ownership registered for the first time as I disintegrated.

My screams were involuntary … the suffering primal, MY suffering primal. This is my life … my wrists … my hell!

I erupted in my shackles.

No words escaped my lips as I screamed behind my eyes: Fuck you, get away from me, fuck you, fuck you! Help! Help, mommy please I am sorry, so sorry, please, where are you? Where is my family? My step-daughter? My mother? Where is my life? I am dying … Mommy, they are killing me … Help me, I am fucking dying!

Exhausted from fighting the heavy, leather four-point restraints, I finally acquiesced. Do as you wish, inject what you want, I give up, it is over, it is done. I am done. Knock me out, please, I am not prepared for this, knock me out. Kill me, just do it now. Do it, do it, kill me, shoot it … that's it, shoot it….

The drug was in me; whatever it was that was forced into my veins started to quiet the fires in my mind. My thoughts slowed with this new chemical glow. Synthetic solace pulsed through my veins while my eyelids searched for closure as the drug sedated body and soul.

Perfect. I had escaped my psych-ward epiphany. A smile slowly dawned on my lips as my breathing deepened. An ambivalent grin better suited for the statues in Zen temples throughout South Asia settled on my face. A bipolar Buddha, trapped in a worthless, psychotic nirvana, hoping never to wake again.

Life | Chapter 2

Two hours after the needle delivered its chemical calm to my brain, I was given my diagnosis of Bipolar Disorder. I was in a private psychiatric hospital in New Jersey even though the last thing I remembered was boarding a plane in Dallas for anywhere in the universe. My addiction and mental illness had destroyed my marriage, so I had loaded my car, said goodbye to my wife and step-daughter in Memphis, Tennessee, and headed to Texas to stay with one of my best friends, Robbie.

I had no idea I was having a manic episode on the drive through Arkansas into the Lone Star state, and was completely unaware that I had been awake for over 13 days when I awoke in four-point restraints in the WHITE room.

The full diagnosis was Bipolar Disorder 1, plus Alcoholism and Drug Addiction. The doctor delivered the news with professionalism, but there was something amiss in his declaration. I was never sure what it was until recently, but now I believe it was a sense of hopelessness or a professional pessimism from dealing with others first notified of their dual diagnosis or co-occurring disorders. There are not many public examples of success for those of us with both serious mental illness and severe addiction.

I did not blame the doctor for this nor do I blame anyone else for my life. I have learned that external blaming leads to more internal blaming which leads to desperation, despair and hopelessness. Instead, since 1996, I have been trying to see past the learned helplessness that ingrains itself into the identity of those in our culture called permanent patients—more specifically, labeled mental patients.

But, at the time, my initial diagnosis hit me hard. It was traumatic. It was a death sentence to me.

While in the hospital, I was always unsure what anyone was talking about, which is not good when all everyone is talking about is you. If you are in a conversation in a maximum-security psychiatric ward as a patient, it is either with a doctor, social worker, or psychiatric nurse and they're all telling you something specifically tailored to your current dilemma.

Because you are acutely symptomatic and the heavy meds needed to treat the symptoms thicken the wall to yourself, you're not always really engaged in the decision-making process. But it is always nice to be invited to observe your own treatment. Instead of being an active participant, you become an audience member watching the movie of your life. You become a rootless other. An "other" without a defining relationship to anything ... you become a nothing, a ghost whispering into your own ears to walk, to eat, to sleep.

Prior to waking up in that psychiatric hospital in 1995, I'd had limited exposure to the specifics of mental illness. My biological father had mental illness, but I had never known his diagnosis. He was diagnosed in the early 1970s when I was five or six and everyone was labeled either schizophrenic or chemically imbalanced. By 1995, I'd heard of schizophrenia, bipolar disorder, and other mental disorders but I didn't really know what those terms meant.

While still in the Navy in 1994, I had managed three sailors who were being discharged for mental illness while we were all on medical hold in Portsmouth, VA. After a couple of surgeries on my feet, I was in charge of a female barracks and these three young men worked as my daily staff to maintain the physical structure. They were great guys; I still think of them often as some of the best our country had to offer. Mike, Lee, and Rich, my boys in the barracks, my first real cause. While I was informally counseling these men on life after leaving the Navy with a discharge for mental illness, I could never have dreamed that I would be diagnosed with bipolar 1 less than eight months after my own honorable under medical conditions discharge for my feet.

I left the Navy as a 20 percent disabled veteran after four years of service due to extensive operations to remove the primary knuckles in all ten of my toes. I still have a broken screw embedded in my left big toe and a severed tendon in my left little toe from complications during the surgeries. I have chronic pain in my left foot and structural knee problems.

Before my discharge, I thought I had my future laid out in front of me. I would go to college on the G.I. Bill and look for intellectual challenges to drive me forward. Instead, less than a year after receiving a discharge stating that I was physically disabled, I was to see what real disability was: acute serious mental

9

illness and active addiction.

There is a time in many people's lives when things seem to be consistently going wrong. I don't know if it is a matter of perspective but it happens to many of us. Some will take this time to come to grips with themselves and begin to overcome these obstacles. Calamity becomes catapult and people fly into new lives where anything is possible. Albert Einstein said, "Adversity introduces a man to himself." That may or not be true, but I was forced to get acquainted with a man I didn't even know existed—the Bipolar Eric Arauz.

What can happen to people with serious mental illness is that our lives can become turbulent and dangerous. There is a time after the first hospital stay when life is apt to fly out of control. There is no more safety net, internally or externally. When your sanity is not a given, you are never safe.

There is only the idea, the acknowledgment: "I am sick."

Not a sick body part, not a virus, not even a bacteria. No, it is the acknowledgment that that which is *me*, all of me, my yesterday, my tomorrow, my dreams, thoughts, blood, relationships, hopes, history, fears, my, mine, my *is-ness* is diseased.

My being is bipolar.

How is that fixed?

What is the antidote for me?

My home, our homes, the homes of people with active, serious mental illness can become the places in society you don't pass through unless you are lost or doing charity work. These are the dark worlds hiding in the shadows of polite society: the streets, the jails, the day programs, the hospitals in neighborhoods sociologists call "service ghettoes." Without treatment of some kind to arrest the acute symptoms, the free fall begins and ends in a multitude of ways, very few positive and even fewer uplifting.

Someone with active, serious mental illness may have asked you for a dollar while lying in a gutter draped in a heavy jacket on a hot August day in Anytown, USA. We are everywhere and we die in ways hidden from open society: in maximum-security hospitals, prison hospices, and on hard city streets at the hands of strangers taking the little we have.

One benchmark of a society's developmental evolution should be how they deal with their weakest, most vulnerable citizens. But mental illness often breeds contempt, not compassion; it becomes an assumed curse somehow deserved by the non-anointed. We are treated as lepers sent to die in modern day exiles, politely called sanitariums, psychiatric hospitals, prison special needs departments, and state institutions which are nothing more than twenty-first century plantations established for the untreatable, the disgusting … me. Places where dreams go to die and souls are buried alive under heavy antipsychotics and anonymous head stones.

I cannot live with that. I won't live with that. My family has psychiatric disease rooted in its biology. My biological father, Einar Gasper Arauz, a first-generation immigrant with a Basque surname who came to America from David, Panama, was a person with mental illness. Remember his name; he deserves that at least. Einar arrived in Manhattan at the age of thirteen around 1950. He learned English and worked hard. I know so little about him that by the end of these next five or ten pages you will know as much about him as I do.

Einar Arauz received an honorable discharge from the United States Army in the late 1960's. I have no idea what he did in the Army, but I do know that after his discharge he used the GI Bill to earn a BS from Fordham University in Business and later an MBA from the same Jesuit institution. He worked full-time during both of his degrees; he was focused, handsome, liberal and funny. These are descriptions from my mother, not me; I was too young to know him in any adult way.

He is not real to me in that way.

He got a good job at a large, international company and started the process of moving from state to state with my mother as each job got better and the fast track got more welcoming. First, Pittsburgh, then Cincinnati, and then back to NYC to be back at headquarters, closer to the powerbase, closer to the top. Instead of moving back to Staten Island where he and my mother first lived, they had a nice home built in a Central Jersey suburb set up to accommodate upwardly mobile business men working in the city. It was happening for my Dad. I am sure there must have been some significant pride burning in his chest in those days.

By the time he had moved back to New Jersey he had two kids, a daughter and a son five years her junior, and by 1973 a third, another daughter. By 1974, he seemed poised on the brink of success. He had worked his entire life. Nothing was handed to him. But things were changing in his mind and he did not know how to handle it.

If you have spent your whole life depending on yourself, fatherless by thirteen, taking care of your mom in a foreign country, how do you come to terms with and focus on a mental illness? The doctors explained that he had a chemical imbalance, but he did not accept the diagnosis. He was trying to do the impossible. He was trying to fix a diseased mind with the same diseased mind.

Various doctors told him, "Just take your medicine, Einar, break the severe symptoms and the results will show that you can live with this disease." He would not.

Acceptance is the key to recovery. Without acceptance you never pass Go, you never advance, never escape, you are stuck fighting the unwinnable fight. A simple word "acceptance," but with mental illness, as well as addiction, it is the Rosetta Stone to understanding the language of resurrection and the vernacular of spiritual redemption. My father never understood the word. He died because of this *existential illiteracy*.

It must have been terrifying for this proud Spaniard. He was alone in the US with no one to depend on except those who depended on him: a pretty, upper middle-class family in a large new home. I have come to know him much more as I have cycled in and out of mental hospitals and felt the terror and paranoia of our shared disorder. He bent his considerable intellect to fighting a battle that was unwinnable without the very help he refused to accept. He would not try medication or any other form of treatment when I knew him. Later in his life—I assume while in the controlled living environment in which he died—he was compliant with a recovery program. But the damage was done, life had been too hard for too long.

The population of people with serious mental illness die fifteen to twenty-five years earlier than the average American according to the National Association of State Mental Health Program Directors (NASMHPD). Einar Arauz fell right in the middle of this bell curve with his death at fifty-seven years old. He did not survive to be the statistical anomaly that I am fighting to become.

The lesson I take from my father's life—and from my own experiences—is simple: There is treatment and there is recovery. Whether it is therapy, medication, Zen, twelve-step programs, religion or anything else. Quiet the cacophony of the most serious symptoms and then try anything and everything to survive. Take your medicine, however you define that term in your recovery, I repeat, take your medicine, not for a lifetime but for today. Break the symptoms, stabilize the disease, and then make the decision on the future of your pharmaceutical treatment day by day. Do not heed witch doctors and charlatans eager to tell you they have the answer or possess some unknown truth about how to defeat mental disease. Swallowing whole the "miracle cures" others have to sell you will kill you.

Untreated mental illness, like addiction, kills. It is not an ailment to be overcome but a truth to be accepted before it kills you or someone you love who is suffering. As a national behavioral health advocate, I go around the country visiting the most secure state psychiatric hospitals and college classrooms looking for my brothers and sisters with my disease and any other mental disorder. I let them know I love them, and, most of all, that I understand and accept them.

Mental illness is a biological disease. It can be brutal and certain degrees of affliction have limits on people's functionality. But it is not a condemnation, it is not a decree from God that your family is to face scourges; it simply is. There are treatments, there is hope.

But the brutal fact is that many will die in the infirmaries of their hospitals. They will die surrounded by men and women wearing long white coats, stethoscopes and name tags. There will be no families at their sides, no one around to see them through the final transition and, to be honest, many will welcome the end of this journey. That is how my father died. He died alone, without his family, without his son, his only son, at his side. It was a slow death that crept up on him while he was being beaten in shelters and while he screamed for mercy in the mental illness wards in New Jersey jails.

My only hope is that he had forgotten me in the decade before he died—in the decade since we last saw each other. I pray that the ruthlessness of the disease devoured so much of him that I became a delusion, that the family he loved and worked so hard to provide for was forgotten. That the disease would grant him a reprieve from the full knowledge of his lethal actions and their ramifications. That his pain was lessened as he exhaled his last breath and joined his parents in the next realm. He didn't deserve his life and he didn't deserve his death. But life is not about what you deserve or you would not be holding this book in your hands.

I now know my father in a way I am sure he hoped I never would.

But by grace, serendipity, medication, abstinence from alcohol and drugs, and the largest and greatest support network a sinner, failure, maniac, and advocate could ever want, I have a life on the other side of the nightmare. And now, I am awake to all the universal possibilities available to survivors.

Life | Chapter 3

By 1982, my dad had been symptomatic for a couple of years. My mom took the kids, and we moved to an apartment in the same town to keep us in our schools. She had not been working while she raised us, but now she was thrust back into the workforce. As is often the case, she had to start at the bottom. My mom is one of the sharpest people I know; she was a valedictorian in her all girls' school in Brooklyn and is still one of the most beautiful Irish women you will ever see. But with no work experience in over a decade, she had to grab whatever she could. I slept on the couch for a few years but we got by, we survived.

As with many people with mental illness, I had a collective life experience centered on the acts of one family member with active mental illness. The manifestations are different with each family and with each individual family member, but the feelings and emotional scars are the same. When my dad stopped going to work and ended up in constant squabbles with the neighbors, I was introduced to the concept and the reality of shame.

Shame coats everything: thoughts, psyches, emotions, accomplishments—everything. It sits behind your eyes like a ravenous toll collector not allowing anything in or out without its touch. It destroys perception, inception and conception. It creates a living landscape of absolute damnation.

Guilt is the easier emotion. If you are guilty, you are guilty of something. At one time, I stood outside a court room in New Brunswick, NJ looking at the agenda for the day and read: *The State of New Jersey vs. Eric Arauz* listed five separate times for five different offenses. It was freeing to see what I was being punished for so clearly delineated in front of me. Whatever sentence guilt imposes upon you, there is a chance for atonement, absolution, for freedom. But shame's sentence is always the same—life imprisonment.

I became aware of a growing darkness and reticence in my mother. She was reluctant to talk to neighbors, and gradually my childhood became something everyone around me wanted nothing to do with but from which I could not escape.

The worst part of this childhood dilemma was the absolute love of the torturer. It is unnatural to hate a parent at an age when you cannot understand yourself, let alone others. My early years should have been a time of intellectual and emotional freedom. I should have been able to trust my dad to protect me from other real world dangers and not to become the thing that was most lethal to me.

By the time I was in sixth grade, he was out of control. Einar had been totally out of our lives for some time—until one day he walked into our apartment unannounced. He continued this behavior even in the face of countless restraining orders. One time, he came right in the front door, took his pants off, and lay down on the couch—my bed.

There was no safe place for me anymore. My home had become just as scary as the rest of the world. I never knew if my father was in the house or not. If he was in the house, would he greet me at the door when I came in? Would he wait until we were all home to attack, or would he simply wait until Johnny Carson was over and everyone cleared from the living room, my bedroom, to destroy me?

I can see most of his actions differently today. Now I understand he had nothing. Manic, confused, and scared, he drove aimlessly across the state. When he would come in the house, he was always trying to sleep or lay down. I'm sure he just wanted a few hours of protection from the world, a minute or two of peace, a refuge in which to close his eyes. He needed to not wake up to a world that was worsening by the moment. He was a veteran with mental illness suffering from a disease that robs the soul before it ruthlessly takes the life. Einar deserved more; he deserved aid. I deserved more; I deserved my dad.

Life | Chapter 4

I t was three in the afternoon in the parking lot of my catholic school, St. Bartholomew's. There was a cold, heavy rain falling. My father had been constantly breaking restraining orders for months. I had been instructed not to go with him when I saw him, but I couldn't help myself. When I saw his gray car in the last row of the parking lot, I eagerly walked past the bus line. I trotted past the parents waiting for their own kids. Nobody noticed a fat kid with a silly grin walking by their closed car windows. My dad's car sat alone; its wipers exposing Einar's face every other second as they slid their way across the windshield.

I was coming up on the driver's side but, because the car was a two door, I had to crossover to get in. I was in front of him, dead center in front of the nose of the car, my head down to avoid the drenching mist when I heard the engine roar. I looked up. I don't know what I saw first, the car or my father's eyes but neither showed any emotion as they both lunged forward at me—*eye to eye, father and son.*

I planted my left foot, hoping to get traction, and dove back to the right. The car went straight over where I had been standing and kept going. Fresh wet tire tracks erased my shoe prints.

What just happened? Had he...? No. That couldn't have happened ... he couldn't have.... He did.

Shame, mortality, and terror flooded my twelve-year-old mind. I was not capable of processing the reality of this situation. I was dizzy and disoriented, crying involuntarily, a bodily reaction without awareness behind it. I was only clear on one thing, one important thing: my father had just tried to kill me.

Before I knew what I was doing, I was chasing the car. With my book-bag and thermos in my right hand, I tried to catch up to the passenger side. The parking lot was packed and there was nowhere for him to go. He would have to drive toward the exit and merge with the buses and other cars driven by parents who didn't just try to kill their sons. About two hundred feet before the street, there is a statue of the Virgin Mary on the right side of the exit. At that point, traffic bottlenecks; you have to commit to a lane by then or you are not leaving.

He was driving very slowly as I caught the car. I looked inside and started to yell.

"Daddy, let me in. Let me in, Daddy! Daddy!"

I was slipping and sliding in the now punishing rainfall. Blue pens and red rulers flew out of my backpack, a trail of classroom debris littered the parking lot.

"Daddy, let me in. Daddy! Daddy!"

Nothing, not a glance. I used to lie to myself and picture a heartfelt look as he drove off but there was nothing. No remorse. Nothing.

I clutched at the door handle and begged for him to let me in. A lane opened in the exit line, and he accelerated out of my grip. The slick silver door handle snapped back against the car as it tore from my fingers. His right blinker signaled, he turned out of the parking lot, and drove off down a rain-blackened Ryders Lane toward Route 1.

From the car next to me, I could hear my name being called by the mother of a girl in my class. At first it sounded like someone yelling while I held my breath underwater, but slowly it got louder as I stopped screaming. There was panic in her voice, and her face could not conceal her sorrow.

I got in the back seat of her car and stared forward. Mrs. P. asked me where I lived and I told her. She kept reassuring me that it would be OK. Everything would be OK.

I remember saying, "Thanks Ma'am. Please just take me home."

Do not underestimate the feelings of a child. Suffering has no age requirement. It speaks in a vernacular known to all at every stage of life and it always asks for the same thing—cessation. If cessation can't be found, then it looks for communion. Communion is found in many ways by many people. Alcohol, medication, denial, acceptance, religion, atheism, intellectualism, therapy, positivism, nihilism, etc.; no matter your route, I have walked a similar one and I understand. You are not alone.

Of course, in 1982, sitting in the back of Tricia's mom's car, I didn't know that. Numb, I watched the windshield wipers rock back and forth ... back and forth … wiping away the tears as the whole universe cried at what it had just witnessed. I knew I had to get home to my little sister. I had to tell my mom. I had to warn my big sister. She was sixteen and always walking places around town. Now walking places was not safe.

My classmate's mom, a true angel of my youth, would chime in now and then, to reassure me. I don't know if she saw my dad try to run me down, but she did see me running in the rain, banging on the window of his car while he just kept on driving. She did see me chasing him, begging, to get in and ride with the man I couldn't stop loving, the man I was willing to beg for forgiveness if he would only allow me to be his son.

Life | Chapter 5

I loved my dad. I had no idea what he was going through and could forgive him anything. Get punched full force in the face for striking out in a little league game? Fine, I stood back up and loved him anyway. Get slapped, kicked, shunned, dropped off in cities I had never been to? Fine, I dried my tears, tried to find my way home, and kept on loving him. All I wanted was for him to stay. As a young boy, I needed him more than I needed anything else.

I had seen the fear in his eyes when the disease was overwhelming him. I had sat on his bed in his tiny, studio apartment in Jersey City sipping orange juice and rubbing his back while he slept for twenty hours at a time. As a child, I felt the closest to him at his sickest, when he looked to me for salvation, for solace, and when I looked to him for love.

As an adult, divorcing his brutal actions from him personally has taken a long time. For years, I was unwilling to see anything but his transgressions. I could not see him as the source of my life and the bearer of my surname. He was my enemy, a monster, something to be condemned or forgotten, certainly never forgiven.

I only saw him one more time before I was notified he had passed away somewhere in North Jersey with a female confidante who was trying to usurp his last will and testament. He had worked in life insurance at the end of his occupational life and must have taken out a policy on himself. Because of mental illness and his disability, the policy was picked up by the insurance company. Two men who had known him and had met me years earlier fought to keep the policy in his kids' names.

They contacted my mother in 1994 to tell us my father was in a halfway house in Paterson in North Jersey. My mom called to tell me in Portsmouth, VA.

I was finishing my enlistment in the Navy with Rich, Lee and Mike.

Despite our history, I was excited to finally know where he was. I was a new-lywed and was helping my first wife raise her daughter. When we met, she had just found out she was pregnant a few weeks earlier—and that the baby's father was married. Life in the Navy is transient and many live with malleable identities, histories and truths. Many others pay the price for that malleability. We had been good friends and I saw a woman who was making a brave stand to keep her baby. I was very proud of her; I respected her and eagerly stepped into the role of hus-band and step-father.

I was excited to write a letter to my own father, and I couldn't wait to tell him that I had served in the Navy, that I had gone overseas on a Destroyer, that I was a step-father and husband. I wanted him to know that my life was coming together. The haunting specters from my past were no longer in control of my future. I had yet to visit my first hospital, experience the trauma of my first diagnosis, live through my first meds call, struggle with my first realization that my life would be something to be survived and not lived.

"Daddy," I wrote over and over again. I worked on several drafts of the letter. I started to picture what my father looked like, how he must have aged. I couldn't remember the color of his eyes or how tall he was. Would his hair be gray? Or maybe he was balding. I tried to imagine him, but I had no sense of him as an older man. I had safeguarded my memories and held onto stories, but I had no real facts. I had images, but not history. Photo albums captured moments in time, not the tangled, trajectory of our lives; they held images not souls.

Besides, I didn't like to look at the old albums. I didn't want to study the pictures. They held pain and they held fear. Each snapshot was a trigger for the traumas of my youth. But now that could change. I was a grown man—a step-fa-ther. We could be whole as a family, not perfect, not together, but actual, real.

The phone rang on the Quarterdeck I manned each day at the mouth of the barracks. It was my mother. She had the sound in her voice when things are very wrong and very real. The same tone she had when I was eight and she woke my sisters and me for the first time to make a late night escape from our home.

"Your father has passed away, Eric," she said.

The years of hard living had led to water on the brain or heart or whatever and it was over. My reaction was hollow. I didn't know if I was happy or sad. I had prayed for his death many times in my life, especially when I was alone on the couch in the middle of the night. I just wanted the fear to go away. I needed him to go away. But he wasn't real then. He was still a dream, a nightmare.

Now, I knew there was no use finishing the letter. There would be no reunion; it was over. I began to think about our last encounter in1984, two years after he tried to run me down. Two years after he tried to end my life, after he killed my adolescent innocence, staring at me eye to eye through a rain-soaked windshield.

Nobody survived my childhood.

Life | Chapter 6

During the time my father was completely out of my life, between 1982 and 1984, I both gained and lost a lot of weight. I was an unbelievably heavy child, and in seventh grade, I weighed in at over 265 pounds. Food allowed me some solace and the extra 100 pounds gave me a buffer to the world. I hid within myself, from myself, and from the constant pain and fear that defined my life.

After about twelve months without my dad in the picture my mother started dating a wonderful man named Bud Powers and I started to believe I could lose weight. Oddly, the kids in my classes in Catholic school never made me feel like an outcast due to my girth. No matter what happened with my dad or my ever-expanding waistline—56 inches at one point—I was always accepted. I loved my classmates. My classroom and the adjoining church where the whole school went for services every Friday always brought me peace.

The beauty of the sanctuary and the mysticism I felt in church was a balm to my wounded adolescence. Transfixed, I would stare at the hanging Catholic crucifix with Jesus nailed and bleeding and would feel it speak to me. At the age of twelve, I understood more of persecution and betrayal than most adults would ever know. I felt I knew what it was like to suffer and lay flayed and dying in public. I loved to survey the Stations of the Cross bordering the church's interior and wonder how Jesus had endured the unimaginable suffering of publicly carrying his cross through the streets of his world. His was a public crucifixion, a public destruction, and I felt that, like Jesus, I would die on display for others to see.

I lost 115 pounds by the end of eighth grade, the year of graduation. The last year had gone by without incidence. For the first time in a long time, I knew what it was like to hope and plan for the possibilities of the future. I felt connected and safe. Along with half of my class, I was starting public high school in the fall while the other half was going on to the various other Catholic institutions in New Jersey. My mom's job was going better, and I was losing that sinking feeling that one more bad event would send our small family into oblivion. We were like modern-day homesteaders who, instead of fearing Indians or struggling to survive amidst famine, were on constant lookout for homicidal husbands and waging war against poverty.

Graduation day finally came. I was confident I was going to do well in public school. I was a great student with a good work ethic and a tremendous aptitude, testing off the charts on state tests from an early age. Advanced verbal and cognitive skills and now 100+ pounds lighter—New Jersey, here I come!

We signed yearbooks all day and I remember observing my classmates, teachers and nuns. Together, they semed to have conspired to protect and shelter me in the midst of my domestic turbulence. These were the heroes of my youth, and I knew I would repay them by loving them forever in my heart and saying farewell to each one silently in my soul.

The school day drew to a close. The graduating class was released a minute or two early to walk the halls one last time as the lower grades lined up for dismissal.

I walked down the back stairs and got to the first floor; the floor that housed the first through fourth graders. The young students were lined up, smiling, divine, innocent; standing hand in hand with each other and with a God they still trusted to protect them. The spring day whispered through the opened windows and I spoke to the teachers, sharing goodbyes and good lucks, as I walked among the students.

I noticed a small commotion at the end of the hall near the first graders. I didn't know what was happening and I didn't care. It didn't concern me—until I heard an adult male voice, yelling. I saw a man pushing through the lines of children, and as he drew closer, I could hear every word he said.

"*Where are my fucking kids?* Where the fuck are they? Where is my son and daughter? I know you fucking whores got 'em, and you better give 'em up. You hear me? Where are my fucking kids?"

He cut an imposing figure in a black beret and gray sweat pants. The intruder was wearing a plain black backpack, and it looked as if he hadn't cut his hair in years. His eyes dazzled with madness, and he kept screaming and coming right at me. I knew the only way to escape was to walk right by him. The only other way out was a fire escape, and even when facing down an imminent danger, I couldn't bring myself to break the rules and go out the fire door. Rock solid parochial school boy that I was, I would take my chances with a madman rather than risk detention.

I was walking straight at him when we locked eyes. A familiar wave of panic exploded in my gut as I recognized my dad's face behind his vagrant disguise. I was standing face to face with my nightmare. Wide awake and looking directly at Einar.

Eye to eye, father and son.

Time stopped and I froze. I prepared for my fate.

But nothing happened. He looked right at me but kept walking, screaming and stalking his delusions. I slipped by free but perplexed. At the time, it didn't register that my weight loss had hidden me in plain sight. I took a few light steps down the hallway when I broke out in a sprint.

My sister! Where was my little sister?

I was in survival mode, and I had to reach her, had to move quickly … I must protect my sister! As I turned the corner to start charging up the stairs against the surge of downward traffic of upperclassmen, I was swept up by a wall of blue— an army of nuns ready to protect a child of Christ. There was no fear in Sister David's face when, like an enlightened Navy Seal in the face of mortal danger, she intercepted me and ran me to the convent. A young man named Tom O. came with us that day. He ran for his life with me, not away from me. He and Scott D., another ally who at fourteen years old squared off with my father, had no stake in my war, but they would not abandon me to face danger alone. These were teenagers that were already men. You hear of courage and heroism, but I saw it for the first time in the compassion and bravery written on their determined faces.

The younger nuns moved quickly, with grace and glory, in search of my sister. Our school, invaded by a man ravaged by mental disease, was being defended by the strongest force known to the world, the collective strength of women. It has been said that it takes a village to raise a child and it took a thousand women to stop my free fall. I may have one birth mother, but I am the spiritual step-son of many, many women who were devoted to my survival on that day as on countless others.

The nuns protected us until my father left on his own and we made our way home. Because graduation was held that night in the school's church, my last hiding place, my panacea, I knew nothing could happen to me. No one caught my dad that day. This was 1984. There was no Amber Alert, no Columbine, no acknowledgement of the fragility and vulnerability of a family or a school under attack from an intruder within. I would be OK. Somehow, I regrouped and prepared for the ceremony.

Life is funny. Sometimes when things start spiraling out of control, places become alive and superstition supplants reason. I believed the church was a bastion of safety, a fortress that my father would not—could not—breach. But the truth is that terrible things occur every day where people feel safest. And it would be at the church's altar rail that I would face down my father for the last time.

Life | Chapter 7

As my tiny family headed out to graduation, I could see in my mom's eyes that she was not going to let my celebration be ruined. She was a fighter who did everything in her power to protect her children. Alone, she would worry about the bills, about her job, her old car, but she never let on how precarious our situation was. That night was no different.

We got to church and I was immediately comforted by the darkened stained glass windows, the candlelight, and the dimmed bulbs. It was beautiful. It even smelled holy. As with most ceremonies, there were a couple of readings from the Bible and some discussion from the priest. I sat in the second row from the front and watched my classmates in their suits and dresses. Everyone was excited. Small secrets were exchanged, but not too much talking. You never knew where Sister David was lurking.

After my father's breach of school security earlier in the day, I was very emotional. I started to cry. I was only fourteen but I felt a tremendous loss at saying goodbye to this cocoon. I truly loved the people around me and needed them more than they knew.

The priest called the graduates to the rails around the altar and we left our pews and made our way to our practiced spots. We turned to face a congregation full of grinning faces and disposable cameras poised for action. Parents were asked to move to the center aisle and come forward to stand with their children. Pairs of parents began to maneuver side-ways out of their pews. There was only one figure not moving in a pair: my mom. She stood up, straightened her shoulders, and made her way solo to the center aisle. My older sister, who graduated from the same school five years earlier, remained in the pew, smiling, with my little sister next to her, not smiling.

I was transfixed by the parade of parents as they made their way toward the front of the church. Then, I noticed a single figure walking up the side aisle to my left. He was staring straight through me at the altar behind me. I looked back at the center aisle and tried to signal my mother that there may be danger. But she was obscured by the larger parents. I looked to my sisters, twenty pews away from me, but neither was looking my direction. I started to panic—it can't be him, it just can't be.

The closer the procession of parents got, the closer he got, until he emerged from the shadows and turned to his left as my mom turned to her right to stand in front of me. As he emerged from the darkness into the candlelight, I could see his face. He was dressed in all black, from combat boots to turtle neck to beret. He reached me first, took his place in front of me and stood at attention, inches from my face.

Eye to eye, father and son.

I was paralyzed. Einar didn't do anything for the first few seconds but settle himself directly in front of me. I glanced toward my mother whose face was contorted with rage. She had not been that close to her ex-husband in years. He had made her life hell and just that afternoon had rampaged through the school trying to abduct her kids. There was hate in her eyes. This was the man to whom she had pledged everything and he, in return, had stolen her dreams.

She moved next to him, close, and began to whisper vengeance into his ear. She was not about to let him ruin the moment for her family. She was not about to let years of sacrifice and struggle be compromised by the one man who had caused all her family's pain. With no other recourse, she attacked verbally.

The other families did not look our way. They were concerned with their own lives—brothers and sisters fidgeting in their Sunday clothes, grandparents smiling proudly and snapping photographs with six-foot subs and box cakes waiting at home under cheap paper streamers hung hours earlier.

From the vantage point of the pews, we looked like any other family, except for my father's choice of paramilitary dress.

My sisters saw him arrive at the altar, but what could they do? They were as helpless as I was. My father once again made me feel like a coward, an impotent little boy. I was crushed by the knowledge that as much as I wanted to protect my mom and sisters, I could not. I was failing at my basic duties as a son and brother. Never allowed to feel the assumed invincibility of an adolescent boy, I was convinced he would kill me right there at the altar in front of everyone that mattered to me.

I wondered: How would I die? Was he going to shoot me? Choke me? Would my father stab me? No matter what he did, I knew at that moment I would not counter it. I was weak and useless and without the ability to help those I watched suffer each day. I was a fourteen-year-old deserter, spineless, hidden, another problem with no solution. I surrendered to fate, accepted my teenage death, and patiently waited for its arrival.

As my mom whispered into my father's ear, he watched me. He didn't move. He didn't acknowledge my mother at all. In a precursor to my future Zen practices and mindfulness training, I breathed into the moment. Inhaled my essence and exhaled my death. In and out … in and out … I raised my glance to meet Einar's eyes.

He did not have that zombie look he had earlier at the school. There was a cognitive presence behind his eyes. He recognized me; he was breathing me in and out.

Our breathing formed a cadence as we stared into each other's eyes. I hadn't been this close to him since he came into my room the night he told me he and Mom were getting a divorce. That night, he sat on the end of my bed and wept. He didn't explain anything. He just cried. He cried for a life that was crumbling out of control, a life he didn't understand. He loved his kids and his wife, but his untreated mental disease had attacked his family just as it had mastered its host. He cried because he was losing what he cared for the most and had no idea how he got there.

As an adult I have cried those tears; I said goodbye to a step-daughter I loved more than life itself without understanding how or why my life had spiraled out of control. My first wife had to get rid of me. My bipolar disorder and active addictions were making her life hell and it didn't matter why. I eventually did to another mother what my father did to mine. Like father, like son, I completed an unholy circle and woke in an institution with a life I didn't remember creating.

The evening of my graduation the look on my dad's face was one I hadn't seen in years. The anger wasn't there, the fear was absent. He looked at me with love. A genuine paternal love, a love I needed to see. I didn't know how to react. I wanted to accept his presence and throw my arms around him. I wanted him to know I still needed him and wanted him in my life. At the same time, I didn't want to betray my mother. I knew exactly how she felt about him and I was very aware that his was a dangerous presence in my life.

It was an odd, quiet forever standing under the eyes of a dying Christ staring at my father. Here, he did not look foreboding, he looked infantile. Einar looked at me as if he was my child, as if I was the provider of his solace. His eyes moistened with tears and his look softened even more. He revealed himself to me, trusted me with his essence, gave himself to me.

I imagined him at five years old on the city streets of David, Panama playing with his cousins and at thirteen coming to America with his mother as a first generation immigrant to New York City. His joys and struggles washed over me as I felt his collective life experience pour forth from him onto his son.

"Know me, Eric, know me. I am not a monster, I am your father. I am you and you are me. And I am sorry."

This phrase whispered into my mind and I don't know if he actually said it or not, but I felt it. I felt him. I wanted to save him, but I could not. I was not spiritually mature and available like Siddhartha from the Hermann Hesse novel and I could not offer him the universal solace of human touch with a kiss to my forehead.

Human Connection.

I would not invite the loving press of his lips to the head of his only son to let him know he was not alone and never would be. I was not capable of breeching his diseased and cycling mind, a manic and isolated thing that sustained, verified, and validated itself.

My father had a moment of clarity and released himself into me. He died to his past and loved me on that altar. He did not kill me or hurt me. He loved me and I loved him, but I could not forgive him. Sadly, I learned early in my life that love is a strange thing; I learned I could love that which I also hated.

In a reversal of the biblical story symbolized by the crucifixion hanging behind me, I felt as though he queried me with his glance and asked in our last moment, "Son, why have you forsaken your father in his time of need?"

Incense and insanity filled my senses as I stood immobilized. I could not answer such a question. Then Einar turned, left the altar, walked back down the outside aisle, and out of my life. Forever.

After the graduation ceremony, the nuns sounded the alarm and a brigade of middle-aged fathers in khakis and penny loafers set out to capture my Fisher King, my forever-wounded father. But he had disappeared into the night. In the years after that evening, I often missed him and dreamed of his return, but I was never to see him again or even hear of him until the weeks before his death in 1994.

His illness scarred and traumatized us. It took a long time, but today I accept the totality of our relationship, and I am proud to be an Arauz. I am proud to carry his Basque surname, the last name of father and son veterans—veterans of our country's armed services and veterans of our shared war against mental illness. One man memorialized and one still fighting.

I am not successful today in spite of my mental illness but *because* of my mental illness. Adversity revealed the true Eric Arauz to me, the Eric Arauz who is a warrior, a fighter, a Bipolar Jedi. Father, I thank you for my strength, my intellect, my fire.

Einar Arauz, I thank you for me.

Life | Chapter 8

I am a disabled Navy veteran, national behavioral-health advocate, recovering alcoholic/addict, business owner, brother, uncle, Ivy League university lecturer, individual diagnosed with bipolar 1 disorder and post-tramatic stress disorder (PTSD), husband, political appointee, son, Olympic-distance triathlete, trauma-informed recovery expert, mystic, faculty member at a medical school, multiple degree holder and professional inspirational speaker. And today, no one of these lables holds any more valence in my self identity than another.

I am considered a successful example for many with severe mental illness and addiction. But if I am an example of anything to others, it is not because of me, it is not because I am stronger or smarter than anyone else. It is because of you. It is because of you and the people like you who gave me the support and courage to confront my diseases head-on and to take control of my life and my destiny.

People from all walks of life ask the same question about my co-occurring disorders: Did the bipolar chicken come from the addicted egg or vice versa? Am I a bipolar man with an addiction problem or am I an addict/alcoholic that later developed a mental disorder?

My answer has been the same whether I am speaking with doctors or consumers/recipients/people with mental illness locked away in state mental hospitals. First, I answer, I don't know. I am not a doctor, nor do I claim to be or want to be. Second, I will speak purely from my personal experience—I am not a therapist, nor do I claim to be or want to be. Lastly, I could not care less about which came first. I am a person with various medical issues that include bipolar disorder 1, addiction, post-traumatic stress disorder (PTSD) from childhood abuse and the secondary trauma of long-term psychiatric hospital restraints, asthma, allergies, Poland Syndrome (a pattern of one-sided congenital birth defects), and arthritis in my surgically repaired toes.

But I refuse to allow those conditions to define me. First and foremost, I am a person. Just like you.

I don't need to understand the "why/how" behind the biochemistry of my brain to be compliant to my recovery plan; I just don't want to be strapped down in four-point restraints ever again. It is that simple.

Tell me and show me what works and I will do it. It may take some tweaking here and there until I get used to my meds for my bipolar disorder, but I don't want to die in a mental hospital. The natural reaction to the extraordinary amount of time I've spent in four-point restraints is the continual need for my mind and spirit to expand, to journey inward and outward beyond myself. I long for the freedom that comes from self-actualization, but I will settle for "actually" not being lashed to a bed.

I have three chronic diseases as listed in the DSM-IV, the diagnostic manual for mental illness. Post-Traumatic Stress Disorder, bipolar disorder and alcoholism/addiction. I was locked away in a Veterans Administration maximum-security ward—a ward reserved for the sickest of the sick until they are ready for a step-down ward with treatment—and was considered beyond treatment. I spent months pacing back and forth along a narrow hallway, cycling in a mania my antipsychotic medications could not abate, never getting placed in a step-down ward for treatment.

I have been shackled in four-point restraints for over twenty-four hours while I screamed and cried into the heartless night. I begged the nurses for mercy. Tethered to the restraining bed, I have lain in my feces and pleaded with God for my death. But the God I asked to relieve my suffering was a power I no longer trusted or even feared. In my highest peaks of pure mania, I believed I had become this power. I had stood at the doorway of the divine, the essence of enlightenment, of creation and nirvana, and welcomed myself in. My mind was bathed in a grandiose narcissism so all-encompassing it became the answer to its own questions.

My bipolar disorder is my bipolar disorder. It attacks me differently than anyone else's disorder attacks them.

I am privileged to be part of a large community of people that have this same disease. It is a common disorder. People in my community contact me from around the country. I meet them in twelve-step meetings, at mental health functions, in grad schools, running 10k races and in supermarkets. They share their stories of suffering, their struggles for rebirth and resurrection. They allow me into the dark places they've closed off to the world because they know I have lived in the same prison cells of the mind that haunt them. They trust me with their suffering.

I am completely asymptomatic between episodes. I show no signs of a mental disposition that can eventually erupt in mania. Before my first episode, starting in Memphis and intensifying as I drove toward Dallas, I had been in active war zones, drunken squabbles from Tijuana to Cairo and other high pressure situations that would tax any human mind. But the door holding my disease behind it had always remained closed. It wasn't until I knew I had to give up my step-daughter that my mania emerged.

Bipolar disorder is a biogenic disease. It sits in your head. Often it needs the proper psycho-social stressor to bring it out to the forefront of your mind. But once it is out and gets a taste of freedom, it will never retreat back behind the door voluntarily. The disease has many manifestations and faces. Bipolar 1 has the most drastic highs, called mania, and lows, called depressions. It used to be called manic-depression, but in the current medical lexicon, you will find it under bipolar disorder.

The lows or depressions are easier to explain than mania. Depression is not a simple sadness. It is hopelessness. It is irritability and anger. It can be a numbing void where life is neither good nor bad but simply something to be endured. It becomes an absolute deadening of the self. You become cemented inside your own skin.

While I have suffered through three manic episodes, I've only experienced one depression. It followed my first hospitalization and it was brutal. It was different than my mania in one very important way—I never lost myself in it. Mania, at the level I experience it, eventually completely subsumes my perception of reality and self. The reference point of me is lost and I become immersed in the counterfeit oasis of my own cycling mind.

In my depression, I was crushingly aware of myself, of Eric Arauz. In the first two weeks after coming home from the first hospital, I gradually realized how my life was changing, that I was getting a divorce, that I would never see my step-daughter again. Her beautiful little face appeared in my mind's eye no matter where I was or who I was with. It went from distracting to abusive. No amount of self talk or antidepressants could dilute the image of saying goodbye to her. It leaked into all my discussions and day-to-day activities. I would talk to my therapists, doctors, friends, and day-program partners, but she was always there. In my depression, my mind focused on the one thing I could not deal with and poured it down my throat until I was choking on it. I went to sleep weeping into an exhausted submission and woke up frozen to a sunless morning. Mania led me into the hospital and depression greeted me with its deathlike embrace when I got out.

I stopped drinking in 1993, while I was still in the Navy, but I didn't use any type of recovery program to help control my addictive nature. Instead, I turned to marijuana to dampen and blur my reality. By 1995, eight months after my discharge, I was smoking pot every day. I had turned into a total jerk-off. I had married a wonderful woman, a woman I admired as a hero. But I had become a nuisance. I couldn't get my act together. I needled her constantly and put her down until she had, rightly, had enough. I had loved her, but it was the act of saying good-bye to my step-daughter that was the psycho-social stressor that pulled the pin on my mental grenade.

After my ex-wife and I finally decided we could not stay together, we existed in a numb, domestic limbo for three days before I left for Dallas. I felt like I was haunting my own house. Those three days passed in slow-motion.

Each morning my step-daughter and I woke together. She was about one and a half, and we would sit on the floor while she wiped the dreams from her eyes as I dressed her for the day. Put your arm through the sleeve. Kiss. Pop your head through the neck hole. Kiss and hug. Put out your foot and wiggle your toes. Kiss. Slip one sock on and start on the other foot. Kiss, kiss, kiss for the angel of my tortured life. I loved her as much with my touch as my heart. I promised I would not cry to her as my father did to me.

On the third day, I walked into her room for the last time. Her crib was to the left when you entered and there was a tall window on the opposite wall. The Memphis sun was slowly creeping up her body as she slept on her stomach. Her face was turned toward me, her eyes were closed, her lips pursed like she was kissing Santa. I watched her for a few moments and tried to burn into my mind this last image of my little girl, the step-daughter I loved so much.

My car was already packed and ready to go. My ex-wife left us alone. I will always be thankful for the undeserved restraint and kindness she showed me.

I stepped forward and placed my hands on my baby's back to connect. Gently, I reached into the crib and picked up her warm body. The sun was fully blanketing the crib. I looked into her now open innocent brown eyes. She made a few morning sounds and stretches and sleepily acknowledged her daddy. My little girl placed her tiny hands on my face and grinned. I kissed her forehead, her cheeks, her little lips and fingers. My body roared from the inside. I bowed my head to hide my tears and let her rub my smooth-shaved crown.

I looked back up at her smiling face and gave a little tickle below her chin to get her giggling. It was my first moment of self-forgetting in a self-dominated life. I knew I was dying, rupturing from the inside out, but she would not know. As the extremes of my addiction and newly blooming bipolar disorder were re-arranging my psyche, I held on to her. Each time she laughed, I smiled and got lightheaded. I kissed her one last time and placed her back in her crib to let her sleep. Her eyes fluttered shut as I rubbed her back. Despondently, I stepped away from the crib. I left my shattered heart on the altar with my baby girl and disap-peared from her life. Forever.

I had no legal rights to a child that was not mine. My ex-wife and I had talked about my role in her life after we split, but I knew better. She was originally from the Midwest and would return after her enlistment. I was planning on returning home to New Jersey. I couldn't keep it together in the same house, let alone 1,700 miles away. As I was leaving, I told her I would be useless to them. I believed my life was cursed. My lightheadedness got worse.

I knew my step-daughter would not remember me. She was too young and I was not worth remembering. I wanted my ex-wife to let me die to her and her daughter, to free them both from my pain. I had done all I could and I had failed. I wanted to be a painless non-memory rather than a misery to be endured. I loved that little girl with all my heart … I love her still.

I got in my car and headed south to Dallas to stay with Robbie, the first Virgil on my journey into the depths of hell and back. As I left Tennessee and drove through Arkansas, I tried to decompress from the emotion of the morning.

A great, open sky sheltered the part of Arkansas I drove through. In the distance, clouds loomed black, grey, and white, alive, crackling with activity. Tornadoes seemed imminent. As I drove, I cried like I had never cried before. Facing up to the pain of never seeing my step-daughter again crushed me and each mile I put behind me added to the anguish. I was used to making mistakes, big mistakes, but this was beyond me.

My mind fought valiantly as I raced through Texarkana. It had not been attacked by bipolar disorder before and was not prepared. My mind gradually slipped from thoughts of despair and loss to hope and grandiosity. Hypomania had kidnapped my consciousness.

I would be OK, my ex-wife would be OK, my step-daughter would be OK. I would take care of them. I would get a job, make a few bucks and send it to them to keep them afloat. I would buy them a house, yeah, a house, something pretty, something they can grow old in, something with land....

And like a run on sentence that never ended, my mind started an internal dialogue that did not stop for thirteen wakeful days. The voice was always my own and it was always talking. I do not have auditory hallucinations, I do not hear voices. But I do have all of the various types of standard delusions: Grandiose, Somatic, Religious, Nihilistic, Persecutory and Reference. I also experience the full range of Bizarre delusions: Thought withdrawal, Thought broadcasting, Thought insertion and Thought control.

While in this delusional state I suffer from Ideas of Reference, which means that my brain adds meaning to everything I think and that the meaning refers especially to me. It is a state of mind in which anything can be a direct message to me to do something. All external information is centered on me. Related to me. For me.

I remember driving on Interstate 35 outside of Dallas and seeing a sign for Waco, TX. It instantly triggered memories of the Branch Davidians and David Koresh. I believed I was being called to head down there to the ruins of another of God's divine warriors to learn from his mistakes. The death, destruction and pain of the tragic events that took place there were not real to me. All that was real was that somehow this particular road sign was placed at that particular spot for me to see and follow.

This is not the same as Carl Jung's "synchronicity." Jung believed in acausal happenstances, non-connected coincidences, which reveal the complexity and congruency of the universe to its observers. In the psychotic state of Ideas of Reference, there is nothing acausal, I am the cause and reference point of the universe. I am the center-point of evolution and consciousness. My mind holds the world in its thoughts and at the center of that world was my mind.

My consciousness became soaked in the disease. I began to drown in the mania. My grandiosity turned to paranoia and terror. I went from Messiah to an enemy of the Lord, any lord, any god. I went from Krishna to Christ, from Kali to Mephistopheles. The disease took control of me. Unlike my depression, in mania I was shaken loose from the moors of being Eric Arauz. I was without name or reference. Robbie knew something was wrong. He put me on a plane back to New Jersey, but the *me* that had a family and friends was already gone. Once back home, I humored everyone. I believed I was going to a top-secret government "think tank" for processing and debriefing, and I knew better than to tell anyone anything. In the final hours before my first hospitalization, I was both enlightened and enraged. Without Robbie's intervention, I probably would have died on the streets of Texas.

My mother cried as the East Brunswick police put me into the ambulance in our suburban driveway. I looked at my family with pity, scorn, and love. If only they knew of my true greatness. I would be generous; I would send for them one day and then they would see. They would understand. I would make everything right. The next thing I remember is waking up in the white room and not being able to move. It was there that, without the guidance of any of my Virgils, I began the journey to the ninth circle of my hell.

In the poem *The Divine Comedy*, written by Dante Alighieri in 1321 C.E., Dante travels through the nine circles of hell while searching for his love, Beatrice. This happens in the first part of the three part epic poem called "The Inferno." He is guided by the great poet Virgil who lives in the otherworld of Limbo and who gives Dante the ability to observe the land of insular devastation without getting lost in the flames of his personal hell. Virgil acts as Dante's guide as they descend into the most brutal circles of Dante's personal damnation and back up again to the surface.

The ninth and final circle of Hell in Dante's masterpiece is Ice and not Fire. The treacheries of those souls buried in this circle are the denials of love and human connection. The brutal encasement in this frozen oasis represents the ice that lives in their barren hearts. These 'sinners' denied God's love and divinity to their fellow man and are banished from all light and succor from the Lord's Sun. The inhabitants of this desolate circle denied connection and care to others and are now frozen out of the world.

Permanently disconnected.

The poem portrays that the worst torment of all is not the pain of the flames but the absolute isolation from our fellow man. The worst damnation is not feeling anything. To be frozen from the inside out staring at a world that doesn't recognize you as a part of it.

Ice is the perfect metaphor for my journey back to the world. To survive being frozen alive you must be saved. You are dead and cannot tunnel out. Your survival is contingent on the heroic efforts of others. If you do make it out alive, you have to acknowledge forever that it was not your effort alone that saved you. A Virgil found you in the ice and grabbed you with his flaming hand and pulled you back.

My battle with mental illness, severe addiction and the traumas of my life have been my own journey into the hells of myself with many loving, dedicated individuals filling Virgil's role. This book describes my fight out of the hell I fell into, a struggle toward the light by a blind heretic. Paradoxically, there was help at every turn, every day. Arms embraced me, hands reached out to save me, but I could not see them. I would not see them. I could not accept the fact that I had a condition that needed treatment and aid.

My combined diseases created a malfunction in my perception of reality—a maniacal myopia turning forever inward, forcing me to walk backwards through a life of "Was" all the while blind to what "Is." I was trapped in an opaque psychic helmet of self-stigma that prevented anything from the real world from entering or being acknowledged by my mind. My self-defeating ideas were bounced back to me and self verified. After I began to cycle in and out of psychiatric hospitals, I lived in a self-narrated "story of atrocity" and referred to myself only in a "language of abomination."

The journey of my recovery has been more about feeling than reason. There was no reason I should survive when so many others—including my father—had not. I needed to find an entirely new way to live in the world and I had to stop using my old failing ideas to guide me. In the tradition of Marcus Aurelius and other stoic philosophers, I came to recognize and understand that philosophical currents course throughout all of existence. By reading widely and thinking deeply about my existence, I immersed myself in these timeless currents of thought. I challenged myself to feel them intensely and purposefully acted on them with intention, and, in the process, I discovered universal lessons for living—an Arauzian *Applied Existentialism* for life.

Life | Chapter 9

The nice thing about your first stay in a mental hospital is that no one blames you for your illness and its genesis. You do not blame yourself too much either. Friends, family and others still have compassion for your suffering and are truly hopeful for your recovery. You even act hopeful as if it a brief hiccup. In my case, my first stay in a maximum-security mental hospital was to be followed by two more. After the second, my family and friends were still hopeful, but less forgiving, and after the third, they were desperate.

I was unable to arrest my addictions while trying to adhere to the life plan laid out for me after my first psychotic break. I was in that free fall common to many in my population—a free fall that all too often leads to more hospitals, jails and, ultimately, early death.

The levels of my individual disorders are extreme. When acute, my bipolar 1 is characterized by manic episodes of the highest level. I don't have a manic phase and get a little hyper and slightly grandiose. I completely step off the precipice and leave reality. I don't sleep for weeks, my psychosis takes me across the state, reading road signs and listening to the radio for hidden messages, and my delusions border on blasphemy and rapture.

I don't know I am having an episode. The false beliefs instantly wipe out my awareness. I am not Eric having delusions of grandeur. I am the delusions. I believe the thoughts and feelings immediately and without question. I could be having a manic episode right now as you read this and it would feel 100 percent real to me.

Because of the nature of my disease, my support network understands and recognizes the warning signs. They look for a number of clear indicators, the first being a break in my sleep patterns. If I stay awake into the wee hours of the night for a couple of days in a row, it is a bad sign. I also will spend money without any real discernment of my current financial situation. My speech becomes even more rapid than it is normally and I will be hyper-sexual. My network consists of my wife, Cheryl, my family, select friends, national network members, and now, you.

Even though there are times when I can be an extraordinarily insolent man, I know my wellbeing is contingent on others. My network is my last line of defense and in surrendering to this knowledge, I have found tremendous strength. To love me is to be willing to hospitalize me. To love me is to know you may lose me.

The arrest of my addictions is also contingent, in part, on an outside spiritual recovery program. In this fellowship, I have found fellow sufferers who accepted me before I could accept myself. I would never have been able to eventually build a real life without my sobriety. Like my mental illness, my addictions were extreme and I did not make a serious attempt to stop until the combination of the two, mental illness and addiction, almost killed me.

Alcohol has never worked for me. I was arrested three or four times before I was even eighteen. I was a short haired, ex-jock stoner constantly facing judges from various towns in central New Jersey. I was always looking to get off easy. Alcohol was a constant in my high school years. It didn't work for me from day one, but I did not have the strength of self to say "No" while others said "Yes." Friends, family, and even strangers have found me passed out in backyards with slugs on my face, in cars that weren't mine on Long Beach Island, and between my best friend's parents—in their own bed.

I had told my wife about waking up in my best friend's parent's bed, but she had never had any third-party verification. After years of ridiculous adventures together, my best friend Matty and I called each other the Pumpernickel Battle Twins (PBT). When I took my wife to the other PBT's fiancé's bridal shower at a bar in Hoboken, NJ, his mom was standing at the door waving to me. As we crossed the intersection toward the restaurant, she waived her hand and called out, "Eric Arauz get over here! Hey everybody, this is the only other man I've shared my bed with besides my husband...." Done and done, another moronic myth verified for my wife's amusement. PBT for life!

No, alcohol and me don't go together. I even ended up in the Navy because of alcohol. It was 1990 and things were finally looking up for my family. A year earlier my mom had remarried and we were living in a great new house in which everybody had their own room. Instead of enjoying the new stability and getting to know my wonderful step-dad, Bud, I stayed out late, drank and, eventually, got a DWI, a driving-while-intoxicated ticket. I wasn't equipped to deal with the ticket so I ran away. I used to make it sound very patriotic that I joined the service in the middle of a conflict in the Middle East. The truth is, I was not man enough to ride out my mistake. The truth is, I didn't even know there was a war going on.

When I got the DWI, my lack of self-control was reaching the epidemic point that leads to destruction. Even after getting the ticket and getting my license suspended, I was still drinking and driving drunk. I didn't care about what happened to me. Consequences didn't matter; consequences were not there to stop me before I did something but to be dealt with later. One night, as we were watching the TV show "Major Dad," about a Marine Corp officer's family, I saw my mom's face light up. My new step-dad, Bud, was a Marine, and I decided to enlist right then and there.

I was feeling low, desperate, and this was a way to get my mom's attention. My whole life had become a series of fake attempts at molding reality to make me look good. I would never build anything. Never work for anything. I could not validate myself from the inside so I turned to others to fill me up. I was empty; there was no me without you, without the external world, verifying me. I had no spirit, no hope. I had no authentic emotion anymore. So when I was at the peak of my addictions, I ducked my responsibilities and joined up simply because my mom smiled at a TV screen and I didn't have the guts to stand up and be a man on my own.

Life | Chapter 10

Within a month of getting out of the first hospital, the mood stabilizer, Lithium, was taking effect and my one and only depression had lifted. Some of the side effects were very severe: there were tremors, weight gain and blurred vision. I had serious problems with acne around the base of my neck, but I had Retin-A to offset the boils. My step-dad had fixed my finances and I was looking for work. My family and I were in agreement on the seriousness of my disease. We examined the reality of my disorder and we all knew how lucky I was to bounce out of it. With this self-knowledge, everyone was sure I would follow my treatment regime. The first mandate was to take my Lithium. The second mandate was to remain clean and sober. I am sure there was a third, fourth, and fifth mandate but it didn't matter because I could not adhere to the second mandate, I could not remain sober.

Within weeks of being discharged from the hospital, I was using marijuana again. Almost instantly, addictions seemed to overpower my survival instincts. I saw no real way to deal with my new reality without the dulling smoke screen of narcotics. I was lost and hurt and the drugs allowed me to not deal with the fact that I had an active mental illness. In twelve-step programs, a follower is asked in the second step to find a power greater than themselves to restore them to sanity. Much later in life I would be able to do that, but not in 1995.

The power greater than yourself allows you to tap into a strength beyond yourself to try a new way of living "a priori," without prior knowledge of it. It allows you to take the revolutionary steps needed for changing the absolute paradigm of your life. As you create this new life, you take new actions and from these experiences you create new reinforcing beliefs. But I was still stuck in the old way of trying to fix a sick mind with a sick mind—just as my father had. And like Einar, I was doomed to repeat my mistakes until they either killed me or I was locked in a hospital forever.

My family knew I was supposed to be clean and sober and kept a keen watch on me. I never left home without Visine and tried to come home as late as I could. I decided after working a couple of security guard jobs that I would try to go back to school. Because I had not adhered to the recovery plan of my doctors, I started to chase outside things to validate that I was either not "that" bipolar or at least the exception to the rule.

I was lying to my entire family, all my doctors, and myself. I couldn't change my life because of the fear of letting go of an old, battered self-image that had been burned into my psyche since my father's illness began to terrorize my family. I was terrified to cut out my friends and stop using and abusing drugs. I was twenty-five. I had served in a war zone and been half way around the world and I felt as lost as I did in high school. Since I gained my identity from the outside, I allowed you, society, anybody to tell me who I was. This was a part of my identity crisis prior to the first hospitalization, but after my release my self-stigma was blinding. I could not see me at all. I was nothing more than the reflection of my assumed whims of the world.

W.E.B. Du Bois wrote a book called *The Souls of Black Folk* in the 19th century. Du Bois explored the identity crisis of the recently released slaves in post-Civil War America. He introduced into the cultural lexicon the phrases "double consciousness" and the "veil." With double consciousness, Du Bois showed how slaves were so spiritually bankrupted by their captors that on release they looked to their hateful masters to define them. Since their identity had been stolen and beaten out of them, the slaves allowed themselves to be defined by what the slave-owners thought of them. They imbibed the negative qualities that their captors projected on them and accepted these external damnations as internal truths.

This veil then stood between the slave and world and prevented any authentic projection of identity. The veil also stood between the slave and him/herself, blinding the individual to any true self-knowledge and worth. It was Du Bois' hope that slaves would be able to see above the veil and exist in the possibility of a world without veils.

The Souls of Black Folk is the first work I read that got close to describing my loss of identity due to my childhood trauma and exacerbated by my release and re-release from mental hospitals. Before the first hospital, I was a disabled veteran with a high aptitude who was merely having some problems. Prior to losing my step-daughter and having my first manic episode, those problems were mundane at best. I had no reason to contemplate who I was or where my life was headed. I wasn't striving to reach my full potential or to contribute to the world, but I didn't feel hopeless, either. I could remain half asleep and live a half-life and that was fine. Despite what Socrates said, there is something to be said for a life not examined.

However, once I had been out of the hospital for a while, the idea of being someone diagnosed with a mental illness forever started sinking in. The reality of not using alcohol or drugs for the rest of my life started to hit me. I looked at my friends from my central New Jersey suburb and they were beginning their lives. They were twenty-five or twenty-six and had all graduated from college. They were getting married and starting careers. They were not trying to come back from a medical discharge from the Navy, a failed marriage, or a stint in a mental hospital. They were not trying to stop the momentum of a life out of control. I had been diagnosed with bipolar disorder and I didn't even really know what that meant. What I did know, though, was that I was not like my friends—I was the quintessential "other."

I felt like I was 1,000 yards behind the starting line of Life and the race had started five years earlier.

Like the slaves discussed by Du Bois, I was so devoid of essence and self-identity, I looked at you when I was trying to see me. I found myself trying to do things that I thought YOU would accept or value. Afraid of what I believed the world thought of those diagnosed with mental illness, I needed to find some way to externally display my intrinsic worth. I wanted someone—anyone—to tell me who to be, because the me I had become was unacceptable.

The biggest stigma against mental illness came from my own biases. My only role models in my battle were my father and the other patients in the hospital with me. My father was the focus and manifestation of all my nightmares and the other patients were, to say the least, not at the top of their games when I observed them in the hospital setting. During my first hospital stay, for instance, there was one patient who walked up and down the hall taking exaggerated crisscrossing steps and waving his arms side to side. "I'm bipolar," he'd sing while swaying his arms in one direction. "Sometimes you love me," he'd take a long stride toward the opposite wall, his arms swaying the other direction, and, with jazz hands for a little lunatic flare, "sometimes you hate me." Over and over again, he marched down a closed hallway dancing and singing.

What I find unique to the experience of people with mental illness, my population, is the thickness of the veil. While we have a lot in common with other populations that suffer from the extreme malady of loss of self, there is a third dynamic unique to my population. We have a tripartite, a three part, dissociation from self.

Everyone has moments where they wonder about who they are. Examining the schism between their subjective, evolving identity-consciousness and that indestructible, timeless, changeless being sitting behind their eyes observing their life. They look at things they have done and question how they could have done such things or have a crazy thought and wonder who just had that thought. Am I me or am I who you think I am, and how great is the distance between the two? Am I the feel*ing* or the feel*er*?

A person with severe mental illness also asks a third question: *Am I the person who gets sick: manic, delusional, psychotically depressed, etc.?* In my case, it was this third person who took over my mind and almost destroyed my life.

Like Dr. Jekyll and Mr. Hyde, I turned into a completely unknown entity, a stranger that I had never met before.

Who is this third person? What part of me is the sickness? Who am I when the disease takes over my mind and drowns my being? When will he/it come back? What will I do? What will I lose? Who will I hurt? What wreckage will Mr. Hyde leave for me when I wake up in another nightmare as Dr. Jekyll in another mental institution?

Since I had no real identity to attach myself to, I was not active in the defense of myself. I would not fight to stay sober or compliant to my medications. I would not fight to save myself. Political theorist and philosopher, Hannah Arendt, talked about the "banality of evil" experienced by German soldiers when they killed their prisoners; the banality built into the system of extermination so one soldier escorted prisoners into the execution chamber while another delivered the deadly gas canister. In this way, the guard that delivered the lethal gas never had to meet or acknowledge the humanity of those he killed. He was simply dropping a canister in a chute, not killing innocent people.

In my life, this "banality of evil" meant that I could deliver the lethal "gas" to myself because I never got to meet or know the manic me, Mr. Hyde. My self was ruptured. I would forever remain an "other" to my known experience.

Since I was lost to my authentic self, I had no problem taking deadly actions against myself. I knew the right thing to do, but had no real connection to the organism fighting for its life, my life. In my oblivious state I became an enemy to

45

myself even without being manic. Until I could eventually stand and stare back into the abyss of my life and accept myself in the totality of my experiences, I was not going to be able to fight my addictions and face my acute mental illness.

This state of dissociation increased my ability to accept greater and greater levels of degradation. I was growing accustomed to failure and shame. I believed I had an unlimited tolerance for self-suffering. I felt like I had died at twelve years old and had simply endured a dead existence since then. The psychic breaks between reality and my "self" that followed allowed a self-flagellation that was potentially lethal. As I tried to make my way in the world after my first hospitalization, I was not afraid of failure. I was used to it.

To live this deadened existence required a lot of lying and hyperbole. No one wants to read a story with an unlikeable, pathetic failure as the main character. So, I created a new main character, a "me" who was a hero, a "me" who was the focus of my grandiose self-promotion. To others.

It is common for residents in the day programs and mental hospitals I visit to have grandiose dreams for life after release, but rarely do they understand the pragmatic steps needed to accomplish their goals. It is not that I think they cannot accomplish great things. I believe they can all do whatever they desire. The point is that although they're telling me about the record contracts and billion dollar businesses in their futures, they never mention writing the songs, playing the instruments, getting the studio time, working long hours to build their business, how they'll land their first contract…. They're doing the same thing I did. They're creating wonderful dreams and living in their fantasies in order to offset the horror of their realities. I could not accept the reality of my life, but had no problem accepting the unreality of becoming an international finance lawyer or famous entertainer. Living immersed in the fiction of a life that would redeem me and make up for all my sins was easy. Facing reality was not—so I didn't.

Instead, I would picture meeting my step-daughter again and paying for her college. Because I would be so rich and successful in my fairytales, I could easily fix relationships from the past and discharge the shame and guilt that was suffocating me. The lying and hyperbole were as powerful as the drugs and alcohol; they allowed me to escape from a life I never imagined and could not imagine changing.

I believed higher education was a place where I could go back and fix some of the mistakes from my past. I was older than that incarnation of Eric Arauz who first went to community college. I was wiser and I was a veteran. So I began attending community college after the first hospital discharge and worked toward an Associate Degree in Psychology after which I planned to transfer to a four-year university.

Like many students in the Social Sciences, I was more concerned about learning about myself than the actual course work. My plan was to finish the school year and apply to the New York University, Applied Psychology Program. I wanted to work in the field. My experience with the men at the barracks I managed at the end of my enlistment, my father, and now my own experiences compelled me to help others. I was drawn to the NYU program because it would allow me to work in Manhattan at places like battered women's and homeless shelters. Attuned to the suffering of others, I used to see the eyes of my father in the frightened and homeless faces on the streets of New York. Now, I saw my own.

If you met me at that time in my life, you would have seen a man who looked like he had the world under control. I was working as a waiter, doing well in school, getting over my first hospital stay, and preparing my application for NYU. From the outside, I looked like I was thriving, but the reality was that I was doing a lot of things that looked good, but I was not invested in any of them.

I still had my friends. It seems that men, as brothers, don't break up. Buddies can ride out anything. I had friends who were girls but few girlfriends. Romantic relationships never lasted long because I put too many demands on my girlfriends. I needed them to complete me, heal me. I needed to open myself up to them, but I didn't know how. The pain and isolation from my past was too great for me to overcome and was too much of a burden for a girlfriend.

To get through the day, I had to lie to myself, and, therefore, I had to lie to everyone around me. No one could know the whole me, the whole problem. My stability—my success—was founded on hiding the deepest part of myself. I had no authentic relationships. People had nine different stories about me from my own mouth. I was unable to fully engage with society after life with Einar. The only time I had honestly tried again was with my step-daughter. I gave her everything, all of me. I loved her and told her all my secrets and horrors while she played with her blocks. She loved and accepted me. Then that blew up and after I got out of the hospital, I was in a level of denial where I didn't even know where I was hiding anymore. I felt like I lived in an elevator with no buttons except 'B' for basement, that just keep heading down into deeper, darker night-mares of existence. The doors opened long enough to spit me out into a new level of hell, and then I'd climb back in and press 'B' again.

Although the people I met in my job at the restaurant were wonderful, my life there seemed fake, surreal. I was looking at the world through a mask and the world was looking back at someone they thought was me, but who, in truth, had no real identity. Beyond that, the masks I wore for the world were multiplying, and then, even worse, I started to wear masks internally. I was moving farther and farther from my own identity. The inner masks were thick to protect me from me. They were welded on by decades of shame and bolted down by despair. I didn't even know they were there.

I did tell my co-workers about my illness, my divorce, and even my surgically repaired toes, but nothing drove them away. They were empathetic, it was OK—I was OK. Today, I look at restaurants and bookstores as spiritual weigh stations. You meet some of the best people in them, especially in college towns and in neighborhoods around universities. At any moment, you can walk in on a discussion about the commonalities between Jasper and Kierkegaard, new breakthroughs in String Theory, Rilke's poems, or how to get a pound of weed into a dorm. They are places of optimism and hope, excitement and dreams. It was at this restaurant that I met my friend Fu and the other members of my kind cannabis clan.

Life | Chapter 11

Fu was a fellow waiter/cannabis genius. He was tall and lanky with deep black hair and dark eyes with a great, full laugh. He possessed a general disdain for authority at a governmental level and especially at the restaurant level—i.e., our managers. Most of the staff were trying to get to the next step in their lives. The majority of them were undergrads at Rutgers University with most of them looking to grad school. We had potential teachers, politicians, lawyers, doctors, and scientists working the lunch and dinner shifts at the local chain restaurant where Route 18 met Route 1.

Everyone got along well enough, most partied together, and we smoked weed as a congregation. I gravitated to Fu and trusted him. He had the sense of self I valued so much in others. He was an Ivy League drop-out disenchanted with the overall game. He had stepped on the over-hyped grounds of his Manhattan campus, knew it wasn't for him, and had walked away. He was dating a kind and gentle woman who was finishing her degree at the Rutgers Agricultural School, Cook College. We all hung in a pack. Me, Fu, E, Kwan and others on the streets of Hub City—New Brunswick, NJ. I would ride in after work, get high, and hang with my team.

Fu knew my history and my dreams and he always listened when I spoke. He never treated me as if I was an outcast, and for that I am forever grateful. He, and the others, were supportive when I submitted my application to NYU. The days at the job and the nights in New Brunswick continued to be enjoyable and I had a few months of stability. But the cracks in my psychological facade were already starting to show.

I had been out of the hospital for almost a year and the only thing I was doing in accordance to my treatment plan was taking my Lithium. I was not one hundred percent compliant, but I took it here and there. I was also running a lot. The operations on my toes had been successful enough initially and I was running five miles every other day, stoned or not. I would run the neighborhood around my parent's house. I loved the freedom. The feeling of my heart racing and my body flying through the streets was the perfect antidote for my life in restraints. I could not clear my mind or my soul but I could get my heart pumping.

Even though I was studying, working, and running regularly, I could not function without being high. My drug use was constant, perpetual. It was not a matter of trying to chase a feeling or add some energy to my everyday situations, it was a defense mechanism—a windshield, a self-imposed veil. I could sense my life fraying around the edges and the drugs gave me distance from the world around me—and from myself. The way my excessive weight did in my early teens. Once my acceptance into NYU was guaranteed, my friends and family believed I was finally moving ahead. But the truth was I could not move forward. Change meant Unknown. Unknown meant Fear. Fear meant Drugs. Drugs meant Numb. Numb meant Dead.

Most days I would show up to work an hour early to make sure I could smoke a joint in the parking lot facing the car wash. I didn't just take a couple of hits and walk in; I banged the whole joint to my head, dropped a little Visine in my eyes, and into work I went.

The restaurant had this thing called a "Crunch Lunch." I think you had fifteen or thirty minutes to get the meal to the table from when the customer ordered it. They even had stop watches on the table. If the restaurant was busy, I could function fine. I could get lost in the flow and in that mindless self-forgetting, I could go on autopilot. I was always comfortable in chaos. The problem with the Crunch Lunch is that at the end of the shift no one is there. Around 2:00-2:30 p.m. most lunches are done and the restaurant is dead waiting for the night shift.

One day when I had performed my pre-work ritual in the parking lot, something went wrong. The restaurant was slow and I only had one table. I took their lunch order, hit the stopwatch, and entered the order in the computer at the wait station. After that, I had a bit of time to kill. It was almost summer, and it was hot in the restaurant. So I went back into the freezer, did about fifty whippets, and sat down to clear my head. The massive amount of carbon dioxide inhaled from the whippets stormed my body. My limbs went numb; my heart was exploding beneath my ribs. Time seemed to stop as I teetered on the edge of blacking out.... I felt great.

After a while, I went back out on the floor, walked right back up to my one and only table, and asked to take their order. They lost it. They started screaming and yelling that they had ordered forty minutes ago. I could see they were not sure what to do. They were going to get their food free anyway, but they felt wronged. They wanted my penance.

At first they probably felt giddy watching the timer run past fifteen minutes. Then after another twenty-five minutes, they probably wanted to get up and go but were trapped by all that wasted time and the prospect of a new-found free meal. Then after a few more minutes, they had gone over the edge into full-fledged rage. Finally, a large, bald, high, nicely chilled waiter walks up and offers to take the same order he took forty-five minutes ago. Nice.

Sorry man, look me up, lunch on me.

Life | Chapter 12

Sleep was impossible. Even with all the weed, I'd spend hours in bed before I would fall asleep. I never felt rested. The spring semester was over at my community college and my daily schedule was empty except for work at the restaurant. I was biding my time, waiting until I started NYU in the fall. But without sleep, time seemed to stretch out before me. My mind was not racing—yet. Just restless. Bothered. The delusions had not shown up, but the first sign had appeared. I couldn't sleep. I wasn't seeing a therapist anymore. Even if I had been, I hadn't been honest with them or with my psychiatrist in a long time. No one knew I was getting high every day except my fellow partakers. My second manic episode was upon me. Once it even gets a little taste of my essence, there is no shutting it down until it locks me away.

With a year free from its grip, the disease took its time and no one recognized my symptoms for several weeks. But once the full onset of mania set in, it was exponentially worse than the first episode. Because I was smoking pot more regularly than I was taking my meds, I was not met with the same level of compassion I received after the first hospitalization. No one could believe I was engaging in such reckless behavior, and eventually my family was told that I was beyond treatment. In fact, they were advised to seek counseling for dealing with a long-term institutionalized family member. It appeared that another Arauz man would meet his demise at the hands of his disease.

Never underestimate the power of denial. I had all the knowledge in the world about bipolar disorder. I read *Mood Swing* by Dr. Fieve, Dr. Kaye Jamison's books about the disorder, Patty Duke's biography and others. I knew why I needed my medication and why I needed to see my therapists. I was crystal clear on the danger of alcohol and drugs with my disease. The problem was that I could not accept my co-occurring bipolar disorder and alcoholism/drug addiction. I couldn't accept what admitting my problems meant for my life. Until I had the strength and help to look completely at my past and accept it in totality, I would not—could not—build a future.

Most people are not prepared to face a future without hope. In 1996, I was not prepared to face a future *with* hope. Instead of doing all I could to conquer my disease, I followed my manic Faustian journey to the bitter end. In order to truly accept what I needed to do to heal my life, I needed to experience all the hells life had to offer a very sick man. So when the flaming elevator doors opened again and Mephistopheles held out his dead hand, I took it. I would follow his merciless lead as we danced the dance of madness on the locked wards of a Veteran's Administration Psychiatric Hospital.

The end began the night before I was scheduled to register for NYU in late spring/early summer of '96. Before I made my nightly jaunt in to see my friends in New Brunswick, I snorted a lot of cocaine. If you have bipolar 1 disorder, doing coke is never a good idea. In fact, it is a lethally bad idea. If you then head into New York City the next morning on zero sleep, you risk never returning.

After snorting the lines of coke, I took off to see my restaurant clan. Everyone was happy for me; they knew how important NYU was to me. We finished the evening laughing and having fun in a neighborhood bar.

As I drove home, wide awake, I began to feel as if I was fulfilling my destiny. For a moment a feeling swept over me that I had been on the planet for ten thousand years and my enrollment at NYU would be the culmination of all things ever desired in all my lifetimes. As quick as the thought came, it left and I finished the ride back to East Brunswick and slithered into my parents' house.

In 1996 my parents' house was full: both sisters, my grandma, my mom, and Bud and I were all living there. It was late and since I couldn't sleep, I stayed up and watched Charlie Rose on PBS. There were a few weird moments during that night. Occasionally, while I was watching TV, I felt as if the person on the TV was talking to me. They never said my name or gave me specific instructions but there seemed to be an inference between us, an acknowledgement. A look to the left by the TV personality and I looked that direction. A discussion on the safety of our country and I knew they were letting me know my services would be needed by Uncle Sam. Any discussion about the future and its coming intellectual, technological, or medical breakthroughs and I knew they were signaling that I was ready … that they would soon pick me up and set me on my course to change the world. The onset of hypomania was creating a fantasy world of self-deception. My low self-esteem and tripartite identity loss were being replaced by a cosmic narcissism; I was going from zero to Zeus.

Of course, I had no idea any of this was happening. My mania has no self-reflection, thought equals reality. I showered before the others awoke and headed to Manhattan to start on the path to my destiny.

In the progression of my disorder, the transition from private fantasy to public fantasy is a grave marker. I could think whatever I wanted and believe I was the center of all things, but a walk back into the sunlight and, again, reality would take hold. Even in my most manic phases, where I have truly believed I am the Divine and all powerful presence in the Universe, I would never open my mouth and reveal to others the truth of my thoughts.

As I made my way up the NJ Turnpike by commuter bus, I could not shake the feeling I had the previous night. I still felt I was going to NYU that day to transgress the chains of my existence, to meet with the ones who knew my truth, who recognized my grandeur. I looked out the passenger side windows of the bus and stared into the morning sun as it leaked out from behind the Twin Towers. I had made it; my suffering had purpose. The thought crossed my mind that "the boy who loved too much" was coming home to the compassionate arms of his national family. My life's story had come together to create a delusion large enough to heal my wounded spirit. I needed the solace of nationwide acceptance for the oblivion I had sunk into since the hospital. I was so, so sorry for hurting everyone and letting everyone down. I thought about my step-daughter and the familiar regret and sorrow washed over and through me. But, at that moment, I knew everything would be OK. I knew the solution to my troubles—I would sacrifice myself for the greater good of my step-daughter, my family, my country, the world. Tears ran down my face as my spirit was overwhelmed with the joy of knowing my true purpose was about to be fulfilled.

I would disappear into the various covert think tanks the US has buried throughout the country. I would let them absorb my genius. The CIA would create a story for my parents and I could repent for my failings by saving the country. The fullness of the delusion sank in as the bus made its way past Exit 13A and Port Newark. I was free now. It was finally over. I sat back in my seat and gazed out at the state I loved.

The warmth of the sun lovingly caressed me through the window. I would miss my mom and sisters, but I had to go, had to leave, had to fulfill my destiny. I actually closed my eyes and slept for the final forty-five minutes of the trip into the city. When I awoke I knew I would be one step closer to my calling. The plan was set: I would grab a cab from the Port Authority to Washington Square Park and there I would find my guides. Like many with mental illness who gravitate to the city, I was heading into the cauldron of Manhattan with its myriad of untold promises—and dangers.

Life | Chapter 13

The diesel air woke me to the city as I made my way from the bus station out to the street. My delusions had crossed the threshold of night into day, and the city was my psychotic paradise. I surrendered myself to the many signs being thrown my direction. A cop at a crosswalk blows his whistle and points for the cars to turn right and immediately I turn right, too. A woman, three people in front of me at a crosswalk, looks abruptly over her shoulder, and I know to now hail my cab. I was immersed in a one-player video game in the biggest city in the world. It is a miracle I stayed focused enough to make my way downtown to NYU. As my cab pulled up at Washington Square Park, I opened the door and stepped back into the game.

The park smelled of street hot dogs and reefer. Perfect. I have no memory of paying attention to my watch, but I know I made it to my registration appointment on time. The city is absolutely the best place to have a manic episode while your delusions are still romantic. No one says a word to you on the seething streets and the stimuli are infinite: one dream layered on top of the next, like hitting restart on a video game that will not end until you are dead or placed in Bellevue Psychiatric Hospital. I often wonder how many delusional astronauts, mystics, wizards, czars, and angels found their wings clipped when they were slapped back into reality in that hospital.

When I came into the Psych Department at NYU I was greeted by other incoming students and a couple of PhD students who were there to orient us on the campus and help us register. I was also greeted by the bulletin boards and office doorways that were stapled, taped, and hung to bursting with overlapping layers of brochures and flyers advertising travel abroad programs, Peace Corps opportunities, internships, jobs, apartments to share, etc. It was awesome. It looked like the inside of Timothy Leary's mind. As the mentors explained the importance of following a strict academic curriculum because this was the professional school in the department, my mind was busy soaking in the room.

Tibetan research into energy healing, Shakespeare's Hamlet and the use of self-revealing soliloquy as the precursor to Freud's psychoanalysis, Reiki and Trauma, the psychology of God and Nietzsche's Zarathustra, studies into the mind of Mushin in ancient samurai ... the options for exploration painted the room and I did not take in a word my mentor said. I was living in the connective tissues of the brain that could simultaneously process all these various topics and synthesize them. The world and its possibilities exploded in my malfunctioning psyche and pushed it further in its grandiose spin.

I realized I was destined to be the hub for all domestic spiritual and mystical progress, my mind would encompass the world: A living Buddha, a Christ-figure, Gandhi with bad feet and a much bigger sheet.

Members of the entering class were introducing themselves. I introduced myself: community college, Navy, disabled veteran, but I did not mention my illness or my destiny as the Global Czar of Interdisciplinary Mysticism. For the first time in a long time, sitting there surrounded by my future classmates and NYU grad students, I felt no shame at being a community college kid because that past was completely offset by the narcissistic delusions of the triumphant future that awaited me.

As I waited for my individual advisement appointment, my delusions bloomed. Finally, they called me in and shut the door. My advisor had my transcripts in front of her and a sheet showing the various classes I would need to complete the degree. She settled into her seat and offered me a drink.

"Eric, you have a little over thirty credits that will transfer into the program. You need sixty to actually begin the field studies, so let's figure out what you need to get going."

She had certain pages creased and others had paperclips in them. She was about my age, mid-twenties and very stylish in that confident city way. It was hot outside and she was in a cream sun dress with yellow trim. This put me in a bad situation. My episodes have a strong component of hyper-sexuality. I believe that I and I alone have the erotic answers for the unspoken desires of the female universe. I observe women very closely and drink in their presence.

Because of the delusions of erotic grandeur, I approach women with the confidence of the gods of Olympus coming to Earth to take a bride. When I find the object of my yearnings, I believe I can make love to her without even touching her. Each word is an attempt to find the soul of the woman and I see her without any restraint. Her makeup, earrings, shoes and jewelry expose her to me and I love her for her choices. I care only about her interests as she sings to my heart with each breath she exhales.

I devour her.

When I finally touch the warmth and moisture of her skin, it sends me ten thousand years back to my first intermingling with the feminine sex. As I psychically explore her, I see all the couplings in my bloodline that ever led me to this place. I am the primordial man mating with his partner for the first time, I am the Roman General returning to his bride after a decade of war with Carthage, the Viking warrior-king and his queen on the night before a journey across the unknown North Atlantic seas. She is the totality of my consciousness, a miracle beneath me. In a universe of boundless possibility, she is enough, she is everything.

She is all.

We have been linked body and soul always and with each movement, sound and sight, the erotic delusions flush through my veins. Mental disease has gone from mind to heart to groin. Serotonin glazes my brain as the universal orgasm approaches and I stop to simply watch the most beautiful of all sites: the female form writhing in ecstasy. Tethered by lip and loin, I have never been as deeply connected with another as I thrust into the oneness, pushing ever deeper, passionately grinding in eternal unity … a cosmic carnal communion … see me … feel me … find me … save me … this is the Soulfuck … she loves me … they all love me … I will Soulfuck them all.

Like a manic Ziggy Stardust, lover and leper messiah, I sucked her into my reeling mind and made love with a diseased and crippled ego.

I snapped back to reality as she continued talking. She was now standing with the window behind her. The backlight of the sun illuminated her figure in her sundress. Naked and vulnerable, she stood before a ravenous animal that had just spent five minutes living in our potential spiritual and physical union, engulfing her body and soul.

I couldn't tell if she wanted me to say something or not when I looked at the book she was working on. It had the list of classes for the whole school and was now mistakenly open to the page about Witchcraft. Although she had actually been working for the last fifteen minutes on the exact classes I would need to take next year, I had no memory of anything she'd said. I only had a few simple questions about my new curriculum.

Each question would be centered on Witchcraft.

I picked up the book and looked at the list of classes she had put together for me to meet the requirements to begin the Applied Psych Program. They were all fine classes, mostly perfunctory Psych, English and whatever else was needed to accrue the required credits. Of course, this would not do for someone as illuminated as myself, so I tried to offer my own ideas.

I asked about Basic Witchcraft first ... just dipping my toes in the water.

She answered that it could be one of my electives. No real animus there. Seemed to roll with punches, nice.

Next question.

I asked, "If I am going to be looking into witchcraft, there seem to be a few classes in White Witchcraft, maybe I could take a few classes in this, maybe a minor?"

She fielded that question acceptably. A little annoyance, but I didn't write the course book, the classes were offered.

She was trying to focus me on the list of classes I needed for the next year and get to the next student when I decided to make my final thrust into a Witchcraft-based psychological curriculum.

Next question.

"So, with the basic Witchcraft course and now the White Witchcraft courses, shouldn't I take some Black Witchcraft courses to make sure I am well-rounded? Not just all White Witchcraft, but some Dark too. Seems bad form to focus too much on one type of sorcery."

Now the amusement left her face and she told me that I could do whatever I wanted. Just register for the classes she picked out. She looked agitated and perplexed.

Perfect.

Final question.

"In your opinion, what would you recommend for conjuring? I'm looking seriously at improving these abilities and NYU seems to have a lot of options."

Fin.

My advising session was officially over. She escorted me out of the office and called in the next student. There were only two more after me. I waited in the department for twenty minutes when the class was told we were going to lunch. We were making our way to the exit when I saw a pamphlet for Eli Siegel, the founder of Aesthetic Realism. It had many of his writings and quotes. I grabbed one and looked at it as we walked outside. The group was herded behind the advisors and walking through the Washington Square Park. Looking at the bottom of the page of my new pamphlet, I noticed a quote by Siegel; something to the effect of how he yearned for the confusion in his grandmother's eyes.

I thought that was awesome.

With my mind fully enveloped by my delusions, it is easy to be sidetracked. It is a type of quasi-mystical ADHD. I experienced all things as the source of all things. My attention span was only as long as the next divine manifestation of "The Way" that crossed my path and Mr. Siegel was that next manifestation. The pamphlet had an address on it that I thought was close. Off to Eli's.

My career at NYU was over.

In four hours, I had gone from searcher to mystic to wizard to prophet for Eli Siegel. That's more than most get done in a couple degrees and I hadn't even had lunch yet.

I started my manic march to Eli Siegel's. I was hoping to talk with him to see if his quote meant what I thought it meant. It meant to me that he wanted the release from his positivistic notions of the world, a de-centering of identity and an embrace of the ambiguity his grandmother recognized in existence. To receive. To abide to the mystery, the unknowns of all existence. I was hashing it over as I got to his address somewhere in the Village. There was a table on the sidewalk with a bunch of his works and different resources surrounding the Aesthetic Realism movement.

I was having a hard time concentrating. Except for my 45 minute nap on the bus, I had been awake for over forty hours and the mania was speeding up my thinking. Thoughts were crashing into each other. I wanted to talk to this guy—NOW! I walked to the front door of the foundation, a very nice brownstone, and turned the knob. Locked. I knocked a few times, soft at first and then more loudly. Nothing. The door had a mail slot and I peered inside. I saw someone sitting at a desk writing. I wondered why they would not answer, so I screamed inside asking for Eli Siegel. They didn't look at me; no acknowledgement at all. I yelled again, but nothing. I walked away confused, but then instantly the whole experience was gone from my mind and I was on to the next thing. I didn't find out until twelve years later that Eli Siegel committed suicide in 1978.

In the early stages of my mania nothing makes me mad. I am the "flow" and each thing "is." Only in the last stages when the paranoia sets in do I get angry because I am terrified and feel trapped. At this early stage, I was still feeling magnanimous. With me, the romantic stage, the delicious stage—hypomania—

does not last long. My mania is so complete and extreme that within days of onset I have to be hospitalized and it takes months to stabilize.

My mania operates the same way the space shuttle does: start with some very quick enjoyable rocket bursts that separate you from the gravitational pull of the Earth's atmosphere, release some dead weight, keep burning and then it's off into space, the final frontier from which no one is returning for a while. I am the unconscious, delusional passenger on the Space Shuttle Eric and all I can do is pray for a safe landing. There are no guarantees and I have never met the pilot.

Life | Chapter 14

Ileft New York and headed back home. It was Friday and my big sister and I had plans to go down the shore the next morning. I don't know if those plans overpowered my delusions or not, but I made it back to my house in Jersey for dinner. When I got back to East Brunswick and walked in the front door, I acted like the day was benign, like I hadn't transcended the barriers of all known human experience and graduated from a four-year university in under forty-five minutes. We all sat down to dinner, and I tried to stay in control. My breathing was being affected by the elevation of my mood, and all I wanted to do was stand on the table and scream at the top of my lungs while passing the salad to my sister.

My grandma sat across from me while Bud grabbed his utensils, salted his food, and headed for his favorite spot watching the news of the day in front of the TV. Grandma peppered me with questions about my trip. More about the city than the school. She had been a dancer in the 1940's and had many memories of Manhattan. Grandma was reaching that age where every conversation was about yesterday. Her todays had become an endless stream of the same thing and she told stories of the good old days, of what was. She was winking and laughing, proud of my success in school. Proud of me no matter what.

When I left for Desert Shield in the Navy, Grandma was beaming and told me all about my military lineage. I wondered if my forebears were slackers like me or real military men. I was a mediocre sailor in the Navy but I was great at the interpersonal part. I would have been a great Viking. I had an advanced job but mingled with every rank. I was a big, weightlifting, heavy drinking, funny lummox who happened to be an Electronics Technician who specialized in fleet-based satellites. Others may have seen me as unique or even interesting; I saw a fraud. I always wondered when I would be exposed. Everybody seemed to be on autopilot while I struggled just to stay on the road. Grandma always alleviated those fears. She had faith in me. Always. *Always.*

A few hours after dinner that evening, I lay on the couch and started to get a little sad and fearful about having to leave everybody. My delicious hypomania, the beginning less extreme form of mania, was turning on me as paranoia set in. The paranoia is always centered on the same organizations: FBI, CIA and NSA. Their clandestine nature captures my manic mind and they become my nemesis. That night, as I was watching the TV, the messages began. There was a security expert on PBS talking with Charlie Rose about a post-Gulf War America. I could feel his eyes looking right at me through the TV screen. I had barely slept in fifty hours and was coming apart at the seams. As I was starting to lose my breath, my grandma popped around the corner and put her hand on my forehead. She rubbed my head for a few minutes and then just stared into my eyes. Grandma Joanie smiled and nodded like we were perpetually in agreement about something. I loved the fullness of her touch. She would leave her hand on my forehead for minutes at a time, let me get used to the connection. My delusions and loss of identity were putting me beyond human reach, but she eased the descent. Her hand was one small respite in my spiral into madness. Her touch kept me out of hell for just a little longer.

There is so much power in touch. It contains the ability to break through most mental constructs. Therapeutic and healing touch assures you of your humanity in a way your mind cannot. "I think therefore I am," means nothing to a person who is manic and who has lost control of their mind and consciousness. Talking directly to me when I am trapped in myself, in my madness, does not work. You cannot usurp my manic shield. But, "I feel your touch, therefore I am not alone"—that is something I can use.

Grandma's touch slowed me down but the disease was not satisfied. It had expanded to saturate everything. The TV was now the portal for my delusions to wash over me. Wave after wave of psychosis. As I watched the security expert talk, I was not listening to him at all. I was only paying attention to the soundtrack of my own thoughts. Every once in a while he would break through my audio blockade and whatever I heard had personal and immediate relevance to me.

I was clear on my mission. The metamorphosis was complete. I knew I had to leave the house to save my family, and that the "authorities" would contact me through the radio and road signs while I drove. I heard him end his interview by saying we must act now and the fate of the country depends on us—on ME. So I grabbed my keys and was off. I did not know where I was off to, but I knew it was time to go.

I knew no one close to me would be able to understand my transition to the world's controlling intellect, and I could see with sick yet compassionate eyes that I could not expect them to be able to see me that way. I had always heard that it was harder for Jesus to convince his family he was the Christ than for him to convince total strangers. It would be the same for me in my religious grandiosity. Jesus and Eric Christ.

I took Route 18 south out of East Brunswick and headed down to Point Pleasant, a beach town on the Jersey Shore. I knew I would be there the next morning with my sister, but destiny was calling. The mission was upon me.

When I stepped into the early summer night, my mind was ripped open by the stars. The temperature was a perfect match to the inside of my parents' place. I would not be shocked into reality with a gust of wind or cold rain. It all seemed like a big reality show, like Jim Carrey's "Truman Show." I would observe myself through the perception of one thousand non-existent, psychotic cameras pouring my identity inward. Fictitiously filming my fall.

Life | Chapter 15

It was after midnight when I got in my car. Mine was one of the only cars heading southbound on Route 18. I started to look at the road signs for affirmation that I was going the proper direction. Like my trip from Memphis to Dallas the year before, the Ideas of Reference were adding meaning to everything I saw. As I drove I would add the numbers of the road signs and create my own code to show things were proceeding properly. After about 30 minutes, I made the turn onto Route 34 South, I took the 3 and 4 and saw the 7, lucky seven, all good.

The first thing you pass on that road after the turnoff is the Naval base, Naval Weapons Station Earle. Of course. My manic mind hinted that the Navy had orchestrated all this. That they had reviewed my military entrance exam, noted my scores, and realized my potential. My disease told me that the Navy encrypted the test with a series of highly analytical questions set up for the average person to get wrong but for the New Age Knower like me to get correct. My mind told me that they had seven or eight of these questions on each section. The questions would build, each forming a prescient mathematical framework for the next question; the question themselves revealing the burgeoning knowledge until the last series of experimental questions that were embedded in the mechanical section.

It was by using the answers that I provided in the mechanical section that the government's plans were realized for an intergalactic missile system and time travel. Through the breakthrough intelligence I unknowingly discovered in the embedded questions, the government was able to find answers to some of the universe's most complicated equations. Each potential recruit would get the same tests but those, like me, who showed the extraordinary capability to think outside of human experience would be labeled and controlled. We represented a higher intelligence, a more evolved species than the others. We were GODS. Since the potential test takers would be servicemen and women, they would eventually be the actual property of the government. Done and done.

This entire system of thought came to me in about two seconds as I drove the length of the naval base. I never questioned it for authenticity but, instead, accepted it absolutely as a universal truth.

I continued on toward Point Pleasant and lit an enormous joint to slow my enlightened flow. As I listened to the radio, I believed each song was programmed for me. Of course, all people relate to music and to lyrics in some way because music is written for humans by humans about the variants of the human condition. But that never entered my mind.

I reached Point Pleasant around one o'clock in the morning. At that time of night, a busy beach town is much more alive than the comfy confines of a central Jersey suburb. During a typical night in East Brunswick, I had two missions: get to a 7-11 for a Big Gulp and don't get another DWI. Down the shore, the world bustled and nobody noticed a blue-eyed Bedouin heading into town guided by the songs playing on the radio, songs programmed from the soundtrack of his psychosis.

The drive felt perfect, divine even, like I was riding a chariot pulled by unicorns. The road felt smooth under my tires and the smell of the sea air woke fond memories of sailing across the Atlantic, the Mediterranean and the Red Sea. I was free, free, free. The CIA programmed the Kansas song, "Carry on My Wayward Son" for my radio and I knew I was following the correct path. As the song played in my ears, I pictured the looks on my family's faces when the whole world recognized my majesty. My shame disappeared and I wept in the car as I imagined my family holding me, loving me, forgiving me.

The 70's rock band serenaded me with the chorus from the song, and I looked forward to the peace at the end of my epic journey when I could finally lay my head to rest and dry my tears once and for all.

Many people have a difficult time giving up their manic episodes. They know that they are killing them. They know the psychological damage could be drastic enough to bury them forever in forensic fantasy. But, they respond, it simply feels too good, or the episode gives them the self worth they never had. I've also heard some say their episodes create a world worth living in, a world in which the manic person is a superhero, and that they would rather risk their lives than receive treatment and go back to a world in which they are merely sick people with bipolar disorder.

Bipolar disorder is considered a spiritual and mystical disease by many. Anecdotally, the people I have talked to around the country, in and out of hospitals, experience some religiosity in their mania and almost all describe states of rapture more often associated with eastern traditions, with states of higher consciousness when people link with their God, the universe, Great Spirit or nature as one—Nirvana (Buddhism), Heaven (Judeo-Christian), Samadhi (Yogic schools-Hinduism, Sikhism), etc.

I don't deny the many facets of bipolar disorder and its altered states of awareness, but I look at the lure of mania from a different angle. My life was so out of focus by the second episode that I lived each day in constant pain and despair. Unlike the protagonist in the 19th century Russian novelist Fyodor Dostoevsky's, *Notes From the Underground*, there was no corner of my "St. Petersburg," my day-to-day world, to make the degradation static, to stop the suffering. Dostoevsky's character used his small Russian apartment to hide from the pain of his existence, to find shelter from his assumed hells. I suffered everywhere. I was burning alive from the skin inward and there was no way to escape the flames.

I was afraid I would work hard to build my life only to have to climb on that elevator and get dumped out deeper in the abyss, on another unknown floor. In my moments alone, I wondered how low the next fall would be. The release in my episodes was not into some super-enlightened life I desired but a freedom from the shackles of my shame-filled, lifelong solitary confinement.

I wanted so badly to be an asset to others, to help others alleviate their own suffering. But my disease and addictions were turning me into the exact opposite of what I wanted to be as a man. I stood as an antithesis to my desired self, fractured, with no real hope or belief in the possibility of redemption or resurrection.

There were very few moments after the first hospital stay when I was not thinking about how fucked my life was. I constantly compared myself to other people and I always came up short. I call it the reverse King Midas Touch. Everything King Midas touched turned to gold, while everything I touched turned to shit. I saw what you had or what I *thought* you had and desired it because you desired it. The problem was that once I acquired whatever it was—a girl, a car, a school, job, point-of-view etc.—it sucked and turned to crap because I had now sullied it. If it was mine, it was worthless.

Being afraid of looking at your life, your memories, your experiences—being afraid of living—is a horrible way to get through the day. I lived with the sins of my father and the sins of my own past and they were repeatedly branded onto my soul with each breath. I believed that if anyone knew the truth of my life, they would see how fucking horrible I truly was. Nothing of my essence could be exposed to the light. I was meant to live in darkness, even darkness to myself.

I had long-ago given up on God and trusted purely my limited and finite mind. He/She didn't help me on the altar and now I had only me. I knew in my heart I was meant to be deserted by both my biological and universal fathers, that even God hated me. I had no Virgil, no guide in my hell, no guide for my insular experience. I would descend alone into myself, my memories, my tortured existence and get lost as I was devastated on each new miserable level. It would be years before I would make any sense out of my life and even longer before I could return to the light of civilization to tell of my journey. I walked the earth frozen in the hell of myself.

Mania was a suicide. It murdered me. It ended me. It stopped the thoughts of the loss of my step-daughter and the pain I caused my family. It was intoxicating for the blackness of its void, its absoluteness. Mania worked for me in a way alcohol and drugs could not. Mania bought universal blackout where alcoholic blackouts were finite. As an active drinker, my last drink of choice was tequila. I drank as much as I could as fast as I could until I was gone. I have blacked out in Mexico, Spain, Italy, Israel and Egypt. But then I woke up.

My mania offered me a way to black out without waking up, to wipe away my past, and to soar ever higher into a future unlimited by the pain of my reality. That is why my life did not turn around until much later when I could look fully into my yesterday and begin to see it for what it was and what it was not. The journey from my second hospitalization to today started with the absolute acceptance I found from the people in a twelve-step program. They allowed me to look at my past through the prism of the program and with a therapist, concurrently. It was like a thousand loving hands held onto me while I leaned over and into the abyss to see—really see—what was true about my life.

That program and those people stopped the backwards pull, the suicidal *undertow*, from reality into a mania that absolved my prior sins. But that program and that therapist were still months in the future. I had a whole lifetime of pain to experience before I could wake up to myself, look into the abyss, and experience resurrection. I made it home from the Jersey shore that night, but it would be the last time I slept outside of a maximum-security psychiatric hospital for months.

It is said you need a death for there to be a resurrection and my demise was imminent.

Life | Chapter 16

I was still awake from my trek down to Point Pleasant when my big sister, Cecelia, got me out of bed the next morning. I was just lying there on top of the covers waiting for the next revelation. She told me we would be leaving in a few minutes. My big sis is very thorough. She had everything packed and ready to go the night before. As I got my bathing suit on and found my flip flops, I thought of how proud she would be when she found out I was the One; the One to solve the universal dilemma of dissociation. How I would bring love and acceptance to a world dying from the inside out. She would weep at the knowledge of my trueness and authenticity. Again the phrase "The boy that loved too much saves the world" swept through my core.

We got in her burgundy four-door car and headed south on the same roads I had haunted less than six hours earlier. I felt like a President-elect being chauffeured to his inauguration. This would be where I would be picked up by the NSA and taken for the good of the country, world, universe.

She talked to me about her week while The Grateful Dead twanged about "Sugar Magnolias" in the background. Cecelia is one of the kindest people I have ever met. She is an uncomplicated and truly considerate person. She ferociously defended me in my youth. I always knew how much Cecelia loved me as her little brother. That moniker never dissolves no matter how many war zones you fight in or tattoos you get. It was true that I was the global force of enlightenment, but I took solace in the beautiful moment of connection between baby brother and big sister. The Dead filled the car with magic and it dawned on me that I had so much already. I had so much. That realization shot through me like an arrow, but it was too late for any epiphany, no matter how powerful, to break the momentum of my fall.

As she neared Point Pleasant, she started to laugh. She has an unbelievable laugh that makes her cry. It becomes a vicious circle, the more she cries the harder she laughs. It is absolutely contagious. I joined in, but I felt miles behind my laughter.

Today, as I prepare to speak professionally, I am keenly aware of the distance between me and my 'mind,' my thoughts, my reactions, the structure of my conditioned biases. The Upanishads describe it as the self (mind), this shroud of identity, and Self (essence, changeless being, universal spirit), the 'You' that can observe your thoughts, the non-verbalized 'You'. I can see a criticism or judgment sit in front of my eyes and be aware not to act on it. It becomes clear that words are mirrors to existence. Tombstones to mark the reality, the *feel* of life.

The fight is internal, to transgress the bonds of self, ego, concentrated memory and known biases, to avoid an action I know is the simple continuation of yesterday. As Eckhart Tolle says, "I am the silent watcher." My thoughts pass by like a panorama and my mood and spirit can be measured by how detached I am from self-centered reactions to the world. To be aware of my triggers, to feel their effect on my physical body and emotions but not act on them. To see that physical feelings and psychological thoughts can be liars put in place by the trauma and hyperbole of yesterday.

But when I am experiencing mania, even the silent watcher is manic. My self and Self are both delusional. My *being* is symptomatic. As the disease progresses from an internal dialogue to an actual total belief system, it moves from the romantic phase celebrated by artists and musicians to the lethal phase. As my mania tries to fight its way into the real world, it is stymied by the fact that I am not Superman or the Archangel Gabriel. My mind panics at my physical limits and the paranoia seethes with this despair and horror.

We parked near the beach and started the ritual of unpacking the car with its chairs, blankets, cooler, books, radio (no umbrella, she loves the sun), suntan lotion and Diet Pepsi. Now ready, we headed to the booth to pay to get our daily beach pass. When we were half-way to the booth, I glanced to my left and saw two young men talking.

Awake for a few days, I tried to look more closely at these men to see if they were part of the retrieval team sent to get me. Would they find a way to approach me and escort me into the unmarked, black government van that was surely waiting nearby? From the van, to the helicopter, to the jet and finally to the covert compound that housed the others like me under the White House. If there were others like me....

While my mind cycled and my sister talked about how the waves looked good for some body surfing, I looked for a signal, anything. My synthesizing mind would make sure it fit into the dream—just give me something. On cue the shorter man with a long ponytail jumped and did a spinning helicopter kick. In the distance, he leapt straight-up in the air, straightened his striking leg, spun around completely, and landed.

Got it. I now knew the Secret Service, Navy Seals and others were peppered everywhere on the beach to protect me. It was real. I had made it. Passed every test. By the end of the day, I would be swept up by our government as a national treasure to be protected.

Life | Chapter 17

Cecelia and I headed down and across the hot sand to the water. I read every glance of this 40-yard march as an acknowledgment. In my mind, the beach was closed and all these people were here to observe me, to guard me, to adore me. My mind's eye poured over the beach and only saw itself. I pictured Route 34 closed so no one could get to the "Answer" beach. Elaborate lies were constructed for the media to hide my presence. They were not sure how to handle an intellect like mine, one that transgressed the bounds of human understanding. I was the generalist. No specialty. I could learn anything. Everything was in my grasp. I reached down to the quantum levels of human understanding and gave birth to a new era, an Existential Einstein. All the outward signs of my greatness were not needed. I needed no degrees, no business success, no authored books that garnered Pulitzer recognition. My infantile intellect was protected by this specialized and self-validated, psychotic hubris.

As the sun beat down on us, I watched my sister bob lazily up and down in the Jersey surf. I leapt powerfully into the Atlantic and felt my fingertips rip the ocean apart as the cold water rushed up my arms and swallowed my body. As I dove headfirst into my global baptism, I was aware at that moment, that my life would start anew. Fully submerged in my saltwater salvation and forgiven of every sin, the sheer weightlessness of the physical experience allowed my body to float free from restraint, like my mind.

Below the cover of the Atlantic Ocean, I sent my mental call to the world's ocean dwellers. I twisted and danced in the common waters of the continents. I saw the world as a large aquarium, one ocean. All things living in the water-drenched atmosphere. From the deepest depths of the darkest seas to the highest altitudes, there is moisture and it is only when there is absolutely none that no living thing can survive. We all live submerged. No animal, fish, mammal, or eagle exists outside of the sphere of the connecting waters. We are a congregation in permanent baptism.

I surfaced to a new world, a Garden of Eden without the tree or the guilt. I made my way up the beach and felt the eyes of the Earth upon me. People were smiling at their "Wayward Son," pleased I had found my way and was now prepared to lead them. Young children from gifted, covert programs throughout the US, watched me, adored me, believed me to be their role-model and their idol. For all my mental posturing about equanimity, I did not really want to be accepted as one of many. I suffered from the problem of feeling so subpar for so long, never feeling equal, that I only wanted to be recognized as better, higher, more advanced than others. At that one moment, with the sun and the fresh memory of my utopia six inches below the skin of the ocean's surface, I felt perfect bliss in my ascension.

We spent a few minutes on the beach towel and went to the boardwalk. We were not there for the day, only a few hours. We needed to play a couple games, get something to eat and maybe enjoy a ride and then head back home. While walking down the hot wood planks of the boardwalk, I was hyper-aware. I could clearly see who was protecting me from the "Dark Forces." They walked to my right and left; in front of us and behind us. They carried beach chairs and sunglasses and acted like they didn't know me. But I knew … it was all Team Arauz.

The shore has a lot of spinning wheel games. The wheel could have five potential things the dial can land on or one hundred. Depending on the number of variables offered on the wheel the potential prizes get better. Cecelia and I came upon a wheel with about four million different ways to lose your dollar. With such little chance of victory, the prizes were great: TV's, stereos, sport jerseys and other random shore based booty suitable for a manic pirate. I looked at the wheel and knew I would win. My disease was fully aware of the outside world and it didn't care. The wheel game would be its first external test against reality and chance.

I dropped my dollar on the tiniest of slivers on the game's board. The booth operator asked for any other bets and hit the button to fire the spinning arm around the face of the board. It spun and spun over the thin blue and white wedges labeled "Mom, Ace, Dad, Bob and others." My sister watched with detached amusement. No one wins and no one *ever* wins the big games. As the arm was spinning I just observed. I did not try to mentally control the arm; I just knew it would land on my dollar. As part of the universe's continuity, it had to.

My disease was breathing fresh air; it was interacting with reality and not backing down in the harsh midday sun. The spinning arm slowed and then stopped, and the operator yelled.

"We have a winner!"

I looked down at the board.

I won.

Of course I did.

Life | Chapter 18

Out of all the prizes in the booth, I immediately saw what I wanted: a two foot tall, green and yellow striped Mad Hatter hat like Dr. Seuss' on mescaline. Even the game booth guy tried to talk me into something else, but I wanted the hat. Cecelia, being as easygoing as she was, just grinned and we kept walking. My confidence in my majesty was growing. The sun, lack of sleep, lack of food and excessive heat were the perfect combination to push my mind to destruction. The cocaine from a few nights before had lit the fuse and my mind had totally exploded.

Without protection from the sun, my eyes were killing me. My sister fished out a pair of her slightly oversized, rounded, Jackie O sunglasses and handed them to me. I was now walking down the boardwalk shirtless, with these feminine, tiny (on my head) sunglasses and a two foot tall, green and yellow Mad Hatter hat. I wanted to go on a little roller coaster that went forward and then backwards. Everybody we passed was looking my way. The sunglasses allowed me to stare right into people's eyes. Every other person gave me a sign that the pickup was soon. If someone looked at their watch, I knew to be careful of time; if they glanced left or right, I knew to break that direction shortly. The game was still in full effect and, like in New York, I was the only one playing.

The ride was empty.

I got on with my sister, those tiny glasses, and that huge hat. We went forward for a few minutes and the ride stopped. I knew they were stopping for me because I wanted to go backwards. The world was responding to my thoughts. Slowly, the ride moved backwards and picked up speed. Even though I had gone over those same tracks ten seconds ago, going over them blindly changed the sensation. The new direction made the ride more about feel than sight. I threw my hands in the air and closed my eyes. The movement was entrancing. The ride's music filled my mind, the motion filled my soul. I was bursting with ass-first epiphanies as there was no division between me, the ride, and the music. I released. On the brink of a boardwalk-ride rapture, I flew through the air, crying. Universal emotion stormed my mind as the cosmic current electrocuted me.

This experience was not one of dissolution, of negation to my being. I did not become one with the universe; rather the ride, the music, the universe and everything around me was connected to me because it was all me, all relative to my experience. When I left the boardwalk, the shore, the entire place would cease to exist. No one and no thing had an independent existence. It was all contingent on me. The future of everything depended on my actions. I was the God Meister Eckhart spoke of in his 13th century, mystical Christian writings. I existed all around you, not contingent on you but waiting for the one second for you to look to me, acknowledge me. In that one moment, I would pour into you completely. I would become you, while you, as an independent entity, no longer existed. I breathed the air in and out of your lungs.

We got off the ride and made our way to the car, packed it up in minutes and left. The guard doing the helicopter kicks was gone, but his replacement seemed suitable. He was bigger, more heavily muscled, probably a ground fighter or machine gunner, maybe Army Delta Force. Either way was fine. Cecelia chatted the whole ride home while we listened to the other side of the Dead cassette. The window was open and the wind dried the salt on my skin. I could not sleep during the mission, but I closed my eyes knowing I was protected while in the care of my big sister. I knew the police in each town were alerted of my presence so I was sure we would be safe.

When we reached our house, Cecelia went inside to talk to Bud. She sounded concerned about something, but it didn't bother me. Her small worries could not affect me, so I continued upstairs to relax when a knock came on my door. Cecelia said Bud wanted to talk to me.

I wasn't worried as I made my way downstairs and through the kitchen into the family room. On the contrary; I was excited. My sisters and my brother-in-law were sitting in the kitchen as I passed through. I hardly noticed the seriousness of their gazes as I moved to the couch adjacent to my step-dad.

Bud was relaxed and he waited a few seconds to speak to me. Maybe he knew. Maybe the government let him in on the secret. After all, he was a Marine. He was steadfast. He could be trusted.

He picked up the remote, turned off the TV and told me that the family thought something was wrong with me. That I was exhibiting the signs of a manic episode again and they wanted to take me to the VA Hospital to get checked out. I had no problem with that. In fact, I embraced the idea. It made perfect sense. I would go to the VA where the government had full control. It was all part of the perfect cover for my entrance into the covert world of espionage. I left Bud and went upstairs to get changed. My journey was near completion. My mom was in Portland, Oregon on business, but I knew she would be proud when she returned home.

After changing into my traveling clothes, I came back downstairs to meet my sisters and brother-in-law. They would take me to the hospital for my coronation. We piled in the car and headed north from East Brunswick to Route 287. No one was talking to me in the car. It was dark and the evening added to the mystery of my homecoming. I pictured the ambulance that would secretly whisk me down the Jersey turnpike, over the Delaware Memorial Bridge, and onto Route 13 instead of Interstate 95, to avoid detection, and, finally, into D.C. I saw the teams of people brought together to investigate and probe my psyche. I could hear the admirals and generals briefing me on the various security threats around the world. I would be revered as the mental master, capable of reading minds, of bending others to my will. A psychic samurai. The Navy Seals and Delta Force would come to me to learn how to infiltrate the psyches of our enemies.

We passed a sign on Route 287 that should be removed just in case another manic driver ever passes that way. The sign is for "The Land of Make Believe." I have gone back several times to make sure that memory is true, and it is. In plain sight for the entire world to see, the sign shows where you can turn for a children's water park. I had probably driven by that sign a hundred times before that night, but never noticed it. Now as I saw it rush past the car, I drank it in. It was one more piece of evidence that the whole thing was real. The mission had gone live, this was not a practice drill.

The turn for the VA Hospital was coming up on the right side as we passed under Route 78, and I sank down into my passenger seat. It was done; I was finishing the race. With little more than a short nap or two in the previous seventy hours, I finally closed my eyes and relaxed as we made the last few miles to the "drop zone."

Life | Chapter 19

The VA hospital stands far off the road with a golf course laid out in front like a welcome mat. You drive up the long main driveway to two separate medical complexes of equal size on each side of the access road. That night, we pulled in and parked at the facility to the left. The hospital parking lot was empty and so was the waiting room. Aloof, I watched as my sisters and brother-in-law started to deal with the admin people. There was whispering and then some masked guy pointed in my direction. My family members seemed very calm and came to sit with me while I waited to talk to a doctor.

They took me quickly into a treatment room, and I was suddenly face to face with a VA doctor. He asked me a few questions and I answered. I tried to see if he was in on the plan. He was not giving me any signals at all, but I was patient. He would tip his hand soon enough. He wrote down a couple things after I answered and looked back into my eyes for a few seconds. My mind was scrambling. Was he or wasn't he in on the mission? Did he know who I was?

My mania was in control for this evolution with the psychiatrist. There was no more Eric Arauz, with my memories and my dreams and shames. There was only the disease as judge and jury, and it was preparing again to challenge reality.

The doctor was making a few last notes in his flip chart when I asked him if I could ask a question. He said, "Of course." It was funny that even though the disorder has swamped my brain I was still hesitant to ask this question for fear of being found out.

I looked directly at him and said, "Am I crazy, Doc?"

He paused, looked at me for a few moments, and very nonchalantly said,

Eric C. Arauz

"No."

There it was—the signal.

The meeting was over and the doctor returned me to the custody of my confused family. He told me to get some rest and sent me on my way. I was disoriented since I was sure that this was my rendezvous point, but, oh well, on to the next mission.

We got back in the car. The mood was a little different on the trip back. My delusions were recalculating, as I was trying to figure out the next step. I had been certain that the VA was the answer. My paranoia was getting more pronounced. Each new thought of my federal actualization had a slight touch of someone being after me to kidnap me. The ride home was filled with delusional innuendo as each set of lights was read as either good or bad. I was having a Cold War in my head with spies, double agents and assassins. I was relieved when we finally got home. I went straight upstairs to my room and closed the door.

I could hear the group downstairs talking. I don't think Bud raised his voice but he did come to the foot of the stairs to summon me downstairs again. When I got down to the foyer he had his car keys. He told me they had made a mistake and that I had to go back to the VA.

I never argued with my step-dad. He was the best of men. The whole family adored him. His power was achieved, not ascribed. You knew everything would be OK if Bud was involved. Being accepted by him and being loved by him gave me my first real sense of safety and security. Although I was as manic as I had ever been, I still respected him. I followed him into the car and back up Route 287 to the hospital. I was actually reassured. It was clear now that the first trip was a test run to throw off the enemy. I would go with my Marine guard and finish the mission. Now it was *really* real.

We pulled in again to the facility on the left and walked into the same waiting room. My dad asked for who was in charge and the same doctor came out. He saw me standing there and he grinned and greeted my step-father. Bud looked at this guy and told him to keep his goddamn "hellos" to himself. Bud went straight at the doctor, telling him what I had been doing and how recently I was hospitalized. He said he was not leaving until someone put me in a locked ward for observation. He said he would not watch me kill myself.

Sheepishly, the doctor acquiesced and told my dad to leave me there and they would take me to the ward.

Bud said, "No."

Bud said he would walk me right to the door. He would wait until they were ready and he would deliver me into the ward himself. The situation was non-negotiable. My step-father was engaged in a life-or-death mission—SAVE HIS SON—and he wasn't about to let anyone get in his way. The last hand I would touch as they locked me away would be his.

Bud was sitting shoulder to shoulder with me when the doctor returned to inject me with something. The doctor looked at him to see if it was alright. I was under Bud's care, and he was not fucking around. I am convinced he would have kicked the doctor's teeth in if he argued anymore. With Bud's OK, the VA doc pushed his drugs into my body. The orderlies approached and my dad got up and intercepted them. I could see them talking, but couldn't hear the words. Bud walked back to me, put out his hand, and told me to come with him.

I wasn't sure what was happening, but I felt completely safe. The father I had always dreamed of, the father I trusted implicitly, was with me, escorting me through the confusing maze to my pick-up point. I knew it was only moments away and the thought both thrilled and frightened me. The walk led us outside to the other facility that sits on the right side of the grounds adjacent to the general hospital. The street lights glazed the pavement as we crossed the main road and made our way to the first building on the other side.

It was a three-story red brick structure that had a central entrance with cement steps pouring out from both sides of its mouth like a mustache. The building was enormous. It looked institutional, like a Louisiana prison or a Connecticut prep school. There were ten or twelve windows on each side of the center partition. They were all dark. From the outside the building looked deserted. As we got up the steps to the front door, I saw the number of the building. 53. Perfect. 5 + 3 = 8. The infinity. The continuum of all knowledge and experience. I was in the right place.

The orderlies walked up the first flight of stairs to the second floor and opened the door to a staging area. The stairs were fenced in like cages. Bud led me onto the second floor hallway. It had to be around midnight and the wards were silent. I heard a heavy lock turn and a latch release as the door on my left opened and the night nurse came out to greet us. She stepped into the hall and immediately locked the door behind her.

The nurse said a few words to my dad and turned to me. She asked me to follow her through the doorway and into the ward. I looked to my dad to make sure it was OK. He nodded and told me to follow her. He walked me right to the door and told me it would be fine. The nurse opened the door all the way and with a compassionate grin waved me into the corridor. I stepped lightly over the threshold and stared down the darkened hall.

The first thing I noticed was that people were sleeping in chairs in the center of the hallway. Every ten feet a man sat in a chair either reading or napping. I thought at first it was the residents. In my mind, this was a holding tank for the gifted, a limbo for the illuminati.

While I was making my way to my room, I got a closer look at the chair dwellers. They were staff, not residents. I didn't understand what was going on; things didn't make sense anymore. Where was my pick-up team? I was expecting the FBI Hostage Rescue Team to liberate me at any moment. Maybe they had run into trouble. Clearly something had gone wrong.

And what was in that shot they had given me in the waiting room?

Turns out they had given me the "Rhino dart," the heavy sedative that knocks you out, and although I hardly felt anything at first, my mind was getting fuzzy. My mania was fighting lack of sleep, pharmaceuticals and reality with a Herculean denial. Panic flooded through me as I realized something had gone horribly wrong with the mission. I might not be rescued. I might not make it out of there.

The nurse dropped me off at my room. She gave me sheets and a few instructions and left. The hallway had dim lights running, and I made my bed in the artificial dusk. I stripped down to my boxers and folded my clothes for easy escape just in case someone came. Except for one short nap, I hadn't slept for days and I attempted to remain awake. I had to stay awake to keep the episode alive. The longer I lay in the hospital bed, the more I thought about my new situation. The smells of the ward started to fill my senses as I began to drift into sleep. I fought the slumber but the sedative was too much. My eyelids fluttered shut and my mind finally slowed when I had one thought: What kind of fucking place needs guards to position themselves every ten feet down the hallway while the inmates sleep? Where the fuck am I?

Welcome to my Death....

Book 2   Death

I say a murder is abstract. You pull the trigger and after that
you do not understand anything that happens.

- Jean-Paul Sartre, French existentialist philosopher, awarded the
Nobel Prize in Literature in 1964 and refused to accept it

Tonight at the Magic Theater, For Madmen only;
Price of Admittance your Mind.

- Steppenwolf by Hermann Hesse, Swiss-German author and mystic, awarded the
Nobel Prize in Literature in 1946. Unlike Sartre, he accepted it

This place has only three exits, sir: Madness, and Death.
- Rene Dumaul, a 20th century French spiritual para-surrealist writer and poet

Death | Chapter 1

Bud walked back down the fenced-in stairs, left Building 53, and walked back to his car across the street at the main complex. Alone. He headed back down Route 287 toward home where he knew he would have to pick up the phone, call his wife who was away on business, and tell her he had just left her son in the locked ward of another mental institution. My mom, out on the West Coast, waited alone in her hotel room, hoping for the best, fearing the worst. My grandmother sat by herself upstairs in her room. She fingered her prayer beads, said the rosary, and tried to understand what was happening. My sisters and my brother-in-law, who had done their best to help and support me, waited downstairs. They had all tried to save me, but no one could stop my fall.

Being the family member of a loved one with mental illness and addiction is brutal. It's like being handcuffed to a roller coaster careening toward a break in the tracks. But my family did not abandon me. Instead, I dragged them down the mangled tracks of my life and, together, as a family, we plummeted over the edge into the abyss.

Everyone had allowed themselves to hope that I was finally on the right path. We had all been preparing for my coming semester at NYU. Now, I was locked up in a mental hospital and they had to cope, like so many other families, with the fallout from having one of their own suffering from an active mental illness.

My childhood home was just minutes from our current residence. My biological father, Einar, and I had both been escorted by the police from our houses, put in ambulances, and taken away. We had both walked the East Brunswick streets after our releases, sure that the whole town knew about our disease; father and son, shunned like monsters by their imagined stigmas. Suburban Frankensteins.

Mental illness is a more selfish disease than addiction. When I was battling addiction by itself, I was always aware of the degradation I was causing myself and my family. I would have blackouts, but they were brief. The oblivion offered by alcohol and drugs could not satisfy the suicidal urges of my psyche. My mind wanted to die and mania was the answer. While my family struggled and consoled each other, I cycled for months in my captivity totally unaware of the situation.

Buried in my psychosis, I was becoming more memory than reality for them. But they came to visit no matter how sick I was. They came even when they weren't allowed to see me because of the scope of my mania. On those days, they would watch me through the small side windows of the ward's main door. Sometimes I would come to the window to wave and other times I would scream and curse at my mother and grandmother as delusions controlled my thoughts.

Yet, they always came.

Each hour-long trip was like a visit to a funeral home for my viewing. I was on display in the communal coffin of the ward, but the Eric they knew was dead. There was no more *me*. On each trip home, they wondered if it would be the last time they would see me before my body was lowered into and buried under the delusional dirt.

In those first days, my mother feared what would happen to her "Golden Boy." Alone in Portland, the City of Roses, her thoughts turned to Einar. She thought of her ex-husband's descent into madness and his death two years earlier, and she vowed she would not let her son repeat his father's destiny. The battle was on: mental disease and addiction versus the combined strength of my family. It would be a fight to the death and all the participants prepared for the coming emotional bloodbath. My family would fight for most of the summer of 1996 to save me. Each time they visited or talked to the doctors, the news was worse than the time before. The prescribed antipsychotics were not breaking the episode. My family was told I was "treatment resistant," and yet they never stopped caring for me. Each member of my family is stronger than I am, and I am blown away by their fortitude in the face of a son, a brother, a grandson whose mania would not abate until it was satisfied, until it had devoured everything.

There is only one reason I did not die the same death as my father: *my family, my family, my family, my family.*

Death | Chapter 2

irst morning on the ward. The bed was stiff like sleeping on a sheeted sidewalk. The mattress wouldn't even indent when I turned on my side to put my back to the ward. I could hear my roommate shuffling around and talking to himself as he got up to enter the main hall. He was much older than me. I was twenty-six and in good shape. He had to be pushing sixty. I didn't want to turn around but I had to, the light and noise were preventing any further cognitive escape.

I had no real memory associated with the past few days. My mind was attempting to right itself within the new landscape. It did not register that I was incarcerated or that I was even in a hospital. It all just seemed new, somehow different, but not necessarily bad. The delusions, which had completely enveloped me, also had the power to evolve and adapt to any situation. Many people have stood in front of me trying to convince me of the fallacy of my thoughts, but the manic mind instantly finds a role for their denial and translates it to fit the new delusional storyline. No one had confronted me yet. I still believed I was in a military-related holding facility, and that while people knew of my past and my bipolar disorder, it did not rule out this place being the think tank I had dreamed of.

I had not one solitary thought for the misery I had revisited on my family. Just sixty minutes south of the hospital, they woke to the same New Jersey morning. But they were not comforted by the delusional protection from reality that I had. The situation was grave and they knew it.

"MEDS!" was the first word I heard that morning.

I was in a room halfway down the ward, between the nurse's station and the TV room, and I watched men from four different wars shuffle down the hallway in the direction of the call. Like a lunatic lemming, I stepped out into the breach and followed along until I joined the end of the long line of absent-minded patients.

The woman at the front asked each man his name and looked at the file to make sure she had the right medication: pills, liquids, shots, patches etc. The soldier, airman, sailor, guardsman or marine obediently received these concoctions and made his way back down the hall. The passageway was not wide enough to allow for a straight line back from the nurse's station, so the line of men snaked back upon itself. We were smashed against each other.

My eyes wouldn't focus. I still don't know what medical concoction they used to knock me out, but I felt blind. I could smell and hear though.

Maximum-security wards in mental hospitals have a distinct smell. It is not good. It is the smell of adults who don't know how to maintain their hygiene any longer. You see things you don't usually see on the average street, in your favorite coffee shop, or bookstore. Finger nails are no longer tended for cleanliness or length. They can be two or three inches long and stained brown from chronic smoking. The meds can cause tremendous dry mouth, therefore many of the patients have a thick film across their lips that cakes white in the corners. Yawns expose icing-coated diseased tongues. Some medications cause chronic tooth decay and most of the men have been receiving treatment their entire adult lives. They are toothless or can actually have blood sheeting their teeth when they speak. My brothers on the ward were physically sick as well as mentally ill. After a couple weeks locked in this mass grave, I took on that same look. You could not distinguish me in any way from my fellow servicemen then and, just because I am no longer behind locked doors, you should not distinguish me from them now. I took my place in the army of zombies that haunted those halls just like the rest of them.

The meds line moved slowly as each man consented to that day's round of cures. One by one, I listened until my turn came up. Strangely, no one had told me where I was, what had happened, or what they thought the problem was. I simply got in line with everyone else and assumed that when I got to the front and announced myself I would be received enthusiastically. I was getting a little lost in my head when I bumped into the guy in front of me as he was given his pills. My breathing echoed off his back. I didn't like the feeling of having an audible signature. I seemed to be getting louder with each exhale, and I began to fixate on the collective breathing of the ward. The sound of the deep, labored breaths of patients in poor physical shape who smoked way, way too much flooded my senses.

I, too, would become a deep breather. Eventually, it was the only thing that verified I was still alive.

My human sounding board made his way to my left and shuffled down the hall. I was face to face with the human meds dispenser. I ascribed power to her because she held all the pharmaceuticals and everyone else seemed to fear her. I didn't know why.

She looked me in the eyes and asked my name. I heard my voice echoing from my mouth and watched for her response. She took out a very thin folder, much thinner than the rest, read a few things, closed it and handed me a liquid and a few pills. She explained what each was and asked if I had any questions. I had no real concept of what was happening. I had never heard of the things being issued to me and she didn't look like she wanted to catch me up on three years of psychopharmacology.

We both acted like our conversation was perfectly normal and the exchange ended. I turned and took in the terrain that would be my whole world for the coming months. Most men entered the ward and stayed until their acute symptoms abated and then they were processed for treatment on less restrictive and less penal wards. I never left the maximum-security ward for another. I spent every day of my stay locked in the VA hospital right there. It was on that ward that I descended the nine circles of my manic hell until I was face to face with myself and my suffering, until I cursed my existence, and, lastly, until I cursed God for casting me into hell and burning me alive as I was strapped down to die.

There were many men in my stay who helped me as my mania continued to cycle, but I took the final steps of my descent all alone. But as the saying goes, every journey begins with a first step, and as I turned left to check out the ward, I took my first step into the society and culture of a maximum-security mental hospital.

Death | Chapter 3

If you ever watch people walk, you will notice they all have different ways of getting around on two feet. Some walk with extra determination to get where they're going and others loaf and lumber from place to place. You eventually get to know people by their walk and can even pick someone out in a crowd by their gait. This is not true in a maximum-security hospital. On the ward we all walk the same way because we are all going to the same place.

Nowhere.

Outside the hospital, each person you are watching is heading someplace different. If they are going to the same place, they will corral their speed and fall in step. When was the last time you went for a walk with a friend or co-worker and you just split up, stayed fifty yards from each other, and met up again at the same exact time at the same exact place you were going? You didn't.

In prisons and boot camp, people's gaits are similar to the hospital march. Teams of humans are led places or are restricted from places and their destinations are predetermined. The only real difference is that their Somewhere's are determined by an outside entity while me and my ward-mates had our Nowhere's determined by our sickness.

The ward was full of people walking from place to place just trying to kill the day. To kill a day you must kill it hour by hour, minute by minute. Each veteran moved down the hall back to their rooms after meds to ready themselves for the occasional medical visit at the main hospital or whatever else the day had in store for them. Many veterans, including me, rarely left the ward for anything. On those occasions when I breached the ward, I was accompanied by two or three staff as I made my way through the conventional VA hospital wing with my own

Secret Service at my side.

As I wandered from place to place on the ward, my delusions struggled to find an appropriate story to serenade my mind. I was not high or low at the time, just diluted and cycling from one feigned reality to the next. My mind took in the surroundings, the people, and the overall mood as it pieced together the next myopic drama.

It didn't look like heaven, nor did it look like hell.

Limbo.

A place to hang-out for a while before you make your way through the pearly gates. My catholic school upbringing added a nice lexicon for my mind to pick from while I waited. It allowed the hyper-religiosity of my episodes to find a congruent voice with which to trick and trap me.

I had never thought much about it before, but I always assumed Limbo was where you sat before you got into Heaven. But that was not my Limbo. My Limbo was where I sat before I descended into Hell. It was the Devil's waiting room, and his helpers were just figuring out where to seat me. The question was how far would I sin against myself before the final judgment would be rendered and my fate decided?

My delusions gave the answer. I would march up to the bitter end where I would identify with the creator. I did not come to believe I was god-*like*; I believed I *was* God. God the almighty, Lucifer the fallen angel, Jesus the savior, and Judas the beloved betrayer. I was all and all was me.

The lethal embrace of my drug induced mania would eventually elevate me to the highest heights and then take me to the falling off place of the original pariah, the first sinner, Lucifer himself. Ultimately, I would stand in judgment of myself while in four-point restraints in the twentieth hour of confinement. I would no longer sing the praises of my enlightened soul but castigate my true evil self. This death, my psychic death, the cycling, diseased and deranged death of a loving madman was the final evolutionary recompense for a corrupted and vicious bloodline of heretics and demons. My death was payback for it all and my suffering would not be complete until the karmic balance was restored.

The main hallway was generic. It had seen many years of misery and loss and had given up much like its inhabitants. The nurse's station with the med closet was at the front of the ward. As you moved down the hall, the right side had a small nook with a few offices where staff met with patients and further down on the same side sat the common room. This room was the entertainment room, bingo room, and dining room all in one. Meals came to the ward: dinner was delivery, never pick-up.

The entertainment/dining room had an old TV with a cracked screen and a few books. Three-quarters of the way down the hall on the right side, the corridor opened to accommodate the first set of patient's rooms in an alcove. The left side of the hall was all rooms but the right side only had a few. These were multiple bedrooms. One room had three beds and they all faced different directions. The other room housed four or five beds. These beds all lined up and faced the same direction like a barracks.

The end of the right side of the hall was the pay phone, a few smaller rooms and the laundry room. I remember trying to do laundry once. I was on such heavy drugs I could not grip the handles. I couldn't close my hands. I couldn't grip the machine's knobs to turn them. Laundry was beyond me.

Death | Chapter 4

The difficult thing about my institutional memories is that I can picture things, but I don't always have a clear soundtrack to go with the memory. I can remember broken thoughts and the feelings that saturated scenes I can still vividly see in my mind's eye, but the sounds of reality are dampened in my recollections. Therefore, my memory of names and exact conversations are hazy.

What I do remember is that I had many allies on the ward. I am unsure how these relationships were born, but they existed. Three men in particular helped me whether they knew it or not. These three men were very different, but they each saved my life in their own way. They were my three wise men, my guides, my Virgils.

The first was an older man I call Bill.

Bill was in his mid-sixties and walked like an aggravated penguin. His legs were short and so was he. He stood five-five at most. He walked quickly from place to place, but his feet never seemed to leave the ground. He was always lost in thought and rubbing his forehead like he was hard at work contemplating life and not getting anywhere with it. Bill looked straight at you when he spoke. His eyes riveted into yours with the egoless stare of a three-year-old boy. Many people on the wards don't look at anyone, but Bill stopped, squared his shoulders, and engaged you. When I met him, it was very early in my stay on the ward. I was aggressively cycling in my delusions, and my physical body had not yet started to deteriorate.

With a rosary around my neck, I would go from room to room doing tilted pushups off the edges of other men's beds. I would lay down with my belly against the mattress and my head hanging off the foot of the bed. I would slowly pull my torso over the edge with my palms on the floor until the majority of my body was hanging off with only my shins remaining on the mattress. The crucifix would be hanging to the ground and I would put my hands next to each other in a triangle formation with my thumbs and forefingers touching. The cross was lowered into the opening between the two hands and my body would tilt forward and down.

I could feel the divinity of the Lord pulsing through my being. I was the incarnation of Elijah, God's warrior, who was so loved for his service, he would ascend to heaven without death.

Bill watched these workouts and talked to me as if we were having coffee in a food court at the local mall. His mouth was always dry and more times than not, he didn't wear his teeth. After two or three words, Bill would lick his lips or open his mouth as wide as he could. He had been on psychiatric meds most of his adult life and his cotton mouth was chronic. Without constant attention, a film would develop over his lips and almost cement his mouth shut. Bill had been in various hospitals since the Korean War and had the weathered look of a lifer on and off the wards. His teeth had rotted away from age, meds, and street living. His hands were stained from a life of itinerant work and his face was deeply wrinkled and scarred. But his eyes were still aggressively alive. He looked like some type of warrior elf nearing the end of his service.

One thing I clearly remember about Bill is that he called me Glenn. He had a way of pronouncing Glenn with such repetition and conviction that I was not entirely sure it was not my name.

One day we were shaving when I heard the name Glenn shouted over and over. Shaving in the hospital setting is not the same as shaving at home. There were three sinks with plastic mirrors over them and patients had to line up in front of each basin. Five men in each line, three lines, fifteen total in the bathroom. You soaped and lathered your own face and the orderly's hand hovered over your wrist while you moved the razor across your neck and cheeks. I don't remember trying to avoid looking at myself while I was in the hospital, but I was all of a sudden very aware of the face staring back at me. As I was trying to get a real look into my eyes, I heard the name "Glenn" repeated with force. When I wasn't with Bill, I did not answer to or recognize the name Glenn. But the chant of "Glenn!" got louder and louder until I turned to my left to see what was going on.

Bill was in the next line over, staring at me. Shaving cream covered his entire head. From the base of his neck to the top of his skull, he was covered in lather. His cheekbones and the bridge of his nose were as covered as was his throat and forehead. He got out a few more Glenns before he realized I was paying attention. His brilliant eyes were sparkling as he said, "Glenn, excuse me, excuse me, Glenn, do you think I missed a few spots?"

He waited for an answer, but his orderly must have decided playtime with the sick veteran was over, and he turned Bill back to the mirror. Bill shaved his face but left the areas above the border of his natural beard lathered up and walked out into hall the with the top three quarters of his head covered in shaving cream. The rest of his face was shaved with military precision.

Mentally ill or not, it is a thing of beauty to watch a man from World War II or Korea shave. They take such pride in this simple action that watching them gave me great comfort. I thought of Bud, who I had never even seen with even one whisker on his face unless it was Sunday. On Sunday, Bud would work on his Jaguar, a cigarette hanging off his lip and a pack of Parliaments rolled up in his white t-shirt sleeve while his perfect silver beard enjoyed its day in the sun.

Bill reminded me of Bud in his physical stature. His age and his old-school way of doing things imbued enough Bud in Bill for me to want more. Bill made me feel safe. He became my refuge in the nameless and faceless ward.

My mental hospital father-figure reminded me of Bud in another way. Bill was in unbelievable shape. When he took off his shirt he looked like a retired superhero. He had the squared pectoral muscles of Tarzan and his stomach looked like it was carved out of cement. It was not a stomach toned for vanity but one earned from arduous physical work. The muscles were full and thick. His core had utility. His was the build of a man that has lifted, pulled, and dragged things around for a lifetime. Bud had the same build before cancer started in on him. Prior to his illness, Bud could wear a Speedo and not look like a European tourist with a death wish prancing down the boardwalk in Seaside Heights.

Bill and I met up at various times throughout the day with no real agenda. I never planned to run into him; it just happened. He moved much faster than I did and would come out of nowhere. We probably spent every day of my first month on the ward together.

Death | Chapter 5

The physical environment of the ward was mind numbing, like living in a broken elevator. The colors were muted grays, browns and tans. The visual monotony dulled the mood and dampened my energy level. There was never any music. This visual and auditory emptiness allowed the manic mind to run free. There were some sounds that did register with me. They were the occasional calls for meds, the loud, hungry breathing, and there were the screams.

The screams varied in purpose. They can be from the strap down/seclusion room as a patient begged for release and mercy. Or from residents fighting each other either verbally or physically. Or, worst of all, there was the scream that represents the last stages of evolution of the psyche of a chronically hospitalized psychiatric patient who finds himself/herself trapped on the wards reserved for those with severe mental illness: my population.

This last scream is a final call from a long-term hospitalized patient who has a last flash of lucidity and screams to their fading reality as it shrinks in the distance. It is the sound of a warring soul that realizes its plight and then fights through the delusion and psychotic encasement to the surface. It knows that the fight may be lost without one last effort, and it rages to find the light. The sound is clear and defines itself to the listener instantly.

It is pure anguish and lament.

It resonates as an archetype to your primal audio memory. It is the sound of parents acknowledging to themselves that their child is dead. It is the sound of an innocent prisoner about to be executed for a crime he did not commit. It is the sound of a warrior lying in a foreign land knowing he will die there without ever seeing his wife and children. It is the sound rumbled in the congested chest of a homeless addict lying on a cold, city street knowing her last breaths are filling and leaving her lungs. It is the sound she makes picturing her innocent infant and the life she had once led. It is the sound this lost mother makes during the last few seconds of her life as she watches the rats scurry around her, awaiting their invite.

In the hospital, the sound of the final scream fills the hall with its cry for another life, another chance, another reality. I have listened as many of my ward-mates acquiesced to this seemingly final step into their frozen, personal ninth circle of psychiatric hell, the circle that represents the prison of eternal mental isolation. The sickest on the ward, the ones without any hope left in them, will live the rest of their days imprisoned within the walls of their finite and sickened minds. They will cannibalize their thoughts and delusions and slowly fortify a wall of ice between themselves and reality, to the point where there is no way in and no way out.

It is not their fault.

Mental illness is not addiction. It is more dastardly, more heartbreaking. If you take an addict and disallow him or her access to alcohol and drugs he or she will physically get better. They may be stark-raving, self-centered assholes but they will not overdose, drive drunk and kill others. They will not further the damage to their internal organs with liquid poison. Many believe addiction to be a spiritual malady but that is not what I am addressing here. I am simply saying you can theoretically stop the physical decline of an addict by removing his drug or drink of choice and his mind and body will improve even if his attitude does not. This is not true of people with mental illness. We are born with the drug that kills us already in our blood, beneath our skin, and hiding behind our eyes.

Mental hospitals throughout the United States are filled with patients that are compliant to their medicinal regiment. Right now, in hospitals across the country, the call for "meds" was just made and members of my psychotic family will make their way to the line for their pills, liquids and various other treatments. They will ingest what is given to them, some with hope for a cure or at least a dampen-ing of their symptoms. Others will be part of another hospital population. This population has lost hope in the benefits of meds. They take them but do not get better. Day after day, month after month, year after year, seasons change outside their windows while inside their illness remains in control and only their bodies experience the passage of time.

When I studied psychology early in my academic career, I was told that I should know one thing: *Not everyone gets better.*

It is when that reality reaches the tangled thoughts of the lifetime patient and surges to the forefront of a cycling mind that the final scream is released. To my knowledge, the three men who helped me survive my sojourn to hell and back never allowed that scream to escape from their mouths. Somehow they each seemed very alive in our treatment tomb. I did not have that in common with these men. I did reach that point of oblivion. That scream did leave my lips and the full essence of its freedom and death saturated my body and my mind—my very existence. Eventually, I experienced the complete immersion of my psyche with the pain and loss of my life experience. I became one with the is-ness of suffering. I personified anguish. I was viscerally torn apart and everything that was me vanished. Eventually, only my disease survived.

But that did not happen to Bill. Bill was too strong.

Death | Chapter 6

Bill's gut was like granite. You could see the jagged ripples of muscle through his skintight t-shirts. It preceded him by three or four inches.

One rainy afternoon on the ward, I had not seen him for the better part of a day. It was nearing dinner time when I started looking for him. I usually didn't think too much about anyone else, but that day I noticed something was missing. The Thorazine, the antipsychotic medicine the VA was treating me with, was not yet in full effect and I still had some physical strength. At that point, my mania could cycle for days without disruption and my body was still nimble enough to act out a few of its manic directions.

I walked out of my room and headed down the ward. As he was always the one who found me, I really had no idea what room Bill was in. While searching, I heard a solid thumping sound about every sixty seconds or so.

THUMP!

THUMP!

THUMP!

Because of the acoustics of the hall, the sound seemed to come from every direction at once as it blended with the rain and the deep inhales and exhales of my ward-mates. The cacophony of these sounds made the hall seem to pulse, to throb, like you were inside a beating heart. As I got farther down ward, the thump localized and got louder. I peered into one room and saw a trio of veterans smoking in the corner. I didn't know these three young men, but I entered anyway.

THUMP!

THUMP!

THUMP!

The noise was close, and, although I was vaguely interested in it, once I saw the men smoking, I wanted in. Everyone seemed to posses cigarettes on the ward but me. If I saw a few guys smoking in their room or gathering in the bathroom after breakfast, I would enter and hover.

I was living so deeply in my head at that point that I never spoke. I didn't talk to the doctor, the nurse, the orderlies, or my shipmates. I was trapped in my own head watching everyone around me speak while attending only to my own thoughts.

The men stopped what they were doing and turned to face me. I stared back blankly. I had lost the ability to smile or show any emotion after the first few weeks on heavy antipsychotics. My face was leaden, frozen. They waited for me to say anything, but I just stood there as my manic mind raced to get my ever-changing story up-to-date.

As I stood watching the tribunal, the story gradually fell into place. I felt they were three Jamaican holy men who had come to find me. They had discovered I was the resurrected Jamaican leader, Marcus Garvey, and they had come to watch over me. The nation of Jamaica had a secret security force that spanned the world looking for the successor to their deceased spiritual leader and I was the one. I was always the ONE.

These men knew the history of my fights for civil rights and equality in the Navy and beyond. They knew of my love and devotion to all mankind. This storyline would explain my lifetime need to right wrongs against others, to confront biases, to fight against racism. I was always looking for that one thing that would explain everything. I could not live in the question of who am I; I required the comfort and constraint of an existential answer. My manic mind was even more of a coward. It was always trying to define itself with the next thought, the next delusion, the next terror. My cycling mind was like a psychic parasite that could not live on its own; it had to kill its host to survive. First mentally, then spiritually, and then the crescendo: physically.

The three Jamaican prophets passed a cigarette to me and lit it. I watched the fire burn off the hanging end of the rolling paper before it could attack the nicotine-laced tobacco. The filter sat on my lips and stuck to the entrance of my cotton mouth. Smoke wafted gently up into my nostrils and trickled through the dry cavities up into my brain. I could hardly wait for the first long inhale. I wanted the cigarette really burning before I pulled deeply on it with my starving lungs. My eyes were shut now. The filter was warm and no longer foreign to my useless mouth. It was time.

I added the slightest amount of extra pressure to my lips to create a seal on the filter and tilted my head back a few degrees to open my airway. My lungs pulled and the heat of the inhaled smoke flooded my inner cavity with its fire. I sucked for as long as I could, filling myself with its cancerous escape. The warmth and comfort of the smoke poured into me with its thousands of chemicals and I held it in. This tropical cigarette was the only thing that made me feel connected to a world outside of myself. The despair and reality of the ward could vanish as I remembered other smokes in my life: sitting on the fantail of my Destroyer watching the wake as we steamed across the Mediterranean, listening to the Red Hot Chili Peppers' "Breaking the Girl" over and over with a beautiful brunette bartender in Haifa, Israel, and laughing with my sisters after a Thanksgiving feast.

At this point in my sickness, the cigarette meant so much more than a simple nicotine fix. It was my friend and my internal ignition, an artificial spark to my dimming sanity. The meds robbed reality from my physical senses and I was becoming numb to my external being, but cigarettes could, in some small way, give me a fleeting glimpse of life before my diagnosis, before the hospital, before the day programs, and the heavy psychiatric meds.

Unimpeded by the Thorazine, my mania deepened and my physical body began to fail as a direct side-effect of the medication. My strength deteriorated, my sense of taste was dampened due to the chronic cotton mouth, my fingers became stiff and uncoordinated, my arms felt like wet logs hanging from my shoulders, and my legs dragged as though two dead men hung from my hips. As I lost the ability to physically experience the world around me, the power of my illness grew even stronger. Since the ward had no distinguishing characteristics that would give its inhabitants a sense of place—no paintings, no music, no color—it allowed the mind to focus on the one thing it needed protection from: itself.

I exhaled the sacred smoke and looked at the Jamaican holy men through a pale veil of vaporized chemicals. I walked to the opposite corner of the large room and sat on the floor next to a made bed. Stiffly, I slid down the wall and placed the back of my head on the cold ground. The beds on the ward had a very high clearance to the floor, and I wiggled my body under one with the cigarette sticking out of my mouth. I could still see the three sets of feet across the room when I tilted my ear to my shoulder. My eyes closed and I finished the cigarette, turning my head to the left and right to inhale without scraping the metal grid that supported the bottom of the bed. The Kingston trio left the room and I ground the cigarette into the tiled floor.

I was sure now that it was not just tobacco that packed the smoke. I was positive it was marijuana. The calm of the fictitious THC flooded my brain and I let the "weed" do its job. Listening to my breathing, I tried to unite my soul to that of Marcus Garvey's and move into a unitary rapture with his spirit. My breathing grew deeper and my spine sank into the tile floor. My feet fell open and the front of my body lightened to experience the ever deepening breaths. As I slipped deeper into the moment, I felt a distance from my thoughts I hadn't felt in a long time. My hands came back to me as I felt the *aliveness* of each finger. My ankles released and I could turn them from side to side, aware of their presence and utility. My breaths bounced back to me from the undercarriage of the institutional bed and their tobacco-scented return was welcomed. I was making my way back to me. The *me* that was not my mind and not my name but the eternal me.

The observer and the observed as one.

I could see me standing in front of myself in my mind's eye. I could make out the back of my head and knew it was my own.

With each new and cleansing breath, I escaped my manic hell and concentrated on the vision of myself. I watched my *self* slowly turn to face me. I was ready to stand in full relation to myself.

When I first saw my own profile, a release of pleasure and relief gripped me. I was somehow coming to the reality of my sickness and could see hope in my situation. My destitute life had meaning; my father's illness and death and his attempt to kill me would give me strength to face my own battles; losing my step-daughter could somehow benefit her and her mother; my greatest transgressions were not death sentences but tremendous life lessons. I was not lost. There was hope.

I was revolving, evolving, becoming. Every inhale and exhale seemed to take a thousand years. The left shoulder of my apparition was making its last turn to be face to face with me.

I could see my father on his death bed. His physical body sickened from so many years of street living and illness. I could see my step-daughter at her third, fourth, fifth and all her other future birthdays I would miss. My soul wept as I tried to come to terms with my lost life.

The vision of me in front of myself made its final turn to face me and I raised my arms to embrace myself. My mind spun my ever-evolving story: I would not need a Virgil. I could survive hell and come back to share the hero's journey as all great heroes do. I was not bipolar; I was a prophet meant to fight the greatest battle—the battle against the self—to show others how to transgress themselves, to guide others to true power, glory, and enlightenment. Once baptized, I would crawl out from under the bed to be worshiped and glorified. Once I broke free from the hospital, I would be the alpha and omega of all potentiality. I would be God.

I was the full embodiment of *all* being and energy and had escaped the part of me that was man. I now knew exactly who I was. I was not Marcus Garvey, nor was I Eric Arauz. I was the first and the last of all the great men of time. I was the light of a thousand darknesses and the answer to every query of a lost soul. I was the son of a carpenter from long ago and knew my final purpose. I was the Lord Jesus Christ returned to the body of a perpetual sinner and lunatic come to right the world. I was he and he was the One. I was the I AM.

My body was pure energy. The completeness of my conversion experience had removed any anxiety from this last turn of my head to stand "face to face, eye to eye" with my true, revealed self. As my inner vision focused on the face of the man standing in front of me, something was wrong. But I continued to move forward with my arms raised to embrace myself. The body in front of me was definitely mine but the face … the face….

My mirrored face was gone.

The visage that looked back at me had no lips, no nose, no eyes. It was skin stretched smoothly over a skull with no facial features. I could see my own reflection in the oils built up on the skin and now I saw the "me" currently lying under the bed in the glazed reflection. I saw my blood shot and crusted eyes. I saw my pasted lips, cracked and bleeding into my blackened teeth. My skin was white and pasty from weeks shielded from the sun. Somehow I slipped back to my father and saw him crying in his bed. Alone, he was breathing in and out in a cheap hospital room saved for the homeless who die alone. His eyes were wide open as panic raped his face. He was writhing back and forth and screaming, but I couldn't hear anything. I watched from above as he tossed and turned in his restraints while machines pulsed around him. He would die the death of the indigent and insane; strapped to a bed, panicked, furious. Alone.

All of a sudden, he seemed to calm and rotate his head in my direction. He focused directly on me and stared into my eyes.

Einar grinned and said, "This is your future, son. How could you abandon me? Why have you not saved me? You are my son, and yet, I die here alone. You will not be saved, Eric, you will pay a greater price than I have, a much greater price than I. I will see you in hell, Judas."

I exploded out from under the bed. My mind had not let my body move like that in a long time. I threw the heavy industrial bed into the air and flew out from under it. My rapture was gone and my mind fought back into control instantly. I looked left and right, unsure how I got into this room and scurried for the door. Wracked with a visceral feeling of horror and despair, I was absolutely terrified of my own mind and did not want to give it a single second to let it wander back to Einar.

I had no clue which way to turn. Do I go back up the ward or down the ward? It all looked the same. I was literally taking a step to the left and pulling the foot back and then a step right and pulling that foot back.

Which way do you go if everywhere is nowhere?

THUMP!

Right ... the thumping ... Bill ... Bill was what I looking for....

THUMP!

It sounded like a bowling ball being dropped off a roof onto a wet shag rug. I walked to the doorway adjacent to the room I just escaped. I saw Bill. He was shirtless, sitting on the edge of his bed with his feet facing the headboard and his legs locked straight. He slowly started leaning backwards over the edge. His stomach muscles were popping out from the effort as his arms hung dead at his side. He had nothing behind him but air and it would be a three foot drop to the naked, linoleum floor.

Painstakingly, he lowered his body until his torso reached a forty-five degree angle. Bill held it for a few seconds and gently massaged his massive core with his leathered hands. It was then he noticed me at the door. Casually, he looked my direction and nodded, "Glenn," and then he released his lower back and fell skull first into the ground. The back of his head smashed into the carpet-less tile floor.

THUMP!

The horror of my under-the-bed revelation was now gone. I turned back to my room looking for something else to do or maybe find another cigarette. I don't have many more recollections of Bill in my time on the ward, although we did run into each other a few times on my return visits to the VA after I got off of the hospital ward.

The last time I saw Bill, I was on my way to visit my old ward after I had seen my psychiatrist and had my Lithium levels checked. I had been out of the VA hospital for a few years and always went back to see my old home and ward-mates. I was lost in thought about my impending transfer to a four-year university when I heard the sprinklers go off on the large patch of grass to my right. I had seen this display often and knew that the sprinkler to my left would trigger in a few seconds. I quickened my pace. It was too late and I was caught in the tail end of the spray. The back of my calves got drenched as I stepped from the dark gray of the wet sidewalk to lighter cement.

"Glenn? Glenn? Excuse me. Excuuuse me, Glenn?"

I heard the familiar call and knew my name was not Glenn but something about it made me turn. The pace of the question, the familiar annoyed yearning for an acknowledgment put me right back on the ward watching Bill shave his forehead. I turned around but didn't see anyone. I looked left and right but no Bill.

"Glenn!"

I looked down and there, lying within inches of the sprinkler head, was Bill. The sprinkler was immediately behind him. With each pass its sounds were muffled as its stream fired directly into his back. He was lying on his side resting on his left elbow, his head lazily cupped in his hand. Bill's eyes were still blazing and he didn't say anything else. He looked much older to me. This could have been for a multitude of reasons. One could have been the simple fact that living in the hospital and bouncing from halfway house to the street and back to the hospital takes its toll physically on a person.

The other reason is particular to me and not Bill. Mania seems to make everything shine. With the serotonin flooding my senses and my mood so elevated, a cosmic glow radiated from everything around me. With diminished self-consciousness and emboldened self-importance, you look people in the eye longer and observe them more closely. It seems like you have never seen anything clearly before and it adds to the delusional optic confusion.

Now Bill looked old. He looked weary. He looked very sad and very short for this world. But like a cagey tomcat, Bill stretched his damp body while still keeping eye contact and then rolled over on his right side to face the sprinkler. He adjusted his body to the natural curve of the earth below him and received his agricultural baptism every thirty seconds.

"Good-bye, Glenn."

Good-bye, Bill.

Death | Chapter 7

My second Virgil was very different from Bill. Virgil #2 was 6 ft. tall while Bill stood 5 ft. 5 in. max. He was black and Bill was white. Virgil #2 was inner-city urban, Bill was more rural. But my first two Virgils had a few things in common as well. They were both Army and both very strong. Virgil #2 was a powerfully built man. The institutions and disease had not stripped him of his muscle, and that can create a very dangerous dynamic on a ward. The floor is filled with men like me who, after weeks of medication and no exercise, could no longer defend themselves from physical attack. There were men on my ward in their late sixties and seventies waiting for their acute symptoms to subside before they could be treated in a geriatric unit. My ward was the bottom floor. Everyone was mixed in no matter what their issue until they were safe to be in treatment wards. My ward was the communal eighth circle of the VA Hospital hell. The ninth circle was always a solo Kamikaze mission.

The threat of attack on a VA ward is great. It is not due to the character or the type of veteran on the ward. The threat is high because these men have been trained to harm other men for their country. They have been taught how to choke, charge, stab, smother and shoot other human beings. A sick mind can take over a body like a drunk driver takes over a car making them both instruments of death. That is why when I entered the ward that first night with my step-dad, the staff was sleeping in chairs lined up down the center of the hall.

My new Virgil could have ended my life at any time. He was a crack addict and had been diagnosed with schizophrenia. He had been taken off the streets of Irvington, NJ—why, I have no idea—and deposited in my ward. I have no recollection of how our relationship began, but I know we spent a lot of time together.

By the time I met Virgil #2, I was having a hard time walking. I lumbered from place to place on the ward. My mania was no longer friendly and life affirming. It was brutal and cruel and led me down paths of despair and hopelessness with a renewed zeal each morning. I firmly believe that if I had not met Virgil #2, I would not be alive. I would have died on the ward. His face and smile sit clearly in my mind, but I never knew his name. His wellbeing weighs on my soul and in the past decade, I have not failed to think of him daily.

My new Virgil had hospital life figured out. We would sit in his room evening after evening while he rubbed cocoa butter into his elbows. It is funny to think he was concerned about his skin getting ashy while I was practically walking around in adult diapers and sweatpants. While he moisturized his skin, he would talk to me, not at me like Bill. Virgil had big expressive eyes and he smiled often. I don't remember anyone smiling on the ward but him. He talked about girls, clubs, the Army, whatever he wanted, and then he would ask me about myself.

He wasn't asking about my diagnosis or my episodes but about me. I didn't even remember there being a "me" to discuss at that point. The mere existence of a life before the hospital seemed foreign, and the facts of my life seemed conjectured. I was becoming one with the ward and my disease. But this man eventually broke the pattern and woke up my spirit. This awakening may have ultimately helped save my life, but it would have a terrible price associated with it.

My mania had left my soul for dead and was readying itself for full control of my body and life. It was not happy to see me stirring under its weight and my awakening, however slight, would ultimately set off the chain of events that led up to the final confrontation: Mind and Spirit fighting to the death on the battlefield of *me* as I lay shackled and helpless in a restraining bed. As in the Bhagavad Gita, the ancient mystical Hindu text, it would be a modern day stand-off on the visceral battlefield of my insular Kuruksetra. But unlike Prince Arjuna from the spiritual tale, I would have no Lord Krishna to lead me into battle. I would fight alone and would be mentally eviscerated, torn limb from limb, and left to die ... a son sacrificed to his father's disease.

Death | Chapter 8

Virgil must have gotten me to say something about myself because he was always calling me "Sensei." During each conversation, he would tell me what I said the day before. I had no memory of any our talks. I just had this need to find him each day and sit down with him. My days did not start until I was with Virgil.

By this time, my disease had stopped looking outward for new signs around which to mold the ever-evolving storyline that now made up my reality. With surgical precision, my manic mind attempted to cut me from the mooring lines of my life. Each day when I left Virgil's room, my mind would send me into fantastic internal trips creating new and false memories. My mania was not simply wiping out today and tomorrow but yesterday. I had no existential anchor and I was beginning to doubt the reality of any of my memories. My past was an ever-changing mosaic filled with true and false representations of yesterdays that may or may have not occurred.

I had recently lost my shoes or they had been stolen. This was a huge problem for me because of my surgically repaired toes. With the broken screw in the left big toe and a severed tendon that left the last toe on my left foot useless, my foot felt like little piggy went to market and got his head blown off. I also have low arches so I put the majority of my bodyweight on my heels causing me severe back pain. The combination of reconstructed toes on my right foot, mangled toes on my left foot, and low arches made walking barefoot unbearable.

The chronic pain added to my delusions. When I told the front desk my shoes were gone they gave me replacement slippers and I spent the rest of my time on the ward either barefoot or with 1/8 of an inch of blue fabric separating my feet from the cold, naked floor. Each step exacerbated my now chronic left hip and knee problems. The pain was dull and throbbing when sitting and acute and piercing when walking. Delusions insulated my mind from reality, but not my body.

With the pain growing and the Thorazine robbing me of more and more strength, the journey from Virgil's room back to my own could take half an hour. Not half an hour where I wandered from room to room socializing with my neighbors and using the pay phone but with constant and directed walking.

Virgil would finish up some story about home or the Army. He would offer me another cigarette from his pack of never-ending Menthols and leisurely finish immersing the cocoa butter into his skin. No handshake or hugs on the ward, just good-bye until the next time we met.

The first steps from his room were painful. We usually sat for an hour or two on cushionless, tan wooden chairs and my whole body would be stiff. Add in the physical toll from the antipsychotics, and my body was a complete mess. When I stood up after our talks, my torso would gradually loosen, but my left foot, knee and hip did not. The pain was searing and I would almost instantly forget anything about my visit with Virgil and focus on home, my room, my pain—and my new delusional memory of being attacked by a shark that was embedding in my mind and body.

At times the pain in my left side was so severe my mania had to construct an elaborate story to explain it. Hence, the shark attack. At first my diseased mind initiates an idea. It's not a voice in my head saying something happened, but rather just a weak feeling, a sense of something. And yet, that is all the manic/delusional mind needs. It grabs that feeling and runs. The false memory, in this case the memory that I had been attacked by a shark, would get stronger and stronger as my ever-intensifying journey of self-verification continued. I was the omnipotent fact checker for my thoughts. As a thought or idea swam across my mind, it would not be tested against outside reality at all.

Pai-chang Huai-hai, an eighth century Chinese Zen Master, has described enlightenment as a state of existence where you are free from unreality and delusion—No more Untruth: No more Non-Reality. It is here that you will have linked your mind to the Original Mind/Cosmic Consciousness/Reality/Pure Unified Energy, in real time with the heartbeat of an evolving universe, and you will be complete in your connection to the whole, to that which has always been and always will be. Living breathing Truth.

True mania and severe mental illness is the complete opposite of this state.

Eric C. Arauz

It is the complete renunciation of Reality, the Original mind, of the ground of existence. The connection is complete with oneself and only oneself and that fragmented and solitary view of the universe. It is pure Untruth, pure Non-Reality.

It is often said that there is a fine line between genius and madness, but I reject that comparison and believe that those who make it do not understand mental illness and its full scope of suffering when symptomatic. There is nothing romantic or creative about the cycling mind of a patient with mental illness residing in a forced stay at a psychiatric hospital. Nothing. No matter how creative the patient is or how high he or she scores on an IQ test.

In my case, my mania was gaining ground and my mind was becoming restless within its constraints. With no external mooring, my mind floated from one idea to the next with no particular destination, no direction, and no distractions. My mind was bored and would grab at any interesting idea no matter how absurd. A bored mind is a vicious mind. And a bored mind being eaten alive by mania will feed off the most intimate knowledge of itself.

Death at the hands of an animal has always been my greatest fear. Animals have no remorse when they kill. Carnivorous animals respond to an evolutionary need to kill to eat and must exert their will over other organisms just to ensure their own continued survival. Animals cannot be bargained with and they don't respond to emotional pleas for mercy, just as mental illness cannot be bargained with and will not respond to pleas for mercy. People can and do end up beyond treatment if the proper combination of biochemistry and medication, if needed, is never found. Mental illness can and will kill its host and it will not ask for forgiveness.

I began reliving the "memory" of my shark attack after my visits with Virgil. I didn't think about them on my way to his room or during our visits. It was only with that first step back into the hallway that they came crashing back—it was like a scuba diver stepping off the back of a boat and into the sea. As I submerged into the depths of the hallway, the physical pain from my injured toes and aching hip and back would trigger my delusional memory. I was sure I had been attacked in the Navy. I was no longer an Electronics Technician who specialized in fleet based satellite communications, which was truly my job. I was now an ex-Navy diver. My injuries and subsequent pain were no longer from a congenital toe problem that was worsened from walking on steel decks and in steel-toed boots. My injuries and subsequent pain were from a Great White Shark attack that occurred while diving off the coast of Norfolk, VA.

112

Virgil's room was at the end of the hall past the washer and dryers. Even though the walk back to my room would take a person with a regular stride under five minutes, it was now an endless journey for me. I would close my eyes to hide my fear, and with each blind step, I imagined myself swimming alongside my fellow Navy salvage divers. I could sense the shark approaching from beneath me and pictured it crashing into me from my left side, its hard, gray nose slamming into my ribs. I could feel the displacement of the water as the two-ton monster with jaws agape ripped into my side. The last seconds leading up to the attack were the worst. I weakly sobbed as I shuffled step by step.

The shark always attacked with its mouth wide open. It not only tore me to shreds but it drowned me in the airless misery of mind. Finally, returning to my room, I would take a few minutes to gather myself. The horror of the journey back was starting to overwhelm what few defenses I had left.

The darkness of my mind's eye terrified me. Once I lay down and tried to sleep, the delusion changed to allow for a different angle of attack. I could see and feel the shark rush up past me and breach the ocean's surface to explode through my sheets. The heartless beast rose into the sky, snout pointed to the sun, but the aquatic serial killer knew there was nothing for him in the waterless sky, so it turned in mid-air as its great tail brushed the mildew stained ceiling tiles of my room. The maneuver was breathtaking. Helpless, I watched from below in slow motion as the terrible shark's gills opened and closed searching for oxygen. The muscles in its massive side flexed to bring its tail above its head and swing around for re-entry.

As it made its last turn to face me, its razor-sharp teeth framed a mouth gaped open to expose the many lives I had led.

I saw my biological father fighting the innards of the monster to stop the descent. A manic Jonah trying to break the cycle Einar could not defeat: the beast in delusion and in life. Next the pictures of my step-daughter filled the mouth of the great fish. She morphed from newborn to toddler and I could feel her infant breath on my neck as she slept, sweet and trusting, on my chest in our living room. I could feel her tiny fingers grasping at my ears to secure herself to the only father she knew and loved. I could see her turn to wave good-bye as I dropped her off at day care in the morning and then as she struggled to walk, fighting with all her will to get to me as I picked her up again after classes. With both palms on the ground, she raised her hips and overcame her fear of falling to get to me, to get to Daddy. I saw her trip the last few steps into me and I loved her wobbly courage.

Right before impact the shark's mouth filled me with one last image. It was my family in the present moment. I saw them no longer anticipating my triumphant unveiling to the world as the great universal thinker and savior. Instead, I saw them sitting around the kitchen table, crying, wondering if I would ever be released. I watched them eat dinner in silence. All their lives on hold. I saw them talking to the doctors, hoping for any word of encouragement. I saw my grandmother begin to cry while my sisters sat stoically waiting for the next torturous phone call. Worst of all, I watched my mother holding a picture of me as a baby in a pale blue onesy that matched my eyes. She held the picture to her bosom as she remembered the sleepless nights with her newborn son; dreaming of his future and the love they shared.

That was enough.

After viewing the visual panorama of my failed life, I welcomed the crushing weight of the shark as he plowed through my torso snapping me in half. I believed I deserved the excruciating pain of each tearing, gouging bite as my blood spilled across the ocean's floor of my room.

That is how I fell asleep each night.

That is how I lived.

That is not a fine line between madness and genius.

Death | Chapter 9

Virgil and I, along with all the men on the ward, spent a lot of our time smoking or thinking about smoking. It was supposed to be a no smoking ward but somehow each day we would find ourselves all standing in the one communal bathroom sharing cigarettes. The circle could range from three guys to fifteen depending on the situation and supply.

I have been in many hospitals, but it was only in the VA that I found patients willing to share cigarettes. A cigarette is not simply a cigarette to my population, actually to either of my populations: seriously mentally ill or addicted. According to the National Institute on Alcohol Abuse and Alcoholism (NIAAA), more than half of the people in treatment for addiction to alcohol and other drugs will die of a tobacco related disease.

Mental illness also has a tremendous link to smoking. While less than 20% of all Americans smoke, 90% of people with schizophrenia, 70% of people with bipolar disorder, and over 50% with diagnoses of depression are smokers. A study published in the Journal of the American Medical Association (JAMA) on "Smoking and Mental Illness" reported that 44% of all cigarettes sold in the United States are smoked by someone diagnosed as mentally ill.

That is an enormous amount of smoking for one population. Obviously, there is a problem.

People with mental illness get more tobacco-related illnesses than anyone else and die fifteen to twenty-five years earlier than the general population. The number one cause of death in the population of patients with mental illness is cardiovascular (heart) disease. I cannot show any studies that show a definite link between the high rates of smoking to the premature death rate of my population, but it is not a hard step to make on your own.

People with mental illness, including myself, are literally smoking themselves to death. I am no longer a tobacco user. I am a recovering tobacco addict who used and abused tobacco on and off for 20 yrs. Cigarettes, cigars, chewing tobacco, snuff, dip—oh sweet, sweet dip, divine Skoal Long Cut Wintergreen — I used and abused them all.

Cigarettes are used in a variety of ways in the hospital. They are currency, crutch, escape, lover, and friend. In some cases they are the only link to an outside world that will never be seen again. They allow a nostalgic escape in locked wards and locked minds. But they are not treatment.

The cigarette is never simple.

I am not judging anyone who struggles with tobacco; all addiction is rough and requires a vigilant, daily fight. But tobacco addiction is particularly complex among my population because it can sometimes be useful for addicts, both narcotic and alcoholic, to keep smoking when they first get sober. The beginning step down the road to sobriety is brutal for many and they don't need the added stress of trying to wean themselves off tobacco at the same time. But rationalizing a reliance on tobacco while battling other addictions leads too many people to smoke themselves into an early grave.

There have been times in my life when a smoke meant everything to me. Literally everything; a chance for a drag on a cigarette was my primary reason to live through the day. I didn't believe in or think of my life outside the ward. The ward was all that was real and cigarettes were my only solace. Since I was not allowed outside to smoke, the specter of missing a smoke circle in the bathroom caused me to shuffle back and forth from my room to the bathroom, always checking to see if a smoke circle had formed in my absence. It became an obsession. Other patients were either allowed by the staff to hold a stash or were given smokes when asked for them. For some reason, I was never allowed my own cigarettes.

The culture of smoking in the hospital by patients with mental illness is rarely explained and often misunderstood. As both a patient on several locked psychiatric wards and later as a national expert on tobacco addiction and mental illness, I have watched dozens of presentations by outsiders coming onto the wards to preach about the horrors of smoking. They set up shop either in a day room or lobby and give out informational flyers and candy. They inundate my population with facts and figures, all the time talking about how addictive tobacco is and how smoking should be treated like any other addiction. They show graphic photos of charred lungs, diseased tongues, and gumless mouths. Pictures of the cruelty of lung cancer and emphysema are displayed as the stats are trotted out over and over again. The final pitch is always the same. Impassioned pleas for everyone to raise their hand and pledge to quit—*Now!* Like evangelical preachers, they beg for patients to stand and witness about their carcinogen-free conversion experiences.

Garbled and confused, while I was on the ward those pitches never even got to first base with me. The only thing I knew for sure was that *They* didn't know a fucking thing about *me*.

I thought, "What kind of bullshit is this? I gotta see some doctoral candidate doing fieldwork for her dissertation to explain to me the evils of smoking and my misguided choice to partake? Some MD/Ph.D./MSW is gonna tell me they know how hard it is to quit, that it even took them a few tries, but hey, they have been tobacco free for years and if they can do it I can do it too?"

As the photos and the stats and the candy were pushed at us, all I could think was, "Yeah Doc, good for fucking you. I lost my family, my kid, my sex drive, my life and MY FUCKING MIND! You got a stat for that? Take solace in your benevolence for opening up to us lowly patients. Go home and tell your MSW friends, in your Ph.D. car with your RN life that you ministered the gospel of tobacco-free living to a bunch of mental patients while I stay locked away with nothing but the hope of a smoke. I got shit in here. Absolutely fucking nothing. Like I need a fucking lecture on how bad cigarettes are from you? No shit. No fucking shit."

To affect proper treatment of cigarette addiction, the culture of smoking in the hospital setting must be understood. Well-meaning evangelists must truly see what the cigarette meant to me and to others like me. Since most of those preaching the gospel of tobacco-free living have never been locked up in a mental ward, they have no idea what it is like and can only guess at it. But guessing at it with a mind that is not blinded by mental illness is like thinking you know all the answers on a test without even understanding the questions.

I didn't necessarily smoke to die, but I did smoke without a real investment in whether I lived. It is this distinction between suicidal tendencies and a simple ambivalence to existence that is the game played in psychiatric hospitals all over the country. It is not easy to express the hopelessness that arises from longtime and repeated hospital stays. If you admit you have thoughts of suicide, you will find yourself under tighter restriction and lose any benefits you have accrued. You could even find yourself with a longer stay in the hospital as they may now see you as a threat to yourself.

Trying to really explain the ambivalence you have about living and dying is not easy for the most advanced mind, let alone a recently fractured one. But it is that nuance that patients need to expose to staff members in order to get proper help. Until then, a perpetual shell game will exist between patient and doctor. One trying to do anything to prove he or she is ready to get out and the other guarding the gate while trying to best understand and treat the incarcerated.

While on the ward, I almost never told my doctors the truth. They would try to reason with me. They all wanted me see the truth of my situation and I would grin and acquiesce to any demand. Ten seconds after the conversation, it was a blank memory and I went down the playing field of the hall looking for adventure.

The base nature of abject hopelessness and degradation must be understood to really get a firm handle on the culture of smoking. It begins with the external loss of all you know, followed by the loss of mental stability, and ends with the visceral connection to this one thing that reminds you of the outside world and at the same time fills you with true warmth and fire and a semblance of community. It is a temporary replacement for the loss of humanity and connection accompanying chronic illness. It forces an acknowledgment of something outside of you and inside you. To separate a person with severe mental illness from a cigarette it must start with the acknowledgment of the tobacco's true place in his or her life.

The call for smoke break or the first sign of someone smoking on the ward would erase any other purpose from my mind. No matter what I was doing it would freeze me and literally pull me to the smoke. When you train a dog to come, one technique is to train her on a fifty-foot rope. This allows you to combine a physical response to the verbal command. It allows the cognitive acknowledgment of the command to be followed by a strong forward lunge that ingrains itself in the dogs psyche and muscle memory. It defeats simple cognition and becomes visceral. This is how I reacted to smoke call. It never stood as second best to any other option. I would literally not even put a foot down in the other direction when the tobacco scented rope was pulled.

I lived to smoke. I crawled on my belly under urinals and across urine-soaked bathroom floors looking for cigarette butts. Lost in delusion, I would chew whatever I found hoping to gain some effect from the damp tobacco, my head buried in the disgusting trough, eating my death.

In other hospitals where you cannot smoke on the ward, it might be the only time you got outside. It may be the only semblance of freedom you have in a place where even your mind is imprisoned. Different hospitals have different ways to allow smoke breaks and in many hospitals cigarettes are still used as a conditioning tool for those with mental illness. Like a parent threatening that you better be good because Santa Claus is watching, the bait of cigarettes can be used to control, punish, reward, and sedate patients on hospital wards.

The staff is not to blame.

The culture of smoking on hospital wards combined with the ever-present stigma has created this routine. Many are fearful to try something new without a guarantee that the next option will work. This is especially true of people who work where their lives may be at risk. The severely mentally ill population, my population, has been deemed to be a threat to themselves and others. So my population is grouped and housed in one confined area, and the staff's job is to lock themselves in with the patients and serve them the best they can with a vigilant eye on their own safety.

These MDs, orderlies, LPNs, nurses, and others put themselves at risk every day. They are, for the most part, great people on the front lines of the war against mental illness who are trying to serve a damaged population to the best of their ability. They are the not the reason cigarettes are available on the ward. Every administrator in every hospital in the US has the power to change and enforce new policy; the culture of smoking is not the fault of those on the front lines.

The culture is predicated on the fact that many believe my population will never get better. Our lives are to be survived and hopefully we will die quietly.

Stabilized, but not recovered.

No other population of patients is offered a cancer-causing agent as part of their treatment. No other population is treated with the diminished hope of an entire system and forced to accept and then imbibe half dreams meant to limit spiritual reach and diminish existential zeal.

A cigarette is not our answer, nor is it yours.

We deserve more and can handle the expectation. It is part of the social compact between patient and caregiver that when someone is involuntarily committed to a psychiatric facility and their liberties are taken away, certain decisions regarding their wellbeing must be made for them. The patient is beyond reason; you could not explain anything to me in mania that I would not wrestle from reality instantly. Simply because it is easy to give a manic man a cigarette is not reason enough to allow the culture of smoking to continue. The families of people with serious mental illness and addiction entrust their most important possession into the system's care because they are out of options. The system must not be allowed to continue to poison the patients just because it supposedly makes them easier to manage.

It is time to see this for what it is and stop the smoking epidemic facing my population. We must step out of the cycle and end the cultural expectations of diminished life span, systemic execution, and the existential demeaning of my sisters and brothers.

Death | Chapter 10

Virgil and I did more than smoke and chat while he lubed up with cocoa butter. We strolled. He moved with the weight of his muscle and created paths that people did not impede. I could no longer hold anything but a cigarette and Virgil looked like he was lifting cars when I was not around.

When Virgil and I stepped out into the hallway, I did not imagine great white sharks. He made me feel safe. I kept my eyes wide open and followed him wherever he went. It always amazed me that Virgil had places to go. If I had a day planner it would have said nothing but smoke and meds all day, every day. If we were walking to walk, I walked right next to him almost shoulder to shoulder. Sometimes I would fall in step with him to relieve the anxiety of falling behind or getting lost. With Virgil by my side, I was secure, anchored. Without him, I was lost and afraid.

By that time, my mania had almost succeeded in completely walling me off from the outside world, and the only time its power was threatened was when my family came to see me.

No matter how hard the mania tried, it could not deaden the gut-wrenching emotional reaction to seeing my family. Even if I thought they were not there to help me and even if my mind twisted each word, look, reaction, and breath to fit my current delusional storyline, the physical reaction in my core was real. It had not killed that. That is what saved my life, that physical reaction that forced a recognition of me when I knew no me.

It is an unfair burden to place on my family, but I am convinced that if they had stopped coming to see me I would have perished. To all families dealing with mental illness, addiction, or both: We, my fellow patients and I, know you have been wounded. We know there is no time to heal as each morning's news may bring additional pain. We know it is unfair to ask any more of you. But we need you.

There is a psychic "failure to thrive" issue in this tragedy. When a baby is born with severe complications and sent to an institution it is often never held. Never touched. It has been shown that a child who is not touched and acknowledged will physically not grow or "thrive." A ten-year-old boy who has been chained to his crib for his life will look like a four-year old. The same occurs to a mind not acknowledged by the outside world. The longer I stayed in the hospital, trapped in my own mind, the smaller my essence became. My whole world, my whole self, withered. Without the visits and forced acknowledgment of my family, I would have been lost in the lands of my delusion forever.

Your brothers and sisters, mothers and fathers, aunts and uncles, veterans and citizens in mental wards across the country are cut off from all outside human contact. Disease is systematically disassembling their connection to you and to their outside lives. It is blotting out the warmth and sunlight of human communion. The door is slowly closing on them and the disease is stealing them away from you. Sometimes their only connection to reality is your visit, your touch, or even just your face through the window. Your presence keeps the door open a little longer and may, in some cases, provide the glimmer of reality that gives your loved one the strength to push back, kick open the door, and to, some-day, walk back out into the light.

But remember, it is not all about your loved one locked behind closed doors. You are suffering greatly also. Both the family and the family member with mental illness need their own recovery trajectories, their own plans to address the drastic changes in their once-accepted identities.

Take care of yourselves. Find support groups, open up to others of the horrors of mind and soul that torment you each night. But please don't stop visiting. Don't stop acknowledging to your loved one that they are still alive and still connected to the outside. Touch them even for one second, one instant, and return that bit of humanity to his or her skin. It means more than you know. It is much-needed air for a loved one who is being buried alive in his or her own skin by addiction, delusion and despair.

Virgil and I made our rounds from place to place on the ward. From the front of the hall where he would kid around with the staff and I would blankly observe from ten feet behind him, to the bathroom to see if anyone was offering up cigarettes to the daily, post-lunch smoking circle. Virgil never seemed out of sorts and was always very open about his diagnosis and addiction issues. He considered these stays "tune ups." There wasn't much fear in Virgil; like Bill, he seemed to thrive on the hall. He had it figured out.

It was late afternoon and the staff was cut down to a few night shift personnel. No treatment after 4pm, just housing. The hall seemed deserted even though at this time of night everyone would be back on the ward. Virgil and I were walking down the center of the hall. He seemed agitated. I wasn't afraid of him, but everyone else should have been.

Virgil started calling me "Sensei" as we marched. Barking it like a Drill Instructor. Even as his voice grew louder and louder, I was not put off by the constant call. It took me back to my abridged martial arts career and to my life in the military. I hated practice in martial arts, but liked to fight. If you lined up every teacher, martial arts or academic I ever had, they would offer the same observation: tremendous potential but not enough practice. I originally took up martial arts because I never learned how to fight in high school and I wanted to learn how to stand toe to toe with another. Virgil's cries only reinforced those memories and my mania kidnapped them.

Virgil's calls got more forceful and I no longer felt like we were playing manic Marco Polo. I seemed to be in a trance; I didn't know if my eyes were opened or closed. As I turned to see my leader, he was already in midair. His massive frame was spinning above me as he released a flying roundhouse kick that pulverized the fire alarm compartment that housed a fire extinguisher mounted on the wall. He retracted his foot from the shattered glass and metal of the mangled red door when he landed and stared at me with an innocent grin.

I could feel my teeth separate as my jaw unhinged from its permanent clamp for a rare, wide open-mouthed grin. I wasn't happy because he had broken something and thoughts of repercussions didn't enter my mind. I just enjoyed the break from my absolute and pre-determined thought patterns. The spontaneity of the act charged through my leaden body.

Virgil didn't stop grinning for hours. He would not succumb to the misery. He had been through it all before and knew a way out for wayward travelers. His optimism was infectious and I felt like I had a real partner in hell.

No one came to investigate that night. I suspect the workers didn't want to confront him alone. He was physically imposing and the enormous cobra tattoo on his arm added to his overall menacing, marauder motif. But that night was a turning point. Virgil's roundhouse kick broke more than a fire extinguisher casing; it punctured the hardened shell encasing my mind and allowed in a glimmer of light. In some small way, the shattering of that glass casing altered my view of my situation from an all-consuming internal-only focused "In-sight" to allow me a glimpse of the world outside of me, an "Out-sight."

Virgil and I called it a night but the next few days would mark the beginning of the end of my stay on the ward. It would get much, much worse before it got better, but the fight was on and the momentum could not be stopped.

Death | Chapter 11

The next day at meds, Virgil was called over by the head nurse. She seemed like a kind woman. I am not actually sure if she was a nurse. She could have been a doctor, NP, LPN or anything else. Titles were interchangeable. I could not concentrate on what she said and what my delusions said at the same time, so I listened to the delusions. (The choice is not hard: one tells you that you have a chronic mental illness and recommends ninety-two things which mean total psychic change—the other tells you that you are awesome, have always been awesome and will remain the stalwart for all awesomeness to come. Not the toughest of my daily decisions to make on the ward.)

She led Virgil down the hall and showed him the broken fire department equipment. They had a short discussion. Everything seemed cordial; Virgil was even smiling at certain points. The morning appeared to be headed back to its monotony when a few orderlies surrounded Virgil and gently led him to a room I had not ever noticed. I waited anxiously to imbibe my medicines and when it was finally my turn, I took my meds, threw them back like a shot of liquor, and snuck over to the threshold of the room into which my guide had been taken. None of the orderlies had come out and I was growing concerned. If they could get Virgil, my future was hopeless.

By that time, my meds were going down well. They were giving me everything in liquid form. One of the meds was reddish, almost purple, and my delusional mind had me convinced it was sloe gin. Sloe gin itself was a kinder, gentler drink from my alcoholic past. It was a high school drink. The last time I drank sloe gin, I stole a moped and flew through the backyards of East Brunswick trying to avoid oak trees, screened-in patios, and arrest. It was a drink that eventually gave way to stronger liquids, like, say, tequila. Tequila is a different mindset than sloe gin.

Quick breakdown of the difference:

A sloe gin night entailed meeting a girl, having some laughs, chatting about what is important to her and important to you, maybe spark a joint and get comfy, put on *Glengarry Glen Ross* and watch Alec Baldwin deliver the greatest speech of all time, fool around, and then fall asleep together.

Now a tequila night (allegedly) went something like this: bang down warm beers you snuck into your room while listening to Nirvana, leave the barracks in San Diego, ride the trolley to Mexico, grab a few Coronas over the border for a quarter, hit Club Escape on Revolution Ave., buy twenty hits of acid for you and your buddies from your Commanders Cup Navy football team, pass out ten and keep ten for later, drop three hits of West Coast White Blotter under your tongue, call the shot guy over and pay him to pull your head back and blow whistles in your ears while he literally pours wholesale, rat-gut Tijuana Tequila down your throat until he is done and slaps your head forward … REPEAT … see your friend running your way letting you know you are busted, eat all the remaining hits of LSD, get your ass absolutely crushed by the security staff in a disgusting bathroom until they leave you there to find the dealer, have large friend scream, "RUUUUUUUUNN!", blast back out onto Revolution Ave. like Butch and Sundance, hail a taxi, yell "To the border!", freak out crossing back over to the FREEDOM of the good, ol' US of A, all the while finding-losing-and-finding your Military ID as you TRIP BALLS three inches from a Federal agent, step outside into the California air, and lay shirtless on the ground in front of Jack in the Box, step back on the trolly and return to base to hallucinate for another thirty-six hours until Satellite Communications school starts again Monday.

Tequila/Sloe Gin, just different (allegedly).

Every time meds was called at this stage of my time on the ward, the Kiss song "Cold Gin" would start a repeating track in my head with sloe gin substituted for cold gin. The refrain was looping over and over. I would hum, sing and sway to the words, "Its Sloe Gin time again." I couldn't wait to take my meds. I thought I was tying one on to get through another day. It would be followed by a quick smoke if I could find someone in the bathroom and let the day rip. But that day, with Virgil in the mystery room and the events of the previous night still swirling about in my head, I was not as entranced by the song and the meds tasted more like heavy psychotic oil: sweet, embalming and foreign.

I could hear Virgil talking to everybody but I couldn't see him. This room was built differently than the others on the ward. It sat directly across from the nursing station. I had never seen or heard of anyone going in or out of it. The entrance was not a doorway that opened immediately to a wide room like the other rooms. The doorway stood at the beginning of a narrow hallway that then opened to a larger room. The hallway IN the room was eight feet long. At the end of the interior hall the room opened self-consciously to the right and hid from sight. There was a window on the left side of the room I could see from the interior hall. It was higher and smaller than the windows in other rooms. The other rooms had windows that were industrial-sized, 6' tall and 3' wide. They were lined with wire to prevent shattering.

One day in an early delusion when I thought my entire stay on the ward was being filmed, I tested the strength of the industrial windows. I put a chair in front of the window in my room and set up to jump through it: chest first. I was still wearing the rosary then and was physically strong. The advanced process of aging under the daily shower of Thorazine had not set in.

I moved back to the doorway leading into the room and started to run towards the chair. I focused on my steps to not trip on the front lip of the seat. I could picture my omniscient Director filming the episode. Reality placed a small anxious fear in my stomach but mania squelched the alarm and I pushed off my right foot to place my left on the slick, naked wood of the hospital chair. Restraint and sanity left at the same time as my arms lifted into a T and I arched back like a surrendering fallen angel as my left foot planted on the chair and fired forward toward the glass. My heart rose as I thrust my body, solar plexus first, into this second story window with all my might. I would birth myself to reality through this baptism of glass. I knew my family would be proud of the finished product: the movie, the coronation, the universal acknowledgment. This would be the behind-the-scenes documentary of the making of my new Bipolar Bible, the Twisted Testament of a Christ in Crisis.

I flew through the hospital air while my family sat an hour away living their lives. Oblivious to my glory.

My chest slammed into the window and bought me to a dead stop. The rosary embedded deep in my skin and the metal crucifix marked my ribcage. I flew backwards and just managed to get a leg on the chair to push myself towards the bed to cushion the blow of the unforgiving floor.

The compressed cross embroidered in my skin signified my divinity and proper course. My bruised knee healed quickly and the episode was forgotten instantly. It was a watershed moment when my visceral voice of survival was first drowned out and I actually acted upon my delusions.

I wasn't satisfied with only hearing Virgil in the hidden room; I needed to see him. After all, he was my safety, my refuge. I was terrified without him and I was terrified just standing there, alone, in the doorway. The little window high on the wall let some sun into the room. It reached the floor about half way down the interior hall. I figured I could get to the solar border without upsetting too many people and calm my own nerves. The opportunity cost of each step was weighed until I could see Virgil. As I inched closer, I could hear him kidding around with everyone. There were even a few laughs. Someone said, "Sorry, but you know we gotta do this. Nothing personal. Just can't let that kind of stuff go on."

He responded with Yeahs, Sures and Uh-huhs.

I was close enough to see that he was on a small bed with his feet separated under a sheet. They were spread farther apart then expected. It looked like he was wearing ankle weights under the sheet. They were telling Virgil to get ready to lie down when I reached the edge of the sunshine and saw his face.

Virgil was sitting up and grinning. The guards were surrounding the isolated bed and watching him with concern and care. Virgil was taking a last few deep breaths when our eyes met. He didn't react. The expression on his face stayed fixed: no wink, no grin, no acknowledgment at all. I am not sure if he didn't want me to be discovered or if he was checked out mentally to prepare for this brutal ritual sacrifice.

He laid down and put his arms out to the sides. An orderly on each side grabbed his wrists and placed them in large leather restraints. They pulled the tongue of the restraints through a loop and like a belt put the metal prong through the hole in the leather. They each asked Virgil if the restraints were too tight and how he felt. He received no pillow for his head.

Before they left, they asked once more if he was "OK." Virgil thought for a second and turned just his head toward the orderly in front of me. I could see his eyes while he asked to have the sheet removed from his lower body. Locked onto my guide, I watched as the sheet was gently pulled back. As it slid off his legs, the ankles restraints were exposed for the first time. They were grotesque in their blatancy of purpose, like leather nooses for the legs. Virgil was foreshadowing my death and how it would occur. I couldn't look anymore. I felt like throwing up.

The room full of restrainers was clearing out. I had to go. I backed out of the narrow hall and away from its instruments of torture. How did I not notice this room before? I walked past this vicious room everyday with no acknowledgment of the horrors of mind and soul that painted its walls. It must have had a number and maybe even a name but it was a foreign land to me until that moment.

The nurses, doctors and orderlies were discussing Virgil and I was listening, trying to get some info about him. I was doing intelligence recon for my shipmate even though I was physically useless. I could not leave my guide in there with no connection, no help or hope. I failed to realize Virgil was still leading. He was not captured as much as he was teaching.

The orderlies were now standing directly in front of the door and the nurses were all agreeing to whatever the doctors were proposing. Finally, I heard the name of the room, it was called the Seclusion Room and patient Virgil would be secluded until such and such time.

The medical staff in the various psychiatric hospitals I have been a patient in have worked very hard to save my life. I know they all went into the field to help my population and I am very, very aware of the toll taken on this group of compassionate MDs. But I wonder what doctors really know about seclusion and restraint. I know in their training they may have to be restrained, but for how long? One minute, thirty seconds maybe even five minutes. Is it during the day or in the depths of the night? Are other MDs in the room applauding you while you give your clinical opinion of what it feels like?

Let's try this:

Lay prone in the fucking things for an hour in the middle of the night— alone. Better yet: let someone grab you, in the dark, for no reason (since in a state of delusion we very rarely know why we are being punished), and then allow yourself to get strapped to a bed for two hours, three hours, four hours, five hours, six hours, seven hours....

Thirty seconds is not an hour and five minutes is not five hours. Try twenty-four hours, try twenty-four fucking hours lashed to a bed, screaming for your family, shitting yourself, and soul-weeping for a dead father that is haunting your every moment. Do that, try that, then tell me where on the scale of wellness that falls.

First, do no harm. Isn't that what doctors are taught in medical school? No one should carry out treatments and punishments without regard for their effect. It is a person in that bed. It is someone's brother or mother or son or daughter or father ... it is someone like me who is begging for mercy. You cannot deduce from five minutes in a bed what five hours feels like and until you are forced to experience what we experience, my population of patients will not trust you. They will fear you, but they will never trust you.

By shackling patients to a bed, by pinning their arms and legs down in four-point restraints, by leaving them with no access to water, no ability to use the bathroom, no ability to move at all, no ability to look into the eyes of someone who cares, you have made the paradigm shift from *Treatment provider to Torturer.*

You have created something you do not understand and never will.

They wouldn't let me near Virgil. So I called to him and he responded, but then I was escorted to my room. The playing field had changed. It had somehow finally sunk in that life on the ward was no game. The hall had a lethal feel to it. With each step I took, I feared for my life. Each step triggered my psychosis, and I fell deeper into a helpless survival mode.

I was at the weakest point in my adult life, and I had lost my guardian. Once back in my bed, I tried to figure some haphazard plan for my survival. Immersed in my broken mind, every sound increased my terror. When would Virgil return? What was going to happen to me? Somewhere in my deluded mind I thought: I have got to get the fuck out of here or ...

I am going to die in here.

Death | Chapter 12

Virgil returned to me that afternoon. I don't know if he came straight from isolation to my room or not. We didn't hug or shake hands. I was dying to ask about the occurrence but he didn't bring it up. Being strapped to a bed for an undetermined amount of time is very personal. You will experience your own terror and despair. Your body's physical make up will determine which muscles tense and spasm. Your relations with your loved ones will determine to whom and for whom you scream in the night. The bed is what it is and you don't know it intimately until you have laid down with it. It is absolute restraint. It is powerlessness. It is fear. It is pain. It is terror, it is an institutional gang rape.

Anxiety is described as the gap between a desired outcome and the present situation. If you are unable to act on the gap between these two phenomena, the anxiety will intensify and can further the gap between the expectation and the actual. In a seclusion room, pressed to a bed you have only one desire and expectation and that is *release*. Your reality is being harnessed to the mattress. You have no control of the outcome other than to acquiesce to the external demands of the staff and hope that grants you a reprieve. Anxiety is instant when you hit the bed and then it only builds. It takes you down the many dark roads of the self and the SCREAM builds in your lungs. The final giving up and what that means is exposed as a reality. The stripping away, the raw, emotional nakedness lurks with each seclusion. It peeks around corners and withdraws letting the awareness of its reality do the terrorizing.

Virgil and I made our way to his room as the evening was starting to solidify outside the hospital windows. The hall lights were brighter and the ward seemed more insulated and confining, more of an absolute, less contingent on anything else.

The staff announced that we would be showering that night. I can't remember how often we showered, but I know it was not something we did every day. There was a single shower room with three large showers. The shower stalls were singles. One person at a time. Each one was big enough to accommodate a wheelchair and built with handles on the walls.

The men of the ward lined up in the hall outside the shower room door while the orderly made sure everyone was accounted for. The last stragglers made their way up the ward dragging their med-soaked muscles and heaving each breath in and out.

When the door was opened, a staff member stood at the entrance and handed out cigarettes. Three each. I watched as I got closer to the doorway and I was thrilled at the opportunity to smoke in a new place. I didn't care what I got: Kent, Newport, Marlboro, Parliament, Camel, Camel Light. Anything was good just give them to me now.

The orderly placed three in my hand, each a different brand, and I entered the room. There were over thirty of us and six or seven light blue therapeutic chairs to sit in. The chairs were used to bathe the vets that could not stand on their own. The room seemed to be used primarily by physical therapists with whirlpools, raised massage tables and various pulley systems to get men in and out of the tubs. An orderly turned on the showers and steam instantly started to fill the room. The water pressure was violent, so strong it sounded like whitewater rapids had been unleashed behind the curtains of shower stalls.

Lastly, the orderly handed out a couple of lighters and left. The oldest men were given the dampened seats. A few of the guys were even older than Bill. Veterans in their late sixties and seventies shuffled to their thrones. It is a brutal place for the elderly. The stages of one path of my life were being laid out in front of me. Men a few years older than me intermingled with men thirty plus years my senior. I imagined myself in my seventies, in a wheelchair due to my surgically repaired feet, smoking Newports with a Marlboro chaser, waiting for my turn to get pounded in the shower.

Our cigarettes were lit as the room filled with steam. The room had lost fifty percent of its visibility as the moisture mixed with the carbon monoxide. The dichotomy of baptizing my lungs with the life-affirming mist and the death-ensuring smoke was left unexamined. The men were naked or had towels wrapped around their waists. It was a very normal and even comfortable feeling to be together with my fellow vets in our Madman's Sweatlodge.

I looked around the room protected by the moist haze and stared at my ward-mates. I allowed the first seconds of my own self-conscious awareness to drop and moved into the presence of those I observed. Patiently, the moment was revealing itself to me. I saw each man as if for the first time: thirty brave boys from numerous wars and conflicts together in the fight for our lives. No one arguing, no one screaming. The mist had created a more palpable atmosphere to swim in and feel connected. As the sweat poured from my body and dripped to the ground, my eyes focused on one patient in particular. He was the oldest on the ward.

During the days on the ward, I would often see him. He was like me; his stay was not a "tune up." The ward was his life. He had the disheveled look of an absent-minded professor in his crumbled sport coats. Grandpa looked perpetually disoriented while he scurried from place to place looking for something that was never there. Always searching like Mr. Magoo in some demented cartoon.

What does mental illness on top of dementia feel like? Insanity x Insanity = What? What is real then? The fear must have been great at times for that grandfather of the ward.

He had all his hair. It was silver, white and thick. It had the puffed up pompadour look of the 1950s. Prior to seeing him in the shower, I had been convinced he was a doctor and so I wouldn't talk to him. It just was so out of place—so sad—to see this Elk, this VFW member on the same ward as me.

Grandpa was given the largest chair. It had a very high back and stirrups for his legs if desired. The steam glistened on his wrinkled face as he leaned his head back and stared into the roaring abyss of the showers. He looked more relaxed in the mist, and I could only imagine a life filled with hundreds of hospitals and homeless shelters, where the fight for life is literal and daily. I willed his life to be not what it was. At that moment, I wanted him to be a dignified serviceman just relaxing with his brothers, his company or battalion. The dialectic of the moist air and a rare moment of compassion tethered me to my mentally ill grandfather.

His true fragility was revealed as he slowly raised the burning cigarette to his mouth. The cigarette shook in his withered hand and he had trouble bringing it to his lips. His neck tensed under its sagging skin as his head struggled to meet the cigarette. Grandpa's eyes closed as the filter reached his yearning mouth. In a room full of men who had traveled the world to serve their country and die if necessary, no help came his way. No one could see this happening. No one was looking for it.

The cigarette finally met his wet lips and the soggy filter disappeared as he pulled on the smoke. He sat back and the ease returned to his face. His shoulders dropped and his jaw slacked with the invisible exhalation of smoke into the pool of gray air. His suffering diminished, he kept the cigarette next to his lips: waiting. The smoke would come easier next time. Soaked in his own sweat, the blood of the moist, brown filter ran down his wrist with a thin trickle of tar. Steam had matted down his full head of hair atop his handsome, distinguished face and it gave him the boyish look of a carefree child running in and out of the sprinklers in a Rockwell painting. I pray that Grandpa found solace in that moment.

God bless the Grandpa of the Ward.

Death | Chapter 13

Virgil and I met up at the end of the shower ritual and smoked again in his room as he dried off and poured more cocoa butter onto his elbows. Where the hell was all this cocoa butter coming from? I could not find my shoes and had been wearing the same clothes for weeks and Virgil seemed to have his own Estee Lauder counter.

Virgil started talking about cigarettes. I believe I actually spoke that evening and asked, "Where do I get mine from?"

Since I never had cigarettes of my own, I believed it was a conspiracy against me. Virgil explained that the cigarettes are kept at the front desk behind the nurse's station in a filing cabinet. Bottom drawer. He had watched them grab the packs before and made a note of it.

Virgil explained that the staff is supposed to take the patients outside to smoke but since the ward houses veterans in their most acute stages they didn't always make it outside. The staff would give them a cigarette or two to share in the bathroom after meals. Some men were even allowed to keep their own packs with them or they snuck them onto the ward.

The mystery was now explained and then immediately forgotten. The only thing that mattered was that I wanted more smokes. I wanted my smokes. I wanted some control, but I was not Randle McMurphy and I was not going to a start a riot to watch the World Series or get my own cigarettes. This *One Flew Over the Cuckoo's Nest* was not a fucking movie and I couldn't yell "Cut!"

Virgil and I discussed a plan. We would make our way up the ward to the nurse's station the following evening. It is totally empty at night. When the coast was clear, we'd go over the wall and rob the cigarette stash. We would grab them all and smoke 'em down to the filter. We pledged to burn every last one of those cancerous motherfuckers to their death between our teeth!

The heist was planned and we were committed. I left Virgil's room that day and no sharks attacked me as I walked to my room. I did not drag my feet or get sidetracked by my mania. I had something I had not had for months on the ward: I had a purpose. I would go over the wall and steal these cigarettes. I would make my move and pay whatever consequence. I was doing something for me. It was a statement of self that could not be washed away by delusion.

I looked at my hands and saw the beauty in my discolored and chewed upon fingertips. I saw the hands of every man and, most importantly, of me. I am Eric Arauz. I am Eric Fucking Arauz and tomorrow I am going over the wall.

I may have had nothing to live for but I finally had something to die for.

Death | Chapter 14

The next morning came and for the first time in months I woke with a mission, a reason to get out of bed. I had a new roommate but we never interacted. He was another older man in his fifties. He reminded me of one of the sergeants from an old World War II movie. He stood erect and looked you directly in the eye, like Bill. More of a threat than an acknowledgment. He didn't say much and he wasn't uncomfortable looking right at you for five or ten seconds before moving on. He slept by the door and my bed was still by the window. I had a tall stand-up locker with nothing in it. I had no idea where anything I owned was. After my shoes were stolen, it never occurred to me to think about it.

I wore the same clothes everyday. If I changed them I have no memory of it. I always wore my blue hospital slipper socks. My hair was growing back in patches because I had found a razor and started to shave my head in the bathroom until I was caught. Large chunks of hair were missing from my scalp. My eyes were crusted together each morning from the constant circulation of hospital air and lack of hygiene. My lips cracked and healed three times a day. The look on my face was constant so my mouth rarely opened and closed. When I did smile, like when Virgil threw his helicopter kick, my lips ripped and bled into my teeth, filling the gaps with the dark blood of the mentally and physically ill. There were no real mirrors on the ward so my general appearance remained a mystery. The shaving stations by the sinks have those plastic shields on the wall that let you make out a few personal details but you cannot see well enough to focus on your physical destruction.

Even though my physical reality was dismal and getting worse, that morning

I had a relative bounce to my step. I heard the call for morning meds and marched up the ward to receive my breakfast communion. "It's Sloe Gin time again ..." pulsed in my head as I watched my fellow warriors take their prescriptions. One by one this mass of delusion, decay and divinity fell in step as we swallowed and departed. My cocktail of who-knows-what went down smooth.

With classic rock in my ears, redemption on my mind and Thorazine in my veins, I turned like the men ahead of me and tunneled back down the ward. The day passed without incident. I smoked in the bathroom with my teammates and circled the ward a few times before my weakened muscles needed rest. I tried to picture the heist but could not hold the image. I was no longer able to think in pictures like I had before I entered the ward. I thought in feelings and emotions. I could not see anything of purpose in my mind's eye. My memory had been erased by the disease.

The sun set on the ward and the evening slid in through the windows. Inch by inch, the homes on the horizon vanished under the blanket of night until darkness settled on the ward. Virgil appeared from nowhere and we moved without hesitation upstream. The staff was cut at night as the never-ending flow of doctors was gone. No treatment after 4:00 p.m. We walked to the edge of the entrance of the seclusion room and acted like we were talking. Virgil was rambling about high school or karate or physics, I have no idea, but he was talking and grabbing my shoulder and grinning.

Virgil talked and talked, the whole time looking over at the nurses station out of the corner of his eye. My back was to the counter guarding the cabinet containing the cigarettes. He was laughing and leering over my shoulder to see when the time was right. I had no idea what the next step was. I was excited about the heist in theory, but hadn't been able to think through even the smallest details.

How exactly were we getting into the station? What we would do with our newfound fortune? Where would we smoke them all? Someone might notice if we were in the bathroom with the other veterans wearing cigarettes like gun belts strapped across our chest—bipolar bandits bearing tobacco-laden bandoliers.

This was the plan: there was no plan.

Little tip: Don't rob a bank with me when I am in a full-blown manic episode. I will shoot you in the face on the way IN the door, steal the deposits slips, staple them to my skull like an Iroquois headdress, and skip back OUT the door like a crazed leprechaun on Red Bull and ecstasy.

Virgil stopped laughing all at once and said, "Go admiral, go, go, go!"

I didn't know what was happening. I spent so much time in my mind I hadn't acted spontaneously in months. I listened to Virgil and spun around. I pushed off my left foot to propel myself up and over the open counter guarding the nurse's station. I remembered doing tuck and rolls in my Aiki-jujitsu days and committed to the dive. I tucked my head and reached my right hand in front of my body. I shot my turning torso forward and landed on the counter with my right shoulder blade and the rest of my body cartwheeling over me. The best tip for a roll, as in life, is to let go to the momentum. It is counterintuitive but it lets forces outside of your control flow freely. My chin tucked to my chest and my legs flew over to complete the circle.

I landed on my feet in the nurse's station.

SMOKES! GET THE SMOKES! WHERE IS THE FUCKING CABINET?

I was so jacked up I almost ran straight into a wall. I found the cabinet and went at it. It was a tall, tan filing cabinet and the smokes were in the bottom drawer. I tore the cabinet open and saw the contents. It was transcendent. Reds and greens, tans and yellows danced on the rectangular cartoons in a swirling maze. The abundance of such a find froze me. I stared at it. It was emancipation from the slavery of the ward. It was the burgeoning freedom of a shackled existence. That moment did not end the suffering, but it was a break, an honest break.

I grabbed the stash with both hands and started my getaway. Virgil was standing with his palms on the counter of the station watching the robbery. I gave him as many cigarette cartons as he could handle and lumbered over the counter with the remaining treasure. There was no repeat performance of the flying roll moments earlier. Encumbered with booty, the bipolar bandit had to secure his escape.

We ran down the hallway as we headed for the bathroom. We had not decided on a final destination to split the loot but there was no other option. We turned into the port side entrance and made our way to a corner not visible from the hallway. We ripped open the cartoons and smoked the panorama of brands at our disposal. One after the other, the various makes and models of disease pulsed through my brain. The carbon monoxide stole the oxygen from my blood as my starving lungs and brain fought for air. My body was rewarded with more and more smoke; each pull on the cigarette, each deep inhale of carcinogens tasted like freedom as I cut days and months off my life span.

Virgil was smoking two or three at a time, his big mouth grinning as he cackled. Every laugh pulsed clouds of smoke out of his mouth and nose. We had done it. Thoughts of repercussion did not enter my mind. I was in the moment, smoking, smoking, smoking, smoking. As we went through cigarette after cigarette, as they became smaller and smaller between my fingers, I stopped becoming and just was.

The ward was getting louder. We could hear yells and doors slamming, but we smoked and smoked and smoked. The floor was covered with the butts of our kills. The rainbow of torn packages, the torn carcasses of our treasure lay strewn on the floor like battlefield dead.

And we smoked.

Suddenly, the bathroom exploded with noise. Orderlies swept us up and dragged us from the room. They yelled in my face and took Virgil somewhere else. They said they had a witness. I was seen going over the counter. They were sure it was all me.

I hardly heard them. I smirked and thought, "Whatever, fuck it, do what you like. I am ready to start my penance. We did it. We did something real, now you can do your worst."

Unlike McMurphy, I would not be lobotomized.

I would be secluded and restrained.

They dragged me up the hallway to the darkest part of the ward. Step by step, we made our way to the restraints. Their grip slacked as they realized I was not fighting.

As we reached the head of the ward, the seclusion room was in sight. Its entrance was smaller than the others and it stood out to me. There was no door on its hinges. Hell is always open for business.

I imagined writing above the doorway, writing scrawled in the blood, and the screams and anguish of a thousand faceless veterans, writing that said: "Abandon hope all ye who enter here." I was about to descend through my nine circles of hell and, unlike in Dante's Divine Comedy, my Virgil had been taken away. I had no guide. I glanced to my left before we entered the room. There was the scene of the crime—the broken cabinet door and packs of cigarettes strewn all over the floor. I knew it was real. I knew I was real.

As they pulled me the last few feet into the room, I looked again at the imagined warning above the door and grinned thinking,

"Go fuck yourselves...."

The staff said, "Sit on the bed and lay down. Spread your arms and legs. You shouldn't have stolen the cigarettes, Eric."

Death | Chapter 15

Four-point restraints are designed to pin you to a mattress by your wrists and ankles. The only other time I had been placed in restraints, I had been unconscious. For this evolution, I was wide awake. The orderlies were not cruel; they only mirrored my level of aggression. If I fought the slightest bit they instantly responded with more physical control. If I relaxed my body and offered my limbs willingly, they lessened their grip and kept at their mission.

While the orderlies were restraining me, someone else was talking to me. I couldn't see him. In restraints, I was only able to see straight up or a few degrees left and right. I couldn't turn my head due to my thick neck and large shoulders. I wasn't able to see someone standing at my feet. I was also completely exhausted from the tobacco, all the inhaled smoke, and the Thorazine.

The room was dark. I couldn't see the walls, but I could feel them. I could feel the room. Sense it. It felt like suffering. It had no utility except to separate man from society, to separate man from himself. It took the sickest and most defenseless patients and caused them even greater suffering.

Trauma masked as treatment.

How many men—how many veterans served their nation only to come home to disease or to grow old in a manic mind—had been sequestered in this room? How many men, unsure of reality and lost in disease, had been lashed to this bed and pushed to the edge of reason and beyond as they turned inward to face themselves? Anyone who has ever found their way to this room, to this bed, or to beds like it in any of the veterans' hospitals around the country, has existed on the fringes of society and on the fringes of the self.

If you are one of those men or women, you are my brother or my sister. You fought for your country and lived to come home. But instead of being struck by a bullet or an I.E.D., you have been struck down by a disease of the mind. Your own body turned on you and held you captive. If you have been shackled to a bed in a secluded room, you have been a *Domestic POW* held in the prison of your mind on the streets of your native land. Your parents, friends, and lovers will never—can never—truly know your, our, pain. You have psychologically turned your back on a reality you could no longer live with and have been forced, physically forced, to face the horror of your life. As you wept and struggled in these leather shackles, your rampaging mind cornered you. And there was no escape as your disease prepared for the death blow.

With the mania in full control and its host defenseless, it would gain confidence. It knew all your deepest fears, all your secret desires, all your hopes, dreams and failures and it would use them to torture you before it was all over.

The team left and I was alone with the darkened room. The walls stood high above me and hovered over my body like surgeons. My restraints were bulky, brown, weathered leather. Each was fastened firmly around my wrists and ankles. My arms were pulled out away from my body. My ankles were pulled apart and stretched from my hips as far as my groin would allow. Horizontally crucified, I adjusted myself to the mattress and looked straight up at the ceiling. The bed was hidden from the open hall. The long narrow hallway to the main ward began next to the foot of the bed. This room was designed to fit one restraining bed—and one victim.

I knew Virgil had been in this same bed. He returned whole, but I was not Virgil. The beds are communal, but the suffering is personal. Like physical death, psychic death is always a singular event. People only truly learn its lessons once. Physical death happens to every sentient being on this planet, and yet cannot ever truly be discussed because each participant is no longer available for correspondence. Psychic death, on the other hand, can be discussed but it is usually hidden, and the suffering associated with the absolute release of one's mind and essence to mental disease has caused many to actively seek their physical deaths.

I was now hyper-aware of my surroundings. I listened to the room. It was trying to be silent as it slowly revealed itself to me. I felt it had killed before and would relish taunting me before the end. Its walls were naked. The floor was empty except for me and the bed. It was dark but not pitch black; there was light coming from some direction as I noticed the right side of the room was lighter than the left. I looked for the source and saw to my right the small, bare window

I had seen before during Virgil's penance. It allowed as much streetlight in as possible. It was my only ally. It would serve as the portal out as I dug deeper inward.

This room is the same in every hospital. There is no sense of time or place. Because I was unconscious the first time I ended up in four-point restraints, I didn't truly understand what I was in for. I hadn't been baptized in its particular pain yet, and I was not sufficiently fearful. I still had enough fight in me to think I was ready for war, but war is never what you think it is. Throughout history, fresh-faced warriors have left their homes to go fight a foreign enemy. Their people celebrated their valor and heroism and they marched into battle with the innocence and naiveté of youth. But once in the fog of war, they discover that songs and awards that celebrate the killing bear no relationship to the reality which, once experienced, cannot be forgotten. Only the uninitiated see beauty in the slaughter. Those who have been there relate their stories of war for what they are: fights for survival in the midst of a massacre.

All war is genocide.

In psychiatric hospitals across the country, we are waging war against our own. When you kill another, you kill yourself. When you physically restrain and then abandon a psychiatric patient to be victimized and tortured by his own maniacal mind, you are waging war on society. The ritual sacrifice of the bipolar, depressed, schizoaffective, schizophrenic and others on these hospital altars does not purify the culture that houses them. It does not rid the culture of people diagnosed with mental illness. It only entombs them alive.

Bury the dead, not the living.

Death | Chapter 16

As I was settling into the feeling of the bed, I heard steps from my left coming down the hall into the room. A nurse appeared. She wiped my face and asked how I felt. Her eyes were full of compassion. I felt true concern in her voice. She told me it would only be for a few more minutes and they would let me out. I was so dissociated from my reality, I had actually forgotten I was even in the hospital. Like in my youth, I hid so deep in myself to stop the pain, I lost myself in the abyss of my mind miles behind my eyes.

She put a cool cloth around my eyes and throat and told me it would be OK. The towel soothed the skin around my wrists as she wiped them down. She was very tender and I found peace in her damp touch. By the time she was done the orderlies were on their way back into the room. The same men who had restrained me were now releasing me. They were all very kind and again asked how I was. They released the straps holding me pressed against the bed. The freedom was perfect as my body returned to me.

I couldn't sit up or move as my muscles were frozen in place. I didn't have the strength to retract my freed limbs. The men, aware of this, gently pushed my arms into my sides and my legs together. I was rolled to my side and eased up onto my sit bones. No one spoke; they let the room do its job.

The room queried, "Will you be coming back or will you start playing by the rules? Will you take your meds and listen to the staff or will you make your way back here for another round? Am I going to have to teach you a real fucking lesson next time, Eric?"

This experience was a warning shot to let me know how bad it could get for me. The cool air settled on my wet face, wrists and ankles while the room listened for my answer.

"I will kill you next time, Eric. Leave now or this will be your coffin."

The walls silently demanded an answer to their queries while I mustered the strength to put my feet on the ground and push off the mattress. Gingerly, with the help of an orderly, I finally stood. The head orderly grabbed me under the arm and led me down the slim hallway leading out of the room. It was dead silent and all you could hear was the collective breathing of the hall getting louder as the vets slept.

As I stepped freely into the passageway to float down to my room, the head orderly gave my bicep one strong squeeze that made me look into his eyes. He was smiling like the rest of them but his eyes betrayed another reality. He was not my friend. He was a servant of the room. He knew the greater good was stability and order and he would willingly sacrifice me for the ward. He was no ally and would throw me back in restraints immediately should I push the boundaries again.

Something in his eyes showed he hungered for more sacrifice and didn't like the decision to let me back into population. He didn't just dislike my illness, he disliked me. Hated me. I was not safe. He knew what longer exposure to the bed had done to other patients. He wanted to grant me that shared experience. He was the human manifestation of the room. He served his master by collecting the patients and bringing them to the ravenous chamber. I could sense that many veterans had been devoured under his supervision; the broken patients make easier work. I would be returning to the room and he would make sure it happened soon.

I needed to make the best of this reprieve and prepare for the next round. I was losing my fear of death moment by moment as the fight progressed. Death seemed to be my only release from this life, this ward. That thought was becoming clearer each day with each burning breath.

He let go of my bicep and blood started to flow back to the arm. I made my way downstream and headed for my bed. The ability to lay down with my arms and legs under my own control was delicious. The breathing of the ward was deafening as veterans fought through their dreams and escaped this place for the night. As the ward inhaled and exhaled, I listened for their calls. Each snore, hack and cough soothed my wounds from the evening. Like many nights out to sea on my Destroyer, the sounds of the Red Sea and my shipmates became home.

I rolled to my left side with my head pointed up the ward to the seclusion room and looked out the window next to my bed. The streetlights warmed the glass and softened the night sky behind it. My breathing fell in chorus with the other veterans and I drifted into the night free from my surroundings, free from my hospital prison. The bell would ring for another round, and I needed rest. I had no corner man to get me ready. Somehow, I had to come out fighting. I knew I couldn't quit. It gave me a certain freedom to know I was fighting for some control of my life, even if it just meant I and I alone would determine how it ended.

It is a very unique state of being—alternating between fighting to live and fighting to die. Tomorrow is another day, another time, help me brothers ... please don't leave me. The breath of my shipmates filled my weakened body and flooded my dead lungs.

Then it struck me. Virgil ... Virgil ... Virgil.... I am not alone here, I have Virgil. With my Virgil epiphany, sleep crawled up my body and lay on top of me. Dreamless, I slept through the night. I would find Virgil at daybreak. I needed him. I slept strong.

I wanted to live even if it meant dying.

Death | Chapter 17

Most mornings on the ward were the same. The call to meds. The stiffened veterans moving like sloths up to the nurse's station and back down the ward to the first non-activity of the non-day. Then forty-five minutes after the meds slid down my throat the hall would fill with the beeping of the meal cart.

Meals were served three times a day on the ward. A large industrial machine on wheels came on the ward for each meal. About ten percent of the patients were allowed to go somewhere and eat breakfast but the rest of us got take-in. The meals were never bad enough to complain about and never good enough to want more.

That morning the breakfast wasn't any better than usual, but I noticed it. I saw what I was eating. I felt its heat. The heavy meds combined with the chronic dry mouth prevented any flavor from registering on my tongue, but I could sense its temperature. The meal warmed my mouth as my crusted teeth attempted to shred it. The tasteless mouthful slid down my throat and I could feel the burn down my esophagus into my stomach. As it settled down in my belly the warmth felt like an ignition.

Last night's strap-down came back to me and I felt like the orderlies were paying special attention to me. On my ward you didn't want to stand out. If you rise up and start taking on the established way of doing things, things can go badly for you. Wards are special places with a very gentle and tenuous culture based on the assumed power of the workers. My ward housed veterans in their most acute stages of mental illness and that made the population very unpredictable. It created a need for an ironclad social contract between the two parties living there, between staff and patient. Life does end on the ward. Usually it is the natural death of an old man at the end of a long run. But there are other deaths, more sinister deaths.

When you are on the ward for long periods of time, you can become helpless. I had no physical strength and as I ate breakfast I felt like I was being circled by lions. The orderlies were definitely watching me. It is hard to distinguish between paranoia and reality with active mental illness, but after the previous night I couldn't take any chances.

Breakfast ended and I made it back to my room. I really wanted to see Virgil. The ward floor had sunlight streaking down its face as I paced my section of the hallway waiting to see my guide. He never came that morning, and my mind was reeling. I was alone. The coming day now seemed longer and more frightening. Most of the ward had some place they went to each day for something to do, but I seemed to always be here.

Housekeeping cleaned the floor daily on the ward. One of the staff would sweep and then someone else would polish the floor with an old power buffer. Once the buffer got going, I usually relaxed as the white noise of the machine seemed to unplug my mind. I laid down and napped wherever I was. At the time, I was staying in a room that was farther down the hall and in its own enclave. My portion of the ward cut in after the bathroom and created a little cul de sac with another room. I could sit on the floor outside my door and dip my toes in the shallow end of the ward.

As I listened to the hum of the buffer, I drifted into a morning nap on the floor. Maybe things weren't that sinister. Maybe. Am I making everything up? I was so removed from actual reality that I was often questioning it on multiple levels. "Is this really happening?" was a question I asked often. In my heart, I knew something was wrong but the daylight softened the paranoia and dissipated my nightmares.

I curled up into a corner of my court and slept. The hum of the buffer helped me slip away almost instantly. When I opened my eyes the buffer was directly in front of me. I grinned at the orderly but he didn't grin back. I assumed he was busy and I just watched him do his chores. Methodically, he swept the buffer to my left, from the center of the hall to the wall in one smooth motion. As he backed away from me, the floor in front of me glistened.

He wasn't looking at me at all, which was not normal for us. I thought we had a pretty good relationship. Not best friends, but if we were one on one, we at least acknowledged each other. Not that day.

He was only a few feet away again, finishing his pass from the center to my left. I knew I should get up and keep moving but I was so tired from breakfast and a brief nap that I just lay there watching.

Unexpectedly, he looked up at me. I could have touched him. Then he started to buff the floor to my right. And, in one fluid motion, I was trapped in the corner. Lazily, he swirled and swayed side to side with the same efficiency with which he had started the job. He moved away from me and disappeared around the corner into the main corridor.

I was completely trapped in the corner lying on my side while the wet floor sat there patiently waiting for me to walk on it. But if I tried to move, my steps would be recorded and I knew I would pay a heavy price.

The floor was cold and my hips were cramping. I turned over on my left side and faced the wall with my back to the ward. Pinned in the corner, I lay like a dead weight on the ground. It wasn't unusual to see vets lying on the floor. The staff didn't like it but it was inevitable. There was an underground system of hallways in the hospital where many of the men went when they were allowed outside for the day. They would get to the other side of the door and find there was no real solace out there. As they wandered the hospital grounds with no car, no money, no job and no friends, their spirits would dim inside them and the solid, comforting pull of the ground called. So they simply laid down.

In the book, the *Life & Times of Michael K,* by J.M. Coetzee, the protagonist, Michael K, is constantly fighting his desire to lie down and die in the landscape of war-torn South Africa. He was born with facial defects and was hated by his mother in the womb. Yet, he spends part of his life diligently carting her around the countryside in an old wheelbarrow trying to get her back to her childhood home. After she dies, his life seems to be without reason, purpose. The hospital grounds in New Jersey were littered with Michael K's wandering the facilities, aimlessly killing time as the ambivalence about their physical existence grew and their limbs withered. The feel of something solid against your body is better than the loneliness of another solitary, upright march; the ground provides solace, connection, comfort. It is not that the men who sought refuge in the basement hallways wanted to lie down and die as much as they just wanted their suffering to stop.

As I lay on the floor with the smell of the cleaner filling my senses, I fought that feeling. I knew there was more to be done and it would not be done by Virgil or anyone else. I had to stand up and fight the urge to sink into a bed of earth. I knew there was a door next to the nurses' station that led to the outside world. I wanted to live on the other side of that door.

But something inside me told me that it wasn't the door by the nurses' station that beckoned; it was the smaller doorway fifteen feet from it. The seclusion room would be my portal. They still thought they owned me and that I was afraid. They thought they had taken everything from me and that I was a non-factor. I needed an escape from the hell of my daily non-life, but I could not kill myself—I needed them to do it for me. I needed it—my pain, my suffering—to be over. I would make them kill me in the restraints: death by doctor.

There is a term for people who get in standoffs with police and then who make the cops shoot them. It is called "suicide by cop." I had no other way to stop my daily torments and saw in the restraints a tool to kill me to this experience. I knew the suffering would be bone-breaking. I knew I would journey into levels of my diseased mind that would turn on me and devour me. I knew it would be a massacre but I also knew it might finally end the suffering, that I could reach the journey's end. In the fact that it was still an abstract to me, it was the only open-ended thing on this ward. So I would use this horror to end me. I would make the hospital murder me. I would make them end what I could not. I would make it a 'suicide by doctor' and my psychotic blood would forever stain their hands.

I pushed my right palm into the ground and straightened up on the floor. I needed a minute to equalize and then I got to my feet. The floor was still wet, but the sound of the machine no longer filled the ward. It was still early and the nurse's station at head of the ward was churning with activity as the doctors, nurses, and other staff would be planning the day's activities.

The floor was wet enough that the remaining patients on the ward were told to remain in their rooms. Once the floor was completely buffed, you were stranded where you were until it dried. I hated this policy, and knew violating it was my way back into the seclusion room for round two. I decided I would rather control when I was going in the restraints then wait for the ambush.

I shoved off the deck, and placed my left foot onto the damp tile like I was testing the ice on a frozen March pond. When it didn't break under my foot the other one followed. Each step gave me courage as I rounded the bend from my tributary into the rushing waters of the main hallway. My steps left discernible tracks down the hall leaving a line of evidence right back to my room if I decided to break off and abandon the mission. I was in deep enough that there was no escape from punishment. I moved from the right side of the hall to the center and pushed full steam ahead to the nurses' station.

The other patients were keeping to themselves and did not join me in my march. Revolt on a ward is rarely communal; we reach our breaking points separately. As I reached the nurses' station, the head orderly had just walked out of his meeting to see me standing at the trailhead of my newly forged path. He was furious. My reception at the front desk was cut short by his curses and threats. He did not bother concealing his disgust. If the doctors liked or disliked me they never let on, but at that moment, the head orderly looked as crazy as me.

It hadn't been twenty-four hours since I had been strapped down and there I was, breaking another rule in front of the entire ward. An attack by daylight, while a poor method in real war, worked to my advantage. The orderlies were quick. They grabbed me and the doctors conducted an impromptu meeting to decide my fate. With a thumb down from a Clinical Caesar, I was dragged to the room. Because the entire staff was on deck the process was again very smooth. With so many witnesses, the orderlies could not take out their anger on me by adding additional time or punishments. My stay in restraints lasted as long as the first time. It was easier than the first time because of the bright sunlight pouring in through the window and because doctors were coming in and out constantly.

It was over before I knew it, and I made my way back to my room. But it would not be my last time in the restraints.

Third time's the charm.

Death | Chapter 18

I had no fond farewell with Virgil number two. One day he was in my life and we were pulling cigarette heists and the next he was gone. When I returned to my bed after my second stint in the seclusion room, I actually ventured down the ward to his room. There was nothing there. I instantly started to wonder if he ever existed in the first place. My memories were not concrete anymore; nothing seemed to be permanent in my head. I wandered back up the no longer shark-infested floor and passed the pulverized fire alarm station my guide had decimated. It was still shattered. My man was real as hell. It was all real. The benign landscape of the ward was starting to show its own cracks and imperfections. It began to dawn on me that I wasn't nowhere. I was right here. On the ward. And I was real, actual. I took a few more aimless steps dragging my feet forward when I decided to head back to my room.

I was not armed for a battle of a physical nature. My battle would be a test of wills. The time in restraints would lengthen and I was not sure what that meant to my personal suffering. It is not a linear progression of torment from one hour to two hours in a bed held down by your extremities. The anguish and despair goes up exponentially. Like being burned for one second or ten, it goes from mildly annoying to a level of pain that will cause your body to shut down and pass out. I wasn't sure what to expect but I knew there would be more. The fight would be much more sinister in the next go-round. I didn't have it in me to go ten rounds for the title. My next trip had to be my last one, my last gasp. I felt like it was now or never and decided that the next day I would make my move. The full force of the ward and the full force of me, whoever me was at that moment, would be pitted against each other. And I didn't know if there would be any more "me" after the face off.

The truth is I wasn't sure that the "me" I was following in my delusions was my savior or my assassin. But I sensed I needed to destroy my mind, my ego, my manic sense of "Eric" in the battle to find what, if anything, was on the other side. My mania had me convinced that they would never release my body, but if I could make them kill me, my spirit would finally be free from the hospital.

I needed full commitment; there could be no reserve chute in this jump. How much could I take? Where was the line between victory and letting out the Scream: That final bellow of horror that condemns the living to the psychic death that entombs them? Would my physical body give out or would I be trapped forever, in the frozen tomb of the ninth circle of the hell of my disease, the hell of the ward, the hell of my life? I had no more Virgils. I had no one by my side, no one to enter into battle with me.

It was just *me vs. me* ... to finally end this fucking life.

Death | Chapter 19

I wasn't sure how I was going to get myself back in the restraint room but I knew it had to happen. This period of my life had to end. *I had to end.* I was so weak that I hardly lifted my feet to walk. I shuffled place to place with my head down. The muscles in my neck were beginning to atrophy and I had a hard time lifting my skull up to face forward. My hands hung uselessly from my arms and they were swollen from all the blood rushing to them. My hips would cramp, forcing me forward and stopping my stride. I would get four or five steps before I had to grab the wall to straighten up.

Each visit with my family was shorter than the last. I couldn't handle seeing them anymore. The anxiety I experienced in the room with a loved one was intense. I would see them and feel like I was speaking a different language. My delusions would flood my mind with what I thought they were thinking. I would be happy for the first five seconds and hate them by the time they were leaving. I couldn't relate to the world any longer. Most of the visiting sessions ended with me yelling or walking out. I wanted to get off the ward and go home, yet the few times I was off the ward, the external stimuli of reality was so overwhelming that I would fight back to the door for re-entrance.

The cycle was killing me and my family. I was not clear what would happen back in the restraints but I knew this reality was worth nothing. I needed back in that room. I needed something that would raise the ire of the whole floor. I needed the whole staff convinced to keep me in the restraints this time. They had to want to kill me as a team. It had to be a group mission.

There was one sure way to get the attention of the whole staff and at the same time break the one fundamental rule that must be obeyed on a ward of patients with acute mental illness.

I would refuse medication.

The next time, I stepped up for the concoction of drugs that were given to me each morning, I would say *No*. Publicly. That would make them furious. If I didn't take my meds and got away with it, the ward would be in anarchy. Patients must take meds on the wards. There is no alternative.

I was going to challenge that rule. I would boldly refuse the cocktail and see what happened next. It seemed like a good plan, but I was having a hard time keeping it front and center in my mind. Without warning, I would cycle through another delusion of my omnipotence and wander away from the plan. A wayward glance from the staff and my mind let me think they were my followers and I was the incarnation of an Aztec god. My mania was reaching its full potential as a mental disorder. It was blowing through Thorazine without losing any momentum. My mind belonged less to me than to my disease, and if I was to execute my plan, it would be with as much luck as planning. If my plan didn't work, I would never leave the ward. Without knowing it, I would become another example of what my old psychology professor had told me—"some people never get better."

Let's be perfectly clear: My fight to get back into the restraints was the best thinking of a fractured and diseased mind trying to determine its own death. The mania had de-centered my mind's ability to see anything clearly; it was all just levels of sickness. It was a choice bathed in psychosis in a landscape of non-choice. My manic mind could dress up the decision to go back in restraints in many ways but it was really one thing: It was suicide.

I had to kill the *me* I had become and the only way was the restraints. In a world in which I cycled from feeling like an omniscient God to feeling I was nothing at all, I finally, somehow, made the determination to control the only thing left I could control: my death.

Restraints are barbaric. They are a device left over from the medieval times and deemed therapeutic. We can put a man on the moon, a robot on Mars, but the strap-down bed is the best we can do for my population. It is not because there are no better options. It is because few care enough about the population of astronauts lost in the 'space' of the psych hospital. Most of the inhabitants of our planet would be happy if those astronauts stayed lost—and invisible—out in the cosmos.

Death | Chapter 20

The morning call for meds came and like a good dog my body jumped. Laying on my left side, I faced the window and saw nothing. I was in the same clothes I had worn for weeks. I hadn't left the ward for any reason in a very long time: no doctor's appointments, no outside smoke breaks, no walks, no anything. Outside, inside, whatever; it was all the same to me.

My feet dangled over the side of my bed waiting for the feeling to come back to them. They were constantly numb. After a few minutes, my feet met the cold floor and I began wading to the nurse's station. The other vets were already lined up. I heard names and agreements and then on to the next veteran. I didn't know anyone anymore. Patients aren't meant to stay on this ward long. Once their symptoms are manageable, they are sent to treatment wards. The average stay was a couple of days, maybe a week. I had been here for months and nothing was getting better.

Bill and Virgil were gone.

I looked around but did not see a single familiar face. The line was long. Either more vets had come on board yesterday or I arrived later than usual. The routine was calming and the Sloe Gin song started to play in my ears. The cocktail still seemed like alcohol to me. I was actually singing the refrain out loud as I shuffled forward. I could picture the plum liquid they would hand me. I would down it like I was going to the worst party ever and "rock on" throughout the ward. The next vet passed to my left as 70's rock was playing an encore in my psychosis when I happened to glance to my right. I was standing next to the seclusion room door.

Through the blur, I started to remember I had a plan. It was hazy with the music blasting in my ears but I fought for a few seconds of lucidity. What the hell was it? What am I supposed to do?

Another vet went by me and I was on deck for my drink of choice. I stared at the doorway and pictured Virgil in the restraints. I remembered sneaking up and watching him. I remembered getting a full glimpse of the torture chamber. The nausea from that moment washed over me.

What was this plan that I had? What was it and why did I care when my shot of sloe gin was about to be served at room temperature?

The vet in front of me was agreeing to his name and getting his numerous drugs. I just kept staring at the doorway, trying to figure out what was bothering me. My mania was telling me it was just another morning. Everything was OK. Drink the sloe gin and run back to the bathroom for a post-meds smoke. The last vet between me and my drink walked off, and I was at the head of the line. The nurse took out my folder which had swollen in size from a thin pamphlet to an encyclopedia.

She read it for a second and asked me my name. I heard her say, "Eric Arauz?"

I didn't answer.

She kept her head down and repeated, "Eric Arauz?"

I didn't answer.

I thought about it for a few seconds. I had never paused at the question before, but at that moment it struck me that I wasn't sure of the answer. The name seemed a little foreign to me. I knew it was a name I had answered to before, but now I couldn't be sure. This was not an existential dilemma. I was not trying to figure out my place in the universe through the negation of personal monikers and labels. I was literally unsure if I was Eric Arauz; I was so dissociated from the collective past of Eric Arauz that I felt a concrete separateness from all the memories of Eric Arauz.

If I am not my memories and not the totality of my past actions, then what am I? Who am I?

She looked up. She was annoyed and maybe even angry. I instantly hated her. Part of the old me was fighting to the surface inside my mind. Looking closer, I could tell she was pissed off.

I looked her in the eyes and locked on. "Fuck you," I thought.

She said, "You are Eric Arauz, and you have to give blood, right now, for a check on your levels."

It all flooded back to me. This was my way back to the bed, my way out. This was the plan. I had one moment to make it happen or vanish forever behind my eyes. All of a sudden, I felt the full force of the flames burning me alive inside my skin. This was my opportunity. I had to take it. *Now!*

The kamikaze mission isn't real until you cover the distance where you can't turn back. As I flew over the line, I waived goodbye to all I ever knew and answered her.

"Fuck you, I am."

Yeah, that felt good. Let's go. Let's see what you got.

It seemed as if this was a set-up because she didn't even repeat herself. The orderlies swarmed me and viciously grabbed me around my chest and both my arms. The other veterans instantly broke from the scene, running every different direction.

There had to be five or six guards. The first one had grabbed my wrist. I spun my hand out and turned to face another. The next one grabbed my other wrist and I twisted it perpendicular to the opening in his fingers and escaped. I wasn't running; I wasn't able to run with someone behind me with his hands clasped together over my sternum. I was just trying to fend them off as much as I could. By now, I didn't even remember why they were grabbing me. I had already forgotten my mission. All I knew was I had never seen the orderlies so mad. They were screaming and circling me. They seemed to be afraid I might hit someone. Even in my most deluded state I never attacked another person, but they couldn't know that.

As they tried to grab me from each angle, I countered. It was as if everything I ever learned in Aiki-jujitsu flowed through me. But it didn't last long—probably only thirty or forty seconds—before they had had enough.

They charged me all at once and dragged me to the ground. The ward was electrified by the brawl. The patients were very anxious, some yelling at me, some at the guards. Everyone was watching.

The patients' screams were not for my release or to extend mercy to me in my struggle. Just panic, terror verbalized. I could see the bystanders over the shoulders of the converging staff as they flailed wildly while the team dragged me into the seclusion room.

They picked me up in the inner hallway and took me to the bed. The men seemed to be a little more relaxed as they started to put me on the floor. The second my feet hit the ground I exploded. I saw the straps up close and the reality of the bed terrified me. I pushed the first man in front of me with all my force and tried to run directly through the man next to him. My eyes were wide open, and I was yelling incoherently.

As they tried to wrestle me to the bed, I countered every move. I was absolutely convinced that these men had made a mistake. In that moment, I was fighting for my life. If given the chance, I would have inflicted mortal wounds on the staff while operating under the influence of my delusions.

Up close, the reality of the bed was too much for me. The straps were so thick and the bed so naked. The pain and horror of my first stay came back in waves. The light of day no longer disguised the room. I saw it for what it was—a torture chamber, a cemetery for the dreams of veterans with mental illness and PTSD everywhere. The room had heard the final screams of my ward-mates for years and delighted in the sound. It was now clear I was on a suicide mission and even though I'd changed my mind, it was too late.

I was fighting so hard to escape my pants fell to my ankles and I was naked from the waist down. The orderlies were verbally insulting and it had become a brawl, a street fight. I was punching and kicking and so were they. I made one last furious push to escape my fate when the orderly I called "Buddha" came forward. Buddha was at least 350 pounds and black as night. He stepped through the mob of men and grabbed me between my naked thighs. His hands went under me and up the back side and he lifted me straight up into the air. I tried to attack him but before I could do anything his other arm went over my shoulder and he hoisted me up over his head in a fireman's carry.

The bed was right behind me and Buddha slammed me powerfully into the mattress. Before I could react, my wrists and ankles were in the restraints and the orderlies were standing around yelling at me and worshiping their God.

Buddha did not smile. He didn't acknowledge their accolades. He just looked at me with his dark compassionate eyes and left the room. Even though he was the only one to really get his hands on me, Buddha was the only one who showed compassion.

As he left the room, the rest of his worshipers followed him. They were all grinning and laughing. A couple looked back in my direction and chastised me one last time. They felt good strapping me down; I deserved to suffer. I was evil to them, not sick. I could hear them taunting me as they walked out. It pierced my delusions and ripped into my mind. I was fucking furious. I wanted to kill every one of them. I wasn't mad at them for doing their jobs. I was mad at the unadulterated glee they took in my suffering. At the worst time in my life, I had hecklers cheering my death.

I was having a hard time calming down in the restraints. My breathing was out of control. I was sweating. The adrenaline of the wrestling match had temporarily numbed my body to the pain, but that was dissipating now. The bed had no pillow and my head was sliding on the bare mattress. The restraints were loose enough to adjust the position of my ankles and wrists without being able to withdraw them from the leather straps.

I began to sink into this reality.

When you keep waking up in new hells, it doesn't take much to get you assimilated. I was a chameleon to degradation. It seemed that my capacity to suffer could not be saturated. It was not that I could not be broken; I could. Repeatedly. Each time worse than the last. I just had lost the belief that my life would ever get better. Without hope you live on death row. It doesn't matter where you live; death row can be anywhere and everywhere. The condemned walk among us everyday, sure that their lives are over.

The room had promised me I would be back and there I was. The fight with the guards had re-awakened me to my mission, and I was sure of my purpose for a few moments. My life on the ward had become physically, mentally and spiritually untenable. I had no friends, no peers, no mercy, no love, no peace. I did not understand my existence anymore. I was scared and agitated every moment.

The romantic stage of mania had been gone for months. My mania was now paranoid and vicious. It attacked every hidden fear and translated it into my daily life. If someone was talking as I shuffled by them, they were discussing the murder of my mother. If I entered the bathroom and someone looked my way, they were sizing me up to suffocate me in my sleep. The disease translated my waking reality into a permanent nightmare. Whether my eyes were closed or open the attack continued. Every miserable moment, a waterfall of dread washed over me.

I hadn't voluntarily touched another person the entire summer.

With my demented plan in effect, I tried to get a grip on the situation. I had to ready myself for the war. It would be me versus the room. Me versus my fears. Me versus my mind. I could feel my back settling into the mattress. I adjusted my hips to displace my weight equally with my legs spread. I was afraid of how my hips would react to a long strap-down. When they cramped, it always felt better to lean forward and compress the hip joint. Now that would be impossible.

The key to being in restraints is not to think about all the things you cannot do. It is to force your psyche into an "endless present." It is not easy, but you will either keep your mind where you are in space and time or you will suffer biblically. It is a primal defense mechanism. I was coated in mania, yet my awareness focused on dampening the panic that could set in while restrained. I had no idea how long I would be in this time. The last time people were cordial and the first time they were damn near chummy as they lashed me to the dilapidated bed. This time they were mad. Very mad.

Someone entered the room, but stayed far enough away that I couldn't see them. Unless you were right on top of me, you were out of my view. I could feel a presence to my left adjacent to my restrained foot. I asked numerous times who was there but no one answered.

I started to panic. I knew it would only take thirty seconds to smother me with a pillow. I could feel the pillow being pushed down on my face as I screamed for breath. I knew that with my arms tied down, I would not be able to fight at all. Frenzied, I was about to start screaming when the person stepped forward and stood right next to me.

It was the head orderly, the servant of the room. He stood so close to my left shoulder, his slacks brushed against my skin. He had no emotion on his face as he stared into my eyes. I knew he was pleased with the situation. He would knowingly and purposely execute me. He would let the room do its worst to my broken body and mind. I would not be able to touch him to let him see we were the same. To him, I was the enemy, not human, a diseased "other."

His eyes never left mine. He neither touched me nor cursed me. He just watched me like a human sacrifice at his feet. I would not beg this man for anything. Nothing.

With one last breath, the servant looked over the restraints and tugged at each one to be sure they were secure. He pulled at the ankle restraints first to make sure the metal post was secure through the thick strap. Then he did the same with the wrist restraints and turned to leave.

I was sure he hadn't left the room. I could still hear him breathing. I could feel the room getting stronger with each moment with him in it. I lay perfectly still while I heard him inhale and exhale in the landscape of my punishment. I wouldn't react at all until he was gone.

Slowly, his footsteps made their way down the truncated hallway leading out of the room. I was alone.

I passed out.

Confused, my eyes opened. What time is it? How long have I been in these restraints? I couldn't wrap my head around a timeline. Did I have breakfast or didn't I? Was I hungry? I don't ever remember being hungry on the ward. You never burned off the calories you ingested during the day. There was no exercise and the constant regiment of heavy meds made exercise impossible anyway. You ate until you were full on day one and you stayed full until you were discharged.

I couldn't remember eating at all that morning. I hadn't heard the breakfast delivery cart enter the ward but it must have come already. I felt like I had been restrained for hours. It was probably closer to lunch time. Had to be.

The pain in my mid-back and hips was starting to register. Having your arms outstretched in a lazy T causes your back to spasm after only a few minutes. It made breathing harder for me plus, I had a history of chronic asthma as a child. It had been bad enough that I was tested for cystic fibrosis. It had been exacerbated with the chronic smoking on the ward and now my breathing was getting very shallow. As if I couldn't exhale at all.

I had to calm down.

My back was getting tighter and my chest was collapsing in on me. How fucking long had I been restrained? I was starting to really hurt. What if I can't catch my breath. What if the cramps have just started and my hips go next? How do you ride out full body cramps? It had to be near lunch time. I wouldn't be so beat up if it wasn't later. They would let me out soon. They knew I hadn't meant anything by my outburst. They couldn't just leave me in here.

The summer sun was shining down through the bare window to my right. I could feel the heat on my right foot. It felt reassuring. I felt less alone. The temperature in the room was going up. I was sweating on every inch of the back of my body. It allowed for a little movement on the mattress but the restraints still had no give.

I could hear the door to the main hall open. A few voices exchanged pleasantries and then the familiar beeping of the food cart started. I needed to believe it was for lunch and that I had been in the restraints for a few hours. The beeps filled my room from top to bottom as the cart passed my door to go to the large break room in the center of the ward where the patients ate all their meals.

As the sound of the beeps started to fade down the hall away from me, I heard one of the patients ask the attendant what was for … *breakfast*. My mind disintegrated. The reality that I had been strapped down for less than two hours and I was already miserable registered with my entire body like a death.

No one had checked in on me like the previous times. I was alone in this room with no idea when I would be released. To add to my overall misery, I was starving. Every morning I stared at breakfast without any interest, and now I envisioned hash browns, blueberry pancakes and bacon being spread around the ward.

Each minute that cart was on the ward and I wasn't eating, my body grew more tense. The presence of the food cart made time real and, therefore, made the rack real. I needed my limbo back. My spine really hurt and the sweat on my skin felt cold and sticky. My feet were cramping forward due to the toe operations and my hips were begging to contract at the joint.

Brutal.

I had just started. Got to hold on, just pain. I lived in pain. It was all pain. It will pass … someone will come in and help me … they have to….

Right?

Death | Chapter 21

I waited all morning for some help: a cold wash cloth to wipe my face or wet my lips or maybe a nurse would sit with me and tell me it would be alright. Even another patient in the room would have been better, but no one came. The next hours passed until the familiar beeping returned: this time with imagined lobster, steak, sushi and fois gras. I pictured an absolute feast down the hall while I starved alone shackled to the bed. My penance had just begun.

I was the kind of exhausted that could sleep with perpetual nightmares and chronic body pain. My breathing slowed and my mind started to paint pictures in my head. As I was about to fall asleep, a clear image formed in my mind. It came from nowhere but it was the first clear thing I had seen in a long time when I closed my eyes.

It was me.

It was the back of my head, actually, and it was slowly rotating to face me. I hadn't pictured this since I was under the bed awaiting my coronation as the King of Jamaica, but it was back. As the head, my head, started to turn, I could feel a strange sensation in my stomach that was moving up my esophagus. I felt as if I might be getting sick, which scared me. Could I throw up and not choke on it? I wasn't able to turn my head with my neck problems, so if I vomited, choking was a real possibility. But it wasn't that. I had no food in my system, so if I vomited, it wasn't an upset stomach. The sickness in my core was something much more.

Like an existential nausea, the feeling was slowly growing. I couldn't place it. It was something I had never felt before but it was very real. I felt as if I was going to open my mouth and … open my mouth and….

Then I knew what it was. It was *The Scream*, the last gasp of a broken veteran.

It wasn't hard to control now, but just feeling it inside me terrified me. It had only been four or five hours and the Scream had already shown up. And I was sure no one was going to free me anytime soon.

I passed out.

When I opened my eyes the room was much darker. The window to my right was no longer streaming sunlight onto my feet. Evening had arrived and I had been tied down for half the day. My lower body was completely numb. If my legs had been amputated while I was sleeping I wouldn't have known. It was a very odd feeling to wake up and not stretch or move around to resuscitate the rest of your body. I just opened my eyes and I was back exactly where I had left off. The nightmares of my sleep were no better than the nightmares of my waking moments so I was not very rested. I was sleeping merely to kill time.

With the room darkened and the work day done, the ward was starting to clear out. The evening darkness insulated me further from reality and let my manic mind run wild. When the light outside was switched off and there were no relative markers of a reality outside of my mind to focus on, the disease thrived. It wanted full control of the host and was nearing its objective.

I had no idea what time it was. I knew it was dark but not late evening. I was not sure if dinner had come and gone already. I hoped it had. My body was actually doing fine for the time being, except for the fact that I was unbelievably thirsty. I hadn't had a drink of anything since yesterday and with the Lithium and everything else they were pumping in me, I was dry mouthed. I wasn't sure how to get a drink so I yelled to the nurse's station to see if someone would come out. They had installed a protective barrier over the open window since Virgil and I had carried out our cigarette heist and I wasn't sure if they could hear me. I waited a few minutes. Nothing.

I did not feel or hear anyone in the room. I was alone.

My mouth was almost cemented shut at this point due to the chronic dry mouth. I was moving my jaws to keep the use of my parched lips and deadened tongue. The initial scream for the nurse sounded foreign to me. I did not use my voice much anymore. The only voice I heard each day was my own, in my head, and it was more of a feeling than a clear talking entity. Nothing about me seemed real anymore. The heavy antipsychotic drugs dampened the sensation of my skin. I felt like I was wearing a permanent wet suit. The body that was strapped down to this bed was already not my own.

Death | Chapter 22

Anurse finally entered the room and asked how I was doing. I told her I was thirsty and she brought in a wet towel. She wiped my face and placed the towel on my lips. The cool moisture made me hyper-aware of the moment. My neck muscles had stopped working and I could not lift my head, so she gently raised it. As the washcloth moved across my face, drips of cool liquid leaked into my mouth. The cake on my tongue and teeth prevented a strong swallow, but the water was revitalizing. It was clean and new and it came from outside the room. It reminded me that the whole world was not in my head. While the towel moved over my chin, I looked up at her and tried to connect with her. She gazed down at me with a genuine compassion and began to wipe my forehead to cool me down.

It reminded me of my childhood. I had been a sickly child with tremendous breathing problems. If I caught a cold it went straight to my lungs. I would have that hacking kind of cough you try to suppress just to avoid the pain. If a cough got through, it ripped your lungs apart and caused bright white flashes behind your eyes.

My mother would prop four or five pillows up behind me to help me breathe so I could go to sleep. She would fill the humidifier and turn the adjustable lever so it would spray the maximum amount of water. Wheezing and wailing, I took tremendous solace in the dainty, loving kisses of the misting waterfall. When everything was set up, my mom would run a wash cloth under cold water and then put her hand under my head and wipe the cool cloth from side to side over my eyebrows to ease my pain. As the towel bathed my overheated skull, she would give me kiss upon kiss and tell me it would be OK. She would take her hands and rub my face and massage my sinuses. She would sit with me for hours. Even though I was sick, I loved those moments. I knew I was not alone. Her touch was more important than any word she said and her kisses gave me comfort.

As the nurse finished wiping my neck and scalp, I began to pull away from the moment. I considered begging the nurse for my release, but stopped. There would be no easy way out of this. The restraints were in place to break me, but they would break the disease also. I had to push further. I had to face the room at its worst and see what was on the other side of the Scream and this life. It would not happen now but it would happen soon. As night set in and the room could step forward from the shadows, the battle would be waged.

The last little wipes and the nurse was leaving. She told me to relax, it would be over soon. "When you get out, we'll give you a few cigarettes and let you relax. Stay calm, Eric."

I just kept staring at the ceiling as she left. Conversation was useless to me. Every word was intercepted by delusion anyway. I wanted the night to come in its darkest power. I was ready. I was ready to die. I knew that now. I still wanted to see my mom, sisters and family one last time. But how? These motherfuckers are never going to let me out. I was willing to risk it all: total psychic death if necessary. By car or by coffin, I had to get off the ward.

It is hard to explain to the un-anointed. After a certain time cycling in and out of hospitals and seeing the same people in the same wards, you can begin to believe life will never get better. You do not see many people step forward who have slithered on their bellies in the gutters of society. Those labeled by our culture as "others" stay hidden and the self-stigma of being a part of the chronically hospitalized population burns deep. It was easy for me to stop caring about living or dying. Neither held much promise except for more pain.

Many patients I have visited on the locked wards will talk about this to me but hide it from the staff. The line between hopelessness and suicidal is not always delineated clearly in the hospital. It should be. If my population is not allowed to voice how low they actually feel, then the journey cannot start at an authentic place.

The game will continue in hospitals throughout the country:

Staff: "So Jimmy how are you? Do you hear voices? Are you considering hurting yourself?"

Eric C. Arauz

What Jimmy thinks is: "I overdosed on crack and have been awake for seven days. This is my third hospitalization for bipolar disorder and even when I am compliant the cocktail doesn't work. The state has taken my kids from me, and my wife won't allow me to see them. I have lost my career as an attorney, and, with this on my record, I can never practice again. My dad killed himself in a depression. I have never even met a person who has been locked in one hospital let alone three, and my whole family is terrified of me. I have no home, no job and no money and I can't guarantee this stay will work either. I hate my own fucking guts. I absolutely see no way to go on another day. It is absolutely futile. Being dead has to be better than this, it has to."

What Jimmy says is: "I'm fine, Doc. No voices, no problems. I'm excited for another chance."

If Jimmy mentions that he is not sure about living and it is misconstrued as suicidal, he will be locked down for six more months in the state hospital. He has answered this question honestly in the past and has been punished for it. The current system is not set up to manifest or support the successes of the chronically ill. My population, those of us who cycle in and out of the state hospitals, VA hospitals, and prisons, is maintained and then discarded only to return again and again. Jimmy knows the system now. He has imbibed its hopelessness.

So Jimmy plays the game and the disease plays Jimmy.

Death | Chapter 23

It was pitch black when I woke up again. The room was cool. Except for the heavy breathing of the patients and guards lining the centerboard, the ward was silent. There was no clock visible, but I was sure it would have moved from p.m. to a.m. It was maybe two or three in the morning. My neck was killing me from the position I was forced to stay in while restrained. I was having a very hard time focusing my eyes. The meds drowning my system and the lack of light in the room turned the shadows into forms. I was not sure if I was surrounded by people or completely alone. I waited a few tense moments, but....

Nothing. I am alone.

I closed my eyes and opened them again. It was the same nightmare. Sleep no longer offered any escape—from my situation or from my life. My dreams were of the hospital; my delusions were of the hospital; my waking moments were in the hospital. There are many men who are defined by place.

I was a man of the mental hospital.

My mannerisms were that of the severely ill. I shuffled from place to place and if I spoke at all, it was only in reply and always in riddles. I could not hold a conversation and had stopped initiating them months ago. I was involved in a never-ending discussion in my head. Like the antagonist in the existentialist Albert Camus', *The Fall*, my mind started a conversation when mania opened the front door, and it wasn't going to finish until I was dead. It was a one-sided delusional diatribe that didn't require an answer from me anymore.

The delusions were so strong they created feelings inside me instantly. Delusional *feel* became distorted *thought* which became immediate *reality* enhanced by the physical reaction my body registered in its tactile memory. The terror or elation from each of these feigned scenarios was so real to my body that I had become viscerally delusional. There was no separation between me, my thoughts, and my flesh. I was the totality of a corrupted mind, my blood boiling with mania, my existence one grand delusion.

Eighteen hours or so into my seclusion, and my entire body was awake with pain. My hips were cramping and pulling forward. This arched my lower back and caused severe pain to my spine. My hands were throbbing and numb. The bed was soaked with my sweat. My legs were worse than my upper body. The surgeries to my toes had made my legs very off balance. I looked down and tried to see the positioning of my feet to get some idea of how I could find some extra space. The light from the moon was illuminating the end of the bed and making the scars across my toes look like each one was split in half and lying open. The more I stared at them out of the bottom of my eyes the more convinced I was that they had reopened the wounds while I was sleeping.

The healed skin still showed the mark of one hundred and fifty stitches and the moonlight made it look like I was bleeding. The harder I fought to look, the stronger the delusion became. I pulled at the restraints as hard as I could, trying to get to my wounds. My neck fought to keep my head upright to watch the carnage but failed. My head fell back to the mattress. Pain shot up my jaw into my temples and down my spine to my mid-back. I rotated my ankles trying to feel my feet. Every twist of the ankle joint was followed by numerous cracks—loud cracks that sounded like bones breaking, not joints loosening. Both feet were cramped across the arch trying to bring the big toe to meet my heel as my calves tightened in a charley horse.

My knees were on fire. The left one was worse. The cartilage was close to being completely gone and the knee was always sore. Now it was throbbing with bone pain that infiltrated every inch of the joint. I couldn't bend it at all. The restraints kept the leg fully outstretched. The contractions of my hips were pulling on my groin which was in effect causing my hamstring to cramp. The only way to be able to cure all these ills would be to stand up and do yoga for an hour.

That was not going to happen.

My broken and disabled lower body was in full collapse, but there was nothing I could do except lay there and suffer in a dim, colorless hell. Every part of my body was in pain. I was on fire from head to toe. With over eighteen hours in restraints, I was fully immersed in so many new realms of degradation that my body and mind were having a hard time assimilating to each burning psychotic damnation.

With all this going on I had a feeling I hadn't had in a long time.

I had to go to the bathroom.

I mean, I really had to go. How the hell was that going to work?

My back!

The spasm was horrible and began to affect my breathing. I had no idea how to prioritize the body aches, but my back was rapidly becoming the worst. My back muscles constricted and refused to expand with each breath. I start to wonder what it would feel like to suffocate in this lonely room.

No matter how I tossed my body from side to side, the tightness in my chest constricted around my lungs. The dryness of my lips and the thick cake on my tongue started to block my airway. With each exhale my inhales got shorter. I cycled from one deadly scenario to the next when the pain in my bowels ripped through my consciousness. I was hit with excruciating stomach pain. I had not gone to the bathroom since the day before, and the heavy meds often lead to painful constipation. The doctors had recently changed my meds, and my body was not adapting properly to the heavy dosages of Lithium. With each new bodily horror, I feared what my body would do next.

As each part of my body fought for attention, nothing could compete with my body's need to release its waste. The room was enjoying this situation. Just when you thought the pain and degradation had reached a saturation point, a new disgusting variable was added to the equation. As the pain rose up and gripped my belly, I let out a loud involuntary scream. As the next pain shot through my stomach and up my throat, another high-pitched scream filled the room. This was a louder and fuller outpouring and I could identify myself in the yell.

Another nurse entered the room and asked what was wrong.

She looked very sad and seemed sympathetic to me. I told her that I had to go to the bathroom. I told her the cold air was destroying my lower body and that hours lying against a cold mattress were putting me into spasms. I didn't want to cry, but I felt my voice crack as I spoke to her ... as I begged her.

She told me there was a standing order to keep me in the restraints. She could not release me. I could see the horror of me reflected in her face. She offered to wipe down my head and neck, but I declined. It would be too small a gesture to quiet the myopic massacre.

Just let me be. Leave me alone. Let me die in peace.

She walked out and sniffled. I didn't know if she was crying or congested. My delusions said one thing and the remnant of my rational mind the other and the debate was too tiring to pursue. I didn't care.

A few more minutes passed.

I was hoping that the stomach pain would stop. All the other pains seemed to subside when I got the chance to interact with another person, so I was hoping the stomach was going to follow suit. But a terrible pull from my intestines dashed those hopes and let me know I couldn't wait any longer.

"I have to go the bathroom!"

No answer.

"I am not fucking around! I gotta go now!"

The room did its best to devour my scream but it was too loud. It must have escaped into the ward.

No answer.

"I will shit this bed right now if someone doesn't help me. I mean right now!"

No answer.

Another minute went by, then another and I couldn't wait any longer.

Strapped down for hours. Suffocating. My body cramped in every way possible, I shit the bed. Once I started, I could not stop. The landscape of my hell was complete, and I felt the shadows of the night reveal a sly, satisfied smile.

"I shit the bed! I did it! I shit the bed, you motherfuckers! You motherfuckers!"

The loudest sobs of my life drenched the soulless room. I was nearing the end. The physical pain was constant and the emotional pain reached a new level of unbearable with each moment.

The fight to tell the story of my life was lost to my delusions. The bottom of my soul was now exposed in this room. These four walls were the pit I would turn to face myself in. As I closed my eyes, I watched my envisioned body turn to face me one more time. With a final twist, my bald head wheeled around. This time there was a face with a nose and mouth.

I was lashing at the restraints trying to free myself, to feel myself. With frantic constant pulls, my left wrist finally slipped from the restraint. My left wrist is smaller than my right. It is on the underdeveloped side of my body. Because of the Poland syndrome I was born with, I have no left chest muscle, pectoral major and minor, and my left forearm, wrist and fingers are all slightly smaller.

As my freed left arm pulled across my body and over my chest, the restraints on my feet restricted my hips from fully turning over to help me gain the leverage needed to free my right wrist. I gave one last twist from my left side and was able to twist my hips over onto the right side. The excrement gave my body the lubrication it needed to move. My lower spine twisted as I desperately reached for the restraint on my right hand, only to be stopped—frozen, unable to even breathe—by the intense pain shooting through my back. At the same time, the twist of my body released the dam on the current of excrement, and a river of shit leaked up the mattress.

I threw my left hand at the other restraint and grazed the thick strap on my right wrist, but I couldn't grip it. I was completely out of strength, and the cold hard leather was too strong for my fingers. Utterly defeated, I lay twisted on my side staring at the permanent restraints on my wrist with my right cheek bathed in my own feces.

Death | Chapter 24

My last effort at survival had come and gone. My physical senses were now slaves to my mental master. The room reeked of human waste. I had the lost the feeling in my lower body with my spine twisted this way and was unable to turn back. My sight was destroyed by the meds and absolute darkness and all I heard was my mind agreeing with the delusions.

The annihilation of the physical Eric Arauz was complete.

I panted, moaned, and begged my mania to spare me, to have mercy on me. As I fought to untwist my torso, my senses were attacked by the smell and I was flooded with overwhelming sadness. I must have felt how the condemned feel when their day of execution actually arrives. You can hide from yourself to a point but at the end, the visceral façade is lifted and you see yourself plainly.

The thought of this being my last memory as I was buried ten feet beneath my psychosis was pain beyond human limits. I felt the noose fashioned around my neck, its coarse weight resting on my collarbone. Hovering over the trap door waiting its release. The bloodstained, burlap beggar's hood placed over my head. Darkness. I am not guilty. I am being executed, and I am not guilty. No one is coming! *Oh my fucking god, no one is coming!*

Even as my anguish overwhelmed me, I was aware of the temperature of the room and the firmness of the mattress. Instead of being knocked out for my last moments, my mania allowed me to feel every last thing. The walls and floor came into focus and the smell of the room became constant. My moans were full of remorse for a life unfinished and unlived. Tears streamed down my face into my waste. Each sob was followed by a bellow as I got one last vision of my loved ones before the lights were extinguished in my head. I've heard that if you jump from a tall enough building, you go into shock before you hit the ground, that you would effectively die in midair. I was experiencing the complete opposite scenario. My death was getting clearer the closer my flaming body came to the crushing impact of the cement. I was not in shock or numb. I was experiencing the catastrophic impact of a one hundred-story fall in a forever moment.

I could see my sisters smiling at me as I told them I loved them. My grandmother next. I walked in her room while she was reading and hugged her in her rocking chair. She told me she knew it would be OK. I let her have that. I made my way to my step-dad in his recliner and we shook hands like I was leaving for war. Each memory became more real and focused as I made my way through my family. The sobbing continued but my body was operating on its own and my mind could not be stopped. I needed this last farewell. I was reading my suicide note to myself in these last images.

The last goodbye was to my mother. I saw her in the kitchen going through the pictures of my childhood. She always kept fighting, whether it was my disorder or her cancer, and she never gave up. She gave me a slow and loving smile. A long hug and then she released me. I turned to leave the house and watched the front of it disappear as my reality came back into focus in this room. My last room.

I was ready. I knew there was no way back to my life through this mind, through this reality. I wept and screamed as my mania made its last move. Its death move. The screams were so desperate I knew the threshold would be broken soon. I was unclear what it would feel like to completely give up, to truly desire death, to beg for it.

I didn't know if there was another side to life but this side had run its course. The last revolution was completed as I truly faced myself. I was focusing on the mouth expecting to hear words of wisdom. Nothing. Face to face with myself, I looked deeply into my reflection.

I had no eyes. No eyes.

The sockets were gaping wounds. I gazed into the interior of my skull. I could see my father on his death bed. He was with a woman I didn't know. He was crying. He knew he was dying and he was begging the woman to not leave him alone. She held his hand and they wept together.

He was saying over and over again, "Why me? How could this be my life? This can't be it."

I felt like an intruder watching this personal moment. He put his head back and his breathing got labored. He would cry and scream when he caught his breath and then fight for more air. Einar was suffocating as his lungs were giving out. This death looked painful. As he was making his last gasps for air, he turned to me.

He said, "Eric, come to me, my only son. Let me hold you, let me touch you."

I walked over and started to cry. When I was within arms reach he grabbed my hand and pulled me close. I leaned into him so he wouldn't waste his breath. As our eyes met, he smiled and spoke.

He said, "How could you not find me? I am your father and for years you wished I was dead. Serves you right to have my disease. You will die exactly like me. You will never have anything. This is your death you're watching, this is you. Die, Eric, just let it happen. You are completely alone, at least I have someone. You pathetic fuck, I don't need you. You need me. You deserved to be fatherless. I wished I fucking killed you while I had the chance. You are a disgrace to the Arauz name and I am glad you are doing to yourself what I tried to do to you."

I ripped my arm back and tried to turn away from my eyeless reflection, but once the image had materialized, it stood between me and everything else. No matter which way I moved it was one inch from my face. I could see one more scene deep in my projection skull and knew I had to look. I focused more clearly on the image as it settled in my mind.

It was a child's room with a crib in a corner. The morning sun was coming in the window and the heat in the room was rising. I knew the decorations and the color scheme but I couldn't place the room. When I looked closer at the crib I saw an infant in it. I stepped to the edge and saw the baby face of my step-daughter. In reality, when I saw her last she had been sleeping on her stomach; this time, she was looking up at me and smiling. I reached into the crib and the forgiveness in her touch slowed my pulse and quieted the sobs. I picked her up. I spent a minute or two with my cheek next to hers.

I moved her away from my face and tried to kiss her but she put out her hands. I tried again but this time her arms were stronger. I looked into her angel face for love but she was looking at me with hate and told me to put her down. I placed her on a couch facing me and asked what was wrong.

With the voice of an adult, she told me she hated me. "You ruined my life, Eric. You're not my father, not my step-father … nothing. I cried every morning, waiting for you to walk in and kiss me after you left. And you never came, Daddy … you never came, Eric."

I could hear myself screaming into the VA night. Bellowing with all my might, trying to drown out my step-daughter's condemning voice, but I could not stop hearing it.

She said, "I am happiest when you don't exist in my memories, Eric. Sit in that bed and die. Die alone."

She told me I was Einar and that she feared that I would kill her someday. She told me I was Judas and that my diseased soul traced back to the original traitor. She told me I was the great fallen one, Lucifer himself, that my selfishness and conceit had destroyed her, had destroyed all mankind.

She moved closer to me. Near enough to see the diamonds of green that seasoned her beautiful brown eyes.

Then she spit in my face and screamed over and over again, "Die! Die! Die! Eric! Die!"

I erupted into a rage. My back arched as my chest flew up toward the ceiling. My entire body involuntarily breeched. I needed my death. I could not go on any longer. The pain …. the pain … it was too fucking much.

And I felt the scream—THE SCREAM—gather in my mouth and it begin to spill out. I needed to let it go, let it be devoured by the hungry walls of the room, let it out into the ward to be documented with the other wails of defeat and surrender that have echoed in these halls.

With no reserve, like King Lear losing a thousand Cordelias, I roared into the murderous darkness of this predawn execution, "KILL ME! SOMEBODY FUCKING KILL ME! KILL ME! I HAVE TO DIE! OH MY GOD! PLEASE, ANYONE! KILL ME! THIS CAN'T BE MY FUCKING LIFE! THIS CANNOT BE MY FUCKING LIFE! MERCY … MERCY … MY GOD PLEASE SHOW ME SOME MERCY! MERCY!!!"

"GOD, PLEASE HELP ME, PLEASE GOD, WHERE ARE YOU? WHAT HAVE I DONE TO YOU? TAKE ME GOD, TAKE ME FROM THIS HELL— TAKE ME! … TAKE ME! … TAKE ME!"

I hyperventilated and had to pause to catch my breath and wait for some sort of reply to my screams. Nothing. No one. Another wave of misery washed up from my stomach into the back of my throat and flew out into the maelstrom.

And then there was the question, the question I had wanted to ask since I was an eight-year-old little boy poured into the suffering of the VA night: "God, how could you do this to me?"

I wept and begged my creator, "What could have I done to deserve this life? This death? Do you hate me, God? You must hate my guts … you must really hate my fucking guts...."

With no answer from the Lord, I mindlessly screamed over and over again until my voice gave out. Mute, I was the embodiment of hopelessness; I was on the other side now. I had given voice to the disease and was completely subsumed by my mania. There would be no more fight, no more dreams. Just sickness.

No longer begging for mercy, but saying farewell, I called for the only savior I had ever known, the one person who never stopped fighting for me, the hero of my life, a life that was finally over.

"Mommy, Mommy, please Mommy. I am so sorry, Mommy. I need help, Mommy. But no one is coming for me. Mommy, where are you Mommy? I am dying, Mommy. I am dying alone, Mommy ... I love you, Mommy. I am so sorry, so fucking sorry. I wanted to be better for you. I wanted to be so much better for you, Mommy. Goodbye, Mommy, I love you Mommy. I don't want to die here, Mommy. I love you so much, Mommy."

I was on my back again. The smoke was clearing and the room was enjoying another victory. My breathing was no longer labored and the cramps in my body had subsided. I turned and faced myself and let out the last scream of a dying mind and was preparing for permanent sleep. But before I drifted off to wake in my new life plugged into the manic matrix, I had one moment of clarity. It was one second to breathe in and breathe out with a lucid mind, or, to be exact, *no mind*.

My eyes made their way to the window above me and I saw the stars. The moon-pale sky glowed with all its lights and I had my first thought in months that went outward. I looked into the cosmos and gently asked, "Mary, mother of God, please help me."

It was the first real request to anyone for anything since I had started to cycle in my disease. It was the acknowledgment that no matter what my delusions told me, I knew for this one last second that I was *not* god. I pictured that sacred mother, my mother, all the mothers I had ever known caressing me one last time. Looking out into the night sky, I finally knew I was not alone.

In that moment, the moment when I had burned through all the levels of me to my core, I knew it was a communal pool of being that rushed and flowed behind the eyes of all living things. A pulsing, loving, passionate universe with no separation, no beginning and no end. I felt the flowing river of this loving unified energy that ran wildly in the blood of stars and sinners. In my hell, for that one fleeting instance, I found my heaven, my Nirvana. I found the connection I yearned for as a child and saw in the various parables of my childhood spiritual teachings, of all teachings. I knew love and breathed in its fleeting essence. I felt God's motherly touch on my cheek and I rested in her loving embrace.

It was over. I smiled at that thought as exhaustion shut down my body. I had cycled to my ninth circle in the seclusion room, but unlike Dante, Virgil was not waiting for me. Dead, my hollow carcass slipped under the ice of my delusions and disappeared from reality and the world.

I was finally baptized absolute into the pain and suffering of the thousands of men in my bloodline who died this same heretic death: the burned, stoned, crucified and hanged saints and madmen that littered my family lineage.

Death | Chapter 25

The morning finally came and the orderlies returned to undo the restraints. The room was stale with waste and sweat. I couldn't feel the restraints or the weathered leather beneath me. I wasn't sure if my eyes were open or closed. They undid the last buckle on my ankle and freed my limbs, but it made no difference to me. The dead don't care how you dress them for their burial.

They pulled me up from the bed and placed my feet on the ground. They had bought in a clean pair of hospital pants and ran them up my legs. I was not a party to the morning's activities. I tried to move my feet but they would not respond. They hung like dead leaves on the end of withered vines. Each time they let go of my arms, I slowly folded upon myself without the strength to fight gravity. With pants in place, they tried to make me stand. It only took a couple of tries before they realized it would not happen.

The staff decided they would have to carry me to my room. Breakfast would be served in moments so they didn't have time to waste. One under each of my armpits, they stood me up and lifted me from the mattress. The daylight hid the room's murderous face, but we both knew what had happened. It had done its job and I was being taken to the garbage to be thrown out forever. Neither one of us acknowledged each other as I crossed its threshold and was carried down the hall. The room faded into the distance of my mind as the guards carried me past my fellow inmates. I was example number one of the power of the room. My spiritual death was to be a lesson for a student population that wasn't paying attention.

They turned into the alcove where my room was and dropped me on my bed. My body was not responding to any of my requests to stand, turn, sit up or roll over. I was paralyzed. I heard nothing. I saw nothing. I tasted nothing. I was nothing.

My breathing came and went without request and my body existed without the permission of its host. I simply was. No more fight, no more plan, no more feeling and no more love. I was in the abstract landscape of a post-suicide existence. The Jersey sun was coming through my window and shining into my useless eyes. I stared straight into its face as it glared behind the thick institutional glass. There was no warmth. Face to face with the source of life that sustains my solar system, I had no subjective thought process to translate the moment. I was a corpse, a manic-depressive mannequin on display for a dying star.

Death | Chapter 26

The Panther
Ranier Maria Rilke
Translation by Stephen Mitchell

His vision, from the constantly passing bars,
has grown so weary that it cannot hold anything else.
It seems to him there are a thousand bars;
and behind the bars, a thousand more, and no world.
As he paces in cramped circles, over and over,
the movement of his powerful soft strides
is like a ritual dance around a center
in which a mighty will stands paralyzed.
Only at times, the curtain of the pupils lifts, quietly—.
An image enters in,
rushes down through the tensed, arrested muscles,
                            plunges into the heart and is gone.

When you can no longer relate to humans it is a common practice to introduce animals into the treatment regimen. This works with the power of touch. Touch allows the transgression of mind and is very important for patients with chronic mental illness. When your mind has broken your connection with the real world due to delusion, depression, psychotic symptoms or anything else, the actual feeling of another living thing will bring some solace to the pain. Separation from society and oneself creates anxiety and anguish to all populations.

While I am in hospitals, I do not touch anyone. I make sure to stay out of physical reach and my delusions like it that way. It removes the speed bumps from their mission and lets my mind run wild. Seclusion is great for a mind bent on killing itself.

At some point after I was taken from the seclusion room, the staff came for me again. I don't know if it was minutes or hours later, but it was the same day. They took me from my bed to the hallway and sat me on the ground. I had to sit on the floor because the ten or fifteen steps exhausted me. Two men stood on either side of me as another called down the hall to say I was ready. I wasn't sure what to expect and didn't care.

I closed my eyes and tried to rest. I had no feelings. After a few vacant moments, I heard loud breathing and opened my eyes. Twenty-four inches from my face was a Golden Retriever. The owner urged me to pet her.

I didn't know if I had the strength to lift my arm. My hands were still clinched and twisted from the restraints. I looked up into the face of the dog. I couldn't understand this, none of this made sense.

The dog seemed kind, almost smiling in the way a dog will do when it opens its mouth and lets its tongue loll.

I tried to lift my arms but couldn't. No one was hurrying the dog or me. The scene was of four or five adult men standing in a hallway watching a dog inch closer to a discolored and slumping man struggling to move his limbs.

I was fighting to keep my head up. My body was still so weak from the restraining bed that I was folding forward without support. As I fell a few more inches forward, I felt the dog's breath on my forehead. The breath was warm and full and pulsed across my eyebrows. I could feel the panting of the animal. The smell of the dog was clean and friendly and her paws were full and relaxed on the linoleum. She was not pacing or fidgeting. She was as calm as the men. Nature must recognize a tragedy. Suffering seems to speak across species if not across borders.

She was so beautiful with her golden coat and forgiving eyes. The longer hairs on her mane wisped across her and made her look like an angel. As I collapsed a little farther forward into my lap, she inched closer. Her loving breath rubbed the back of my neck. Each canine breath made its way down my spine and eased my night's torture. Her breath, the breath of a living, loving animal, coated me and protected my lost and fragile spirit in that moment. I had no coherent thoughts, but I wanted to reach up and hug her. I wanted to feel her fur in my fingers. I was a monster but I still wanted some connection. I knew salvation was gone and I was not dreaming of rescue, but just a little touch would be nice. Like Frankenstein and the girl he killed by the pond, I only wanted a moment of connection with something soft and peaceful.

The orderlies reached down and straightened me up. She was a foot from my face and her eyes were fixed on mine. Even though my mind was telling me I was worthless and hopeless, her soft, wet eyes told me otherwise. Instead, she let me look at her without guilt or shame. I found the strength to lift my right hand up to the thick coat under her neck and my gnarled fingers dove into her lush hair. The coat washed over my hand and past my wrist as I separated my fingers. I could feel the warmth of her body when my hand came to rest on her throat. I gently rolled my fingers in her golden curls and kept looking into her face for the first sign of repulsion.

It never came.

I could feel something warm roll down my face as I spent the last few moments with my only friend. She moved forward and licked my cheek as that first tear trickled into my mouth. The wet salt registered on my skin as the coarse tongue moved around my face. My left hand could finally mobilize itself and reached up to wrap around to the other side of her neck. Gently, I pulled her to my face and hugged her while I wept. She did not pull back or tell me to stop. I was not crying with a clear feeling inside me. I was beyond crying for things. I just held her to hold her, just kissed her for connection while she bathed my face in her kind divinity.

Those who suffer the greatest human atrocities often push beyond the rational limits of human degradation, past the mind and its capabilities. Therefore, the mind-made panaceas leave us lacking. I would need much more than some scriptures or high holidays to find my way back to civilization. No one could scare me with talk of hell and damnation any longer. I was past that. I have lived in hell since the day my dad tried to kill me. My capacity for suffering and degradation knew no bounds. I had spent my life with a shotgun in my mouth, lying to myself that it would get better tomorrow. Negotiating with myself daily to spare my own life.

People like me are the truly sick and broken. We are the ones who have seen hell and wallowed in it. We are alive because our bodies refused to die even though our minds had us acting in suicidal ways. If we are granted some sort of salvation, some sort of solace, it is that of connection. Everyone needs connection—to themselves and to the world around them.

I was disconnected from the world with 10,000 bars separating me from myself.

I held my golden guardian angel for the next few moments and only let go when they made me. She backed away from me and made her way to another veteran, but the power of her touch remained with me. The staff picked me up off the floor, and I went back to my lifeless state. But I had found the answer to my dilemma in that embrace. I did not know it yet, but the simple touch and absolute acceptance of that dog would be at the core of my rising from the ashes.

Connection was the key, and separation, in all its forms, the disease.

They dropped me back on my bed; the sun was still shining through the window. I rolled onto my right shoulder and relaxed. Sleep was coming. The sun was warm on the back of my corpse. I hadn't slept since the twenty-four plus hours in restraints and the ability to move in a bed to get comfortable was appreciated. My eyelids started to droop and I was ready to begin the dreamless sleep of the dead when I smelled my hand. It was under my right cheek, wedged against the mattress. I breathed in through my nose and re-lived the smell of the dog. It registered somewhere in my cemented mind and the frozen muscles of my face tried to smile. With her eyes locked onto mine in my mind's eye, sleep washed over me. My lost heart felt acceptance in her stare, and I slept in her canine care.

Death | Chapter 27

When you have a family member in a mental health facility the stigma of the disease becomes real, tangible. My family could not tie a yellow ribbon around the tree in the front yard to symbolize my inner battle with my myriad of behavioral health issues. No rescue team searched for this *Domestic POW*. My family could not call the base to check on the status of my ship to see where I was. I was deep in the jungles of the VA hospital and all contact outside of official visits was effectively cut off.

My mother met with the doctors and they informed her of the full nature of what I was doing on the ward. She sat there and had to listen to stories of my insanity. The cigarette heist, the strap downs, the public masturbation—the list grew longer with each visit. She was not just losing me; she was being tortured along the way.

After my 24-hour stay in the seclusion room, the doctors told her the Thorazine was not slowing down the disease at all and that it was taking a horrible physical toll on my body. I was not eating or bathing. The seclusions were getting longer but she was not told exactly how long. They wanted my family to be prepared for what families with loved ones diagnosed with mental illness hear all too often: "There is currently no treatment available that seems to be working." They are effectively untreatable.

It must be hell to hear that about someone you love.

Active mental illness is a selfish, hateful disease in that it allows you to live. With its symptoms, it has the ability to kill your mind and spirit and leave your body to continue on. I was now fully encased in my disease but I was not suffering the way my family was. I didn't even think about them anymore. They were familiar to me but almost no emotion registered. It must be like dementia or Alzheimer's. Your family is dead to you, but you are not to them. Your continued existence never allows them to move on.

My disease was particularly selfish because if only I had stayed off alcohol and drugs my relapse may not have occurred. But I wouldn't stay clean and sober. I had made the decision to kill myself and my addictions opened the door to let my mania in to do the job. My family was handcuffed to me again and I was headed to the same hole in the tracks at full speed. But they never reached for the key to un-cuff themselves and get off the ride. They would have plunged ever deeper into my madness. From my grandma to my step-dad, their resolve was absolute.

In the waning moments of the meeting between my mother and the doctors, she started to ask why they were able to break my episodes in weeks in the last hospital. She would not drop this and wasn't going to take any pithy answer from the doctors. I don't blame the staff. I am sure they get a million emotional pleas for some miracle for each of their hopeless cases. They listened and explained how aggressively Thorazine works. They gave her a brief explanation about biochemistry and attempted to return to their regularly scheduled day.

But Nadine wasn't satisfied. She may not have had a medical degree, but she was a Valedictorian, and she was not done with the discussion. She wanted to know about Haldol. Haldol had worked at the first hospital and she wanted to know if they had tried it with me.

Now, I am not exactly sure what happened next, or if the drug had been given to me before in my VA hospitalization. But something amazing did happen. After that conversation, while I was complete in my maniac metamorphosis, they changed my meds. I have no memory of it, nor do I remember what the break initially felt like, but it happened. While I was singing "Sloe Gin" and listening to my shipmates mouth breathe in the med-line, Haldol was administered and the frozen shell between me and reality was cracked open.

All I know is that I woke up one morning slightly aware. My mind was not racing, and I knew I was in a hospital. More importantly, I knew who I was. My feet hit the cold tiles beneath my bed and I shuffled forward to the head of the hall for meds. I knew something had changed, something was different. I did not sing in line this day and the breathing seemed more disgusting and phlegm-filled to my ears. I looked at the nurse dispensing meds and saw her for the first time. The glow of delusion was gone, and she looked old and worn out. She looked human. I saw care and compassion, not scorn, in her eyes.

I feebly wrapped my tobacco-stained fingers around the small cup containing the red liquid and tasted my meds for the first time in months. The medicine was thick and industrial and it went down slowly. After ingestion, I turned to make the long walk back to my room. With mania's veil dropping from my eyes, the veterans looked so sick to me. Some had their heads down and were swaying from side to side. Many were just leaning against the wall or lying on the floor until they were told to get up.

I could smell the hall again. It reeked of urine. The smell was everywhere, from the bathroom, to our pants, to our beds. I tried to make eye contact but I couldn't focus. My eyes were stuck in the Dreamer's stare of the chronically delusional. I hadn't focused my eyes on a book or newspaper in a long time and the little things moved too quickly for my vision to capture.

The main bathroom was filled with my ward-mates and they were passing around a few cigarettes. The men had them in their socks and pants and were sharing their smokes. I had never before captured this scene. I had only seen the smoking. Now the ritual was more mundane and pathetic. But at the same time it was much sweeter. I could see that these men had nothing. They were in their twenties, thirties, forties, fifties, sixties, and even seventies. They, too, were locked up and, therefore, something had gone very wrong in their lives. Their lives had been wrecked by some unseen force and they were institutionalized with me. The one thing they had to share was their smokes and share them they did. By the time the cigarette reached me, the filter was coated in saliva and blood. It was wet and smelled stale, but I put it between my lips and inhaled.

I was not hopeful for any kind of life. I was still buried a thousand miles deep in the hole of my disease, but I felt connected. I felt connected to the other patients for the first time since I had been in the building. As I scanned the vacant stares of my brothers, I saw them as men. I didn't see devils or spies. I saw brothers trying their best to make it another moment. I saw veterans who had worn the uniform of their country proudly in their collective past and refused to stop fighting today.

I saw heroes.

I saw my biological father and my step-father. I saw myself. One more pull on the soggy cancer stick, and the familiar warmth burned my lungs.

I knew I was alive.

I turned and walked to the doorway to finish my journey back to bed when the thought crossed my mind, "How long have I been here and where is here exactly?"

Death | Chapter 28

There are a few terms that are uniquely part of the vernacular of mental illness. One of these is the "Thorazine Shuffle." This is when a patient is on enough Thorazine for an extended period of time that he or she loses the ability to walk with any strength or purpose. With me, Thorazine took all my strength, and when I wanted to go from place to place, I was unable to lift my feet. The best I could do was to make a decision that I wanted to go to a destination and force my body to get there. I would drag my legs forward and shuffle from place to place. If I attempted to throw the other foot forward too quickly, I would lose my balance. My arms were of no use at this point and they wouldn't even rise up to break my fall. I would hit the ground with my shoulder and just lay there until someone picked me up. Even then, I wasn't always strong enough to stand.

The "Haldol Shuffle" is much different. After I had been on Haldol for a few days I couldn't sit still. I was in perpetual motion. The staff informed me they would let me out soon on a pass to walk the grounds unattended. Always on the move, I was able to find a window that had a good view of the acreage surrounding the hospital. I was scoping out the terrain. No sooner did I sit down than I had to get back up and move to the next place. There was no rest for me now. I had gone from a dead body pulling itself around the ward to a man without pause.

Virgil 1 and 2 were long gone. I missed Virgil #2 very much. I remembered how safe he made me feel. I didn't understand what was happening to me. The guards were still not nice to me, but at least I didn't feel helpless now. One of the other veterans actually asked me if I wanted him to help me stretch. Even with the Haldol, my limp was terrible from having no shoes and my hips were still constantly cramping. Every few minutes I would double over like I had been shot in the stomach, and he must have noticed. He took me in his room and had me sit on the floor with my legs spread. He sat in front of me and pulled my arms to make me fold forward. I felt as though my hips had ruptured as loud cracks filled the room. I could only bend half-way before I had to stop. I hadn't done any physical work in so long that the sweat felt strange, alien. It raced down the icy skin on my back like a sentinel waking the parts of my body I had forgotten about.

The Haldol tore my hands from his grip and forced me back to the hall to start pacing again. I didn't care which direction I went as long I was moving. My three minutes of calisthenics had me ready for another antipsychotic induced marathon, and I was off. Back in the main hallway, a man walked up behind me. I heard him before I saw him.

I turned, and he held out his hand and said his name was Dale.

Virgil #3.

Dale was in his mid-forties. Tall and lean, he looked like any of the dozens of other Vietnam Vets I'd met over the years. Hardened. I knew his branch of service and war zone before he even told me he was Army and that he served in Vietnam.

He said he was on Librium for alcoholism and other things. That he had to be detoxed for a while before they would put him in the VA alcoholism program. He told me about his family, his service and anything else that came to his mind. The hall seemed smaller with Dale next to me. He looked at me without scorn or judgment. If I was laboring for breath, he would slow us down a little. Dale was patient in our interactions. He seemed to know I was terrified and he took his time with me.

Dale had asked me a few questions that I couldn't answer. My voice hadn't come back since the night in restraints. I hadn't had a real conversation in so long that I had lost the ability to use my voice at the spur of the moment. The dry indoor air and heavy meds had sealed my throat. I was hardly aware of it before, but now I wanted to talk; I wanted to talk to Dale.

Dale didn't make a joke or demean me as I tried to push a few words into the conversation. He asked me how long I had been on Haldol. I gave him a look of surprise, How could he know about my meds?

He moved into his next sentence quickly. He saw me constantly pacing and knew instantly that I was on Haldol. He had seen me come into a room and try to sit in every chair in the place. Haldol's side effects look like someone trying to stay in a chair with an invisible force pulling him or her out of it. I would rest in a seat and feel the cushion compress against my body weight. Within seconds the chair was not comfortable and the arm rests were pulling at my hands. It wasn't a thought so much as a full-body reaction to get back up and start moving again. Before you know it, you are up and looking for the next magic place that will stop this frenetic journey.

It is really inconvenient for a person who has to go to any kind of group therapy. While other members are on medicines that keep them seated in their chairs like ancient oaks with deep roots, the Haldol patient is bursting out of his skin to start pacing, to keep moving.

We walked the night away, my Virgil #3 and I, down our ever shrinking hall. Dale pointed out things I hadn't seen in this barren landscape as if he were a tour guide. We'd both been around the world, but Dale had seen combat. He was the kind of man you could drop off in the middle of nowhere and he would come back with stories of women and war. He seemed so at ease with his surroundings on the ward, I suddenly felt like it was the place to be. He was a mentally ill Fonzie and I was happy to be Richie Cunningham following his lead.

He told me he had been in ten or twenty rehabs since he was discharged from the Army. He had been in VAs all over the country and used them to dry out when he was in a little trouble. He had the yellow jaundiced look of a man whose liver was beginning to shut down, and his face was gaunt. The other Virgils in my stay were back lit by my mania and delusions and seemed angelic. Dale got no such treatment from my senses. I saw him clearly. I saw the age in his skin and eyes. He was a younger man than his body suggested. He was losing the war of life, one drunken battle at a time.

Dale discussed the litany of his failures with the candor of a cook discussing a recipe. Families lost and children scattered around the country. He exposed his damaged spirit to me and as I listened, I also began to hear my own past speak. We walked for hours that night and he spilled the story of his life over me. As I listened, my awakening senses drank him in. Through him, I began to realize—to viscerally acknowledge—that I was not alone.

Dale had been living in his own hells for a very long time. I now had my guide for the journey out of my own flames, and he was steadfast in his mission. I never knew what prompted a hardcore drunk to walk with me for the first time that night. Maybe he saw himself in me and decided to make an attempt for a rescue. Maybe he knew his days were numbered and decided to pass on his knowledge of wards, war, and meds. Or maybe he saw past himself, past his own suffering, and saw a way to share himself and live longer than his reeling liver would allow. Whatever his reasons, his full disclosure and compassion were the exact thing I needed to begin to climb out of my solitary hell.

Dale set himself *on fire* for me and showed me his burns from a life burning alive from the skin in. He opened himself up and showed me that pain need not be avoided or suffered in silence, alone. He showed me the cathartic solace of sharing one's story with another who suffers and how the act of sharing your journey to another can be a part of healing. My last mental hospital Virgil, my savior Dale, cared for me as is. He didn't wait for me to get better. Instead, he put his charred hand on my shoulder and would walk me back up the circles of my psychiatric hell to the exit door of my nightmare.

Death | Chapter 29

Suddenly, it seemed, the doctors and nurses began talking to me a lot more about my situation. I couldn't figure out what they were saying, but at least I was aware of the conversations. They were one-on-one conversations in which sometimes I was very engaged and other times I observed the whole discussion as if I was having an out-of-body experience. I had no idea what everyone was talking about, but I did know they seemed hopeful.

Something had changed, but I didn't understand what it was. I had no idea that I had cycled for months in a full-blown manic episode. I didn't understand why my fingernails were black or my teeth bloody. I still felt dead. I was not excited by anything but smoking. The word excitement may be too strong. I felt the need to smoke and nothing else.

One morning, I headed to the main room to wait for breakfast. The beeping of the meal cart got louder and the vets piled into their chairs. As the cart turned into the room, a nurse asked me to follow her to the nurse's station. Nothing registered as out of the ordinary in this request. After all, life on the ward meant you did what you were told. You ate when were told. You bathed when you were told. You were tethered to a bed when you were told.

When I reached the nurse's station, the head nurse told me I wouldn't be eating with everybody else. I had no idea what that meant. The doorway to the seclusion room was behind me and I started to tense up. She reached for my hand and looked at me and said, "Eric, you are going to the main cafeteria for breakfast."

Alone.

She took out her keys and reached for the lock on the exit/entrance door to the ward. I had stopped even looking at that door. I had stopped thinking of ever walking out of the ward. It hurt too much to dream of such things. It hurt to hope.

Casually, she moved around me and pushed her key into the lock. The door swooshed backward into the hallway, and the smell of the outside world washed over me. I didn't move. I heard her say, "down three flights"… "into the basement hallway"… "over to building number such and such and make a right." And as quickly as the discussion started, it ended. I was in the hallway looking at the door—from the outside.

Through the small side windows lining the door, the ward looked safe, benign. You couldn't see the suffering, the pain or the anguish. You couldn't see the hopelessness. You had to step back through the door and into Hell before the insular fires could consume you. And, for the first time in months, I was on the outside, looking in.

I turned and faced the elevators and the door leading to the stairwell. I fought to remember all the directions to breakfast, but I was already lost, muddled. My mind hadn't been mine in months and I hadn't been forced to remember a single fact since I walked through that door with Bud next to me.

I knew I had to go downstairs but that was all I remembered of her directions. So I stepped forward and tentatively rubbed the tip of my index finger on the elevator button that showed an arrow facing down. My finger glided in little circles caressing the down button, slightly pressing in but not committing to activating the mechanism. I tried to remember what it felt like to be behind those heavy silver doors in the little room moving up and down. I could picture doing it before, but the thought of a closed little office was too much for me.

Making up my mind, I stepped to my right and walked into the stairwell heading down stairs. You think the journey out of hell is upward, but I was burrowing down into the belly of the building. I remembered my first journey up the stairs with Bud and the orderlies. The stairs led down past the main floor and into the basement. As I came out of the stairwell, I could only turn right. After that, I needed some direction, so I looked for anybody walking anywhere. I just wanted to follow someone somewhere. I stood still and listened for the familiar sound of voices congregating for a meal or a meeting.

I found my way to the main hallway where I had to make a choice: go left or go right. If I went right, it looked like the hall ended again, to my left the hall rolled out of my sight. I turned left and started down the next underground tributary. I could see the morning light pouring into the hall ahead of me from windows that were street-level at the top of the walls. I kept walking.

Up and down the hall were veterans laying on the ground, washed up against the walls. They were from other wards, but we shared a common condemnation. It was like being on liberty in a foreign country when you enter various random bars only to run into sailors from other ships. You eat and drink together and then go back to your own command, brothers in arms going our separate ways. In the hallway, we paid our respects to each other as I kept sailing to my breakfast. I felt rejuvenated by this passing and surged deeper into the darkened halls waiting for the sirens of the chow hall to call me in.

The hallway got darker the deeper I moved into its bowels. I hadn't seen a veteran in over ten minutes and was beginning to lose faith in the journey. I wasn't hungry but the novelty of the experience kept me moving onward. As I got to a four-way crossing in the hall, I had to decide whether to go left, right, backwards or continue forward. The instructions from the nurse were completely gone. I felt as if I had been born in the hall, without a memory of anything outside of it.

I stood in place for a few moments when I started to hear the din of metal clanging against metal. Listening intently, I heard the familiar sound of massive amounts of cutlery clashing loudly like a boot camp scullery. I followed the noise to an open double door with a massive industrial staircase winding upward behind it. The steps were ten feet wide and made to accommodate large numbers of people coming up and down them at the same time. The windows on the walls stood high above the steps and flooded the stairwell with torrents of light. If I was actually the mentally ill messiah, then this was my stairway to heaven.

I still saw no one, but I could hear the voices of the morning crew getting chow. Slowly, I started up the stairs. Step by step, I made my way up the illuminated path. Each step got lighter as the noise of hard plastic, metal and psychosis filled my ears. At last I reached the top and found St. Peter in a hairnet holding a clipboard and yelling at me for my name. I wasn't sure at first if I should tell him. I didn't see how he could have it on the list. The thought of interoffice phones didn't register and I couldn't fathom the ward calling ahead.

I looked beyond him into the maelstrom and saw hundreds of my service sisters and brothers carrying trays of food and drinks like chow on my Destroyer. Each one swaying in line like the ship rocking in the swells of the western Mediterranean. All had the look of delusion, disease and decay on their face as they pointed at their breakfast choices. None had the fresh-faced glow of their service days and very few looked up. They shared nothing and everything at the same time. There were only two common denominators here: mental illness and hard metal utensils. Perfect.

I stepped into the large room and over to the hard, plastic trays. I looked at the silver utensils and tried to grab one, but my fingers wouldn't wrap around the slim metal. I could hold the tan tray upright with the palms of my hands underneath, but my fingers would not curl around the cold steel. I fished around for a few moments and left. It wasn't as if I cared if I ate with my hands or not. But when I looked ahead of me in the line and saw my fellow residents shifting, twitching, ticking, spitting and swaying with their knives and forks, I wished I, too, was armed.

The meal itself was uneventful. The food was the same as they took into our wards. I sat alone in a corner of the room away from the windows. They were high on the walls also and the sun shone through them like a cathedral. It was too bright for me. I was a cave creature now. Darkness and solitude called to me. A couple of licks of the grits compartment and some cold pinkish meat and I was off.

I couldn't believe I was going to knock on the door to let me back in less than thirty minutes since my liberation. Yet, the Haldol pushed me forward and I felt as if I would rip my skin off the bone if I didn't get back behind the safety of the door to Hell. Sweat poured down my back as I finally reached home and began pounding on the door.

The nurse looked up from her charts and came around to let me back on board. I stood there for a few moments and took in the surroundings. I wondered why I had been so eager to return. I thought of the day I ran alongside my father's car in the wet parking lot. Rather than running away from mortal danger to save my life, I chased it. Like that day in the rain, I was begging to get back in with what was trying to kill me.

Death | Chapter 30

I spent another week going to the gladiators' breakfast with the other knife- and fork-wielding inmates and then running back to the safety of the ward. During the day, Dale and I walked for hours as he warned me about what to watch for when I got out. I realized Dale didn't know I was diagnosed with a mental illness as well as having an addiction disorder. He'd talk about all the hopeless crazies and then turn and wink at me like we were better than those other men. Didn't matter to me. I couldn't have cared less if he punched me in the face every half hour as long as he walked with me. Just listening to, just being with, another person tamped down my growing anxiety. I wasn't mentally healthy enough to work on me yet, but at least the blinders of mania had been thinned enough for me to see another, to hear another without some psychotic translation. He was not a god or a superman or a demon; he was just Dale.

I liked looking at him, his skin, his hands, his eyes. He was real and he was different from me. My mind could still convince me I didn't exist, but it could no longer convince me he didn't exist. Turns out Haldol is the antidote and the poison for me. It makes living almost unbearable when I have to be on it, but it breaks the mania. It is worth it. I know that now, and I was beginning to understand that then.

I woke one morning and put my scarred toes on the ground and worked my legs out to get them going. I took my meds. KISS no longer serenaded me, and I knew it wasn't sloe gin I was drinking. I was alert and able to follow a conversation and even answer a few questions.

I went into the sitting room to watch TV. I can't remember the TV ever being on except for some political thing in 1996 during the election campaigns. I do remember thinking the whole show was for me. Like a pep rally given by the world to let me know they hadn't given up on me. But on that morning, it was off and the screen cracked. I was staring at the reflections captured on the screen when a nurse came in and told me to follow her.

Dutifully, I hobbled down the hall toward the nurse's station and there they were—my parents. My mom was smiling and talking with the staff. Bud was next to her, absolutely not smiling. He was watching me. He never took his eyes off me. As the doctors and nurses discussed my case with my mother, my Virgil, *The Virgil*, was already protecting me. He turned to the staff and interrupted.

"Where are his shoes? He has ten reconstructed toes. Somebody get him his fucking sneakers!"

Everyone stopped talking.

Bud didn't have anything against the staff or the men hospitalized with me, the *Domestic POWs* trapped in their personal wars, but he looked like he was ready to kill someone right then and there. He was Sergeant George Powers, United States Marine Corp, and he would not put down his weapon until the war was over. He was still fighting for his son's life, and he was bound and determined to lead me off the battlefield the same way he led me onto it.

I had sneakers put on my feet while my dad watched. Bud carefully looked me up and down to see if I had any bruises. My mom picked up some paperwork, hugged me and we made our way through the door, down the caged steps, and out the front exit of Building 53. As we got to the car my mother got in first. Bud drove a large cranberry Jaguar and if we were anywhere else we would have looked like any other well-to-do family heading to the country club. But we weren't. We were a family leaving a maximum-security mental institution for home with all the fears and doubts that come with that very difficult, domestic situation.

Always the gentleman, Bud opened the door for my mom, helped her in and closed her door. I followed him around to his side of the car when he turned to face me.

Eye to eye, father and son.

He pulled me to his chest and hugged me deeply, with no reservations. A hug he had never given me before, a hug I had never known he could give. Bud stepped back, adjusted his sunglasses, and got in.

We headed home with Bud at the wheel, the way he was at the wheel of our family. He was the greatest and most faithful man I have ever known. My mom seemed to decompress in the car and was so happy to have me back. She told me stories of what I had missed and asked each moment if I was OK. Bud didn't say a word. He knew the fight for my life had just begun. We had survived the ocean journey, now it was time to take the hill. My Marine was ready. I was determined to follow his command. Bud accelerated for home, and I knew my life was in the balance.

I needed to prepare myself for a battle to survive these two chronic diseases and commit myself to listening and obeying Bud. My thinking was wrong, my mind crushed, shattered. I needed a total psychic paradigm shift: from failing thoughts to failing actions *to* new life-changing actions and therefore, new manifestations that would create new beliefs based on these revolutionary experiences.

I left the ward alone, but would eventually return for my comrades. I would start fighting to rejoin life and society. I would be fearful, and even terrified at points in the journey, but I would not quit, and I vowed that if I succeeded, I would return for my brothers in arms. I am the son of George (Bud) Powers, and we leave no one behind.

As my mom talked and Bud drove, I pledged to do whatever needed to be done. Exhausted, I lay my head back against the seat and looked out the window as we made our way back down Route 287 and left the Land of Make Believe behind.

Book 3   Resurrection

The dead only know one thing: it is better to be alive.

~ Sergeant James T. "Joker" Davis, USMC, from the film Full Metal Jacket

Do not be conformed to this world, but be transformed
by the renewal of your mind.

*~ Paul of Tarsus (Romans 12:2), formerly Saul the Pharisee prior to
his conversion experience on the Road to Damascus*

...there must be something greater than anything I've known.

*~ Jason Schnatter, frontman for the group Mean Venus,
a brother from Hell ... a Jersey Virgil*

Resurrection | Chapter 1

St. John of the Cross, the 16th century Spanish-Catholic mystic and author of the *Dark Night of the Soul*, was tortured by his captors and held in a ten-foot by six-foot cell for over nine months. After each meal of bread, water and sometimes sardines, St. John was forced to strip and was then whipped across his shoulders by each individual present. This caused him such agony that it led to a rapturous state of oneness that divorced him from his self/ego and that opened his being/spirit to the unity and truth of his God. His book captures those epiphanies as they occurred in Toledo, Spain in 1578.

My suffering was not rapturous. It was disgusting and brutal. While I was in the hospital, oblivious to the reality of my own disease let alone life outside the ward, my family suffered in its own way, each member locked down in their own torment. And when I returned home to face them, it was the darkest time of my life. The shame was palpable, smothering, suffocating. The Haldol only allowed for fifteen-minute respites before I was up and pacing the house again. As I walked around the house through its familiar hallways, I would pass by my family members, and I could feel their fear—they were scared both for me and of me.

That afternoon, a couple of hours after I was released, I stood in my parents' backyard and smoked by myself. The neighborhood was littered with bay windows and barbeques, children's toys and patio furniture. I thought to myself: *I am not of this world. I am something different. I am a monster. I am disease itself. And the next time, I know I won't make it out alive.*

I tried to remember if I had ever heard of anyone who had gone through what I had gone through and who made it back. Really made it back. I had already read the standard books of the bipolar canon, but they didn't seem to relate to me. My disease seemed different. I didn't understand the severity of my particular brand of bipolar disorder. I didn't understand how to stop the addiction issues that accompanied it and I didn't understand any of the trauma symptoms that interwove themselves through it all.

When my mania struck, it took everything from me. It took a marriage and a step-daughter the first time. It took NYU, my job and all my money the second time. The second episode broke me—body and soul. I prayed there would not be a third time. I didn't think I could live through a third hospitalization. But how could I make sure? How does one fight an enemy that lives beneath the skin?

I took another long drag of my cigarette, and the VA bathroom instantly came back to mind. I could see the men still on the ward passing around smokes, hear the urinals running as the vets wheezed through the cancer-filled air. I was home, but I had no idea what to do next.

The whole world was my ward now.

I still suffered from low-level delusions, and I had a hard time getting used to coming and going as I pleased in the house. What I needed was someone to convince me that I would and could make it. I had no "stereotypes of success" to look to, and I was beyond inspirational quips. I needed a revolutionary roadmap for saving a man who was seriously mentally ill and severely addicted—a man who knew that using drugs would trigger an episode but who was still unable to abstain. A man who lost his father from the same disease and who absolutely believed he was meant to die the same heretic death.

Hope has become a throwaway word used in love songs and on greeting cards, and it is ridiculed as the stuff of fairy tales. But hope is everything to those who don't have it. Hope is spiritual oxygen. The most brutal state of human existence is the absolute absence of hope. Without it, the heart suffocates and the mind deadens.

I told myself: I am twenty-six. I am divorced. I have been in two maximum-security mental hospitals and have been strapped down in seclusion rooms over twenty times. I have screamed into the night immersed in my disease, pleading for death while swimming in my own feces. My biological father died of the same mental disease and attempted to kill me while in its clutches. The only thing I ever loved absolutely was my step-daughter and she is gone forever. I am a drug-addict and an alcoholic. I have tried twelve-step programs and have failed. My feet are fucked. I have never in my life met a single person who was ever in a ward like mine and who survived and thrived after he got out. I have thirty community college credits. No car. No job. No money.

No life.

Standing in the backyard, I felt completely disconnected—from the world, from my hometown, from my family, from me. I didn't know who or what I had turned into. I was an "other" to myself and I didn't understand how to communicate with what I had become. Who was this third person who appeared in mania to blow out my whole life? I could not relate to the part of me that was killing me. My blood was teeming with manic hand grenades, and I never knew when my mind would pull the pins.

My tripartite identity crisis made it impossible to accept my problem. I knew there was a me—the actual me, changeless, behind my thoughts—and I knew there was an Eric—the image/ego, identity, the man the world sees, the image of myself created by my memories—but I still couldn't link to the third part, the manic ERIC. Since I could not fully accept the identity of the third me that was killing me, I would not take real actions to save myself. Even after everything I had been through, I still hadn't "bought in" to saving my own life. I needed to accept that the bipolar disorder was not an "other," but, instead, that it was a real part of me. I would have to change how I defined the disease, how I defined who I was. And that meant I had to change how I defined my biological father.

Many of us diagnosed with mental illness grew up with the disease in our families. We dreaded being just like the family member we simultaneously feared, loved, and hated. My diagnosis was more than a medical recognition of the disease; it was a death sentence because it transformed me from Eric into Einar and I knew how Einar's life story ended. I needed to truly believe that if I was to become successful in life it would be because of my mental illness, not in spite of it.

But those realizations were far in the future.

At that moment, I couldn't see any way to get better. Because I had no hope, I saw no reason to believe I even had a chance. I was not suicidal, but I had no reason to live.

Dr. Robert Lifton discussed Hiroshima trauma survivors in several of his discourses. He wrote that some survivors had what he called a "death imprint." These survivors of the bomb believed that death had tattooed itself to their entire existence. Rather than feeling grateful that they had been miraculously spared from the horrific effects of the bomb, they believed that they were also meant to die along with their kinsmen.

I sympathized. My life, too, was imprinted with death. I had been a dead man walking since I was twelve.

The only discussion I remember towards the end of my hospital stay was about a halfway house and social security, about some kind of job program and a partial care program. The myriad of half-dreams were laid out at my feet, and I embraced them with the half-hopes of a half-man.

How hard would you work for a half-dream?

How much would you sacrifice for a half-life?

I stubbed out my cigarette on the grass and headed back inside. My parents were waiting for me and asked me to sit down and talk. Mom kept things simple. She said I was going to die if I didn't change. She said if I didn't go to a twelve-step program for drug and alcohol abuse, I would have to leave the house and move into whatever living situation the state offered. Bud didn't speak at all. He just looked at me and nodded. I said "yes," of course.

The conversation with my parents ended, and that evening I was at my first twelve-step meeting on the Cook Campus of Rutgers University in New Brunswick, NJ. It was there that I began my relationship with two of the most important things in my journey out of this lifelong darkness and into the light: a twelve-step program to control my alcohol and drug addiction and Rutgers University, the State University of New Jersey.

Resurrection | Chapter 2

The recovery meeting started at 8 p.m. on a Monday evening. Bud dropped me off at 7:50 p.m. I was terrified, but my parents made it clear that I could not live in their house without attending. I had him drop me off at the corner by the Agricultural Museum and the horse farm, away from the mass of people already gathering for the meeting. After he drove away, I smoked by myself until the others disappeared inside.

Like a man walking to his own execution, I made my way across the street to the green double doors guarding the entrance to the meeting and pulled the one on the right. It didn't move. Locked. I instantly thought about calling it a night and smoking another twenty cigarettes across the street until my dad came back. As I turned away to leave, I heard a huge laugh, a thunderous group laugh that sounded like one hundred people laughing at once: a boot camp laugh.

I hadn't heard laughter in months. It had been so long, I forgot it existed. My body reacted to the sound; my hand shot out and instinctively tried the other door. Open. I pulled the door out of my way and stepped across the threshold into the coffee, cookies, and redemption of a recovery meeting. It was the single greatest turning point of my life. It was that literal step, those people, and that program that allowed me to arrest my addiction and give me the space to treat my mental disorder. Over time, I would come to immerse myself in that community of alcoholics, drug addicts and saints. I did not know it at the time, but by opening that door and crossing that threshold, I officially left the Emergency Room of my broken life and entered the long-term care of my *Burn Unit*. It was there that I found the healing salve of mercy and miracles.

I would have never been able to recover from my mental illness without remaining clean and sober. It is a very common occurrence for people with mood disorders to also suffer from addiction. There are many reasons for the link. What I liked about the twelve-step program was that it wasn't concerned with the "Whys" but was much more concerned in the "Hows." The people I met were fellow sufferers and they wanted to help me stop my suffering. When you arrive unconscious, burned and bloodied in the Emergency Room, they don't ask you why; they just need to stabilize you long enough to get you to the proper treatment. Triage and stabilization comes first. Treatment and rehabilitation for your particular illness or injury comes after that.

The twelve-step program was not the answer for my bipolar disorder but it did stabilize me long enough to have a clear idea of exactly what it was I was dealing with and how to treat it. Even if someone with severe mental illness is not an alcoholic or addict, I believe they should refrain from alcohol and drugs forever because of how those substances influence moods and counteract the efficacy of psychiatric medicines. The problem is that people link those substances to more than just recreational substances. They are escapes, coping skills and crutches for the addicted. Many are more concerned about feeling left out at a party than actually living their life.

If it were any other substance that was causing the absolute destruction of your life then abstinence would be much easier. If it was fudge, toothpaste or candy canes, the quit would be easy, but alcohol and narcotics are real and lethal addictions. They physically and mentally tether you to the non-reality of an addict's life. Recovery happens, but relapse is common and scorned by outside observers. The outside world doesn't understand the stigma and torture of addiction, but the community of recovering people share the common weakness and can offer strength to those who falter. There are many paths to recovery for alcoholics and drug addicts and I have no opinions on which are better or more effective. I used a twelve-step program and can only speak to my experience, but there is no wrong answer for the cessation of the insular degradation of my addicted brothers and sisters. Help is the key, from the outside, from a fellow sufferer, from a Virgil.

I call recovery communities for addiction *Burn Units* because of the sensitivity and scarring of the patient. When a person enters a recovery program he has just come through hell. He has been on existential fire, burned alive from the inside. His disease has run rampant and the wreckage and destruction can be overwhelming. The pain and shame are tragic. He enters the *Burn Unit* in different states of destruction and those who have been on fire for long periods of time may need to be put into a "coma" just so they can survive the initial treatment.

Eric C. Arauz

Physical burn victims are sometimes put into medically-induced comas to help them survive the pain of their burns, the pain of the treatment, and to protect them from the pain of their survival. Each breath tears newly formed skin, and it is like being on fire without the flames, every nerve ending exposed.

For addicts and alcoholics these "comas" must be self-induced in order for them to be successful—that is, the patient must be a willing participant in the treatment. The self-induced comas are the detoxes and rehabs that provide the space and time needed for healing from their worst burns before waking up to the real world. The addict's body, mind and spirit are so damaged and tortured that he would not survive the scars of a life lived in addiction. He needs time to become strong enough to confront the damage without dying from the treatment, dying from the reality of the damage.

Both types of burn victim must prevent diseased skin from building up over their wounds. They must live with their wounds open to the air. For those victims who have lost their actual skin, doctors tend to the infection; for those victims who have burned their souls, other addict/alcoholics tend to their spirits to prevent more spiritual decay.

When both victims return to society, they will have to live with their wounds. Both the physical and the spiritual burn victims find strength in the examples of other victims who stand publicly exposed to the world. They learn to find beauty in their damaged skins and singed souls. They can discover meaning and utility in their suffering and share that with other burn victims.

In recovery, we not only expose our wounds to the air, but we purposely share our wounds, setting ourselves *on fire* again and again to show others there is hope in such suffering. We burn for others and for ourselves, and we greet each new charred victim at the green double doors of the *Burn Unit* with our flaming handshakes and smoldering hugs.

Resurrection | Chapter 3

When I entered the twelve-step program, I was not ready to hear anything about how to recover. My mind was still reeling from the mental hospital I had walked out of only twelve hours earlier. The cacophony of the large group deafened me to any singular voice. The twelve steps and twelve traditions at the front of the room were blurred by the side effects of my antipsychotics. Names came and went as each person announced themselves to the group. Various announcements were read and applause greeted members who made their way to the front of the room all the while the Haldol was still trying to tear me out of my chair. Paying attention was difficult. The frenzied screams from the healing antipsychotics were demanding that I get up and start moving, walking, pacing.

The room broke up into two smaller meetings. The person leading the meeting said the group in the back of the room was for beginners, so I got up and grabbed a chair back there. All around me people seemed relaxed, chatting and occasionally laughing in response to something the person speaking had said. I clutched the bottom of my chair and scanned the room to see where the next speaker would come from. The last speaker finished, hands went up, a name was called, and the room quieted. I locked in on the face of the person about to speak as my body was convulsing to be freed from the chair. She looked up and said, with no apprehension, that her name was _____ and that she was an alcoholic.

My body relaxed a little and my hands released their death grip on the bottom of the chair. I would have loved for her to say she was a bipolar alcoholic, but that was not the primary purpose of this organization. She started to share, and I started to listen. My mind quieted with each sentence of her five-minute oral catharsis. I began to hear my own breath. I could feel my heart beat. She spoke my language, she knew my suffering even if she didn't know me. I heard the *vernacular of suffering* infuse her didactic: degradation, hopelessness, sin, self-hate, loneliness, otherness, worthlessness, and suicide. She spoke in the "language of the heart."

I knew two things at that moment: 1) I was an alcoholic and a drug addict and; 2) that I was not totally alone. She may not have had all the problems I had, but she certainly had enough.

What moved me most from her speech that night was that she didn't just complain about her problems, she shared her successes. She talked about how she had taken action to address her addiction, her life. She spoke in a vernacular in which I was illiterate, the *vernacular of resurrection*.

She spoke of freedom, guiltlessness, hope, love, connection and forgiveness. That night, I didn't understand how that could happen for me, but she made me believe it had happened for her. I had never seen anyone so open about suffering and so confident that there was life beyond the suffering. In Dale, I had found a person to relate to, but he gave me no answers. My Virgils in the hospital could lead me close to the ninth circle of my own hell and deliver me to the doorstep of the real world but were unable to show me how to live outside of the burning circles.

The people I saw that night had the answer to the beginning of my resurrection. They were veterans of the *Burn Unit* and were not afraid to show me their scars. That is how early recovery is for the alcoholic. We may have survived, but we are not equipped to begin living. We are self-lacerated and our flayed skin and broken souls are exposed to the world. The panacea we used to protect our open wounds is gone as we are denied alcohol, deceit and drugs to hide our burns. We are traumatized and in a state of shock and we come to these programs and these rooms looking for safety, solace and salvation.

There is no skin graft for our disease to lessen the burn. We must learn to live naked and exposed and not use any bandages to hide our wounds. We heal by exposing our wounds to the other burned addicts. We show each other the power of a shared weakness, our Jamesian "torn-to-pieces-hood," and how our burns lose sensitivity with exposure. The *Burn Unit* functions as a place to live in the pain until you are ready to hear, understand, and then live your healing answers. The problem is not the fire; fire with any extended exposure will burn anyone. Many people use alcohol and drugs without turning into raving lunatics and criminals. It is in the *Burn Unit* that we show the patient that the first step will be the only one that mentions alcohol or drugs; the next eleven and a half are about your thinking, about your choices. The fire and alcohol or drugs are not the problem. The problem is: Why would someone run back into the fire of addiction to try and heal their burns?

Why would a twelve-year-old boy chase his father's car immediately after it almost ran him over?

Why do we chase our deaths?

We need a new way of thinking that will come from new actions—revolutionary actions.

The twelve-step program, the *Burn Unit*, is where I discovered the tasks I needed to change my beliefs. I would learn to negate my assumed identity step by step. The true power of the community was in the communal negation, being surrounded by others who were peeling off layers of themselves and living with new raw skin. This collective strength gave me the power and courage to keep trying to live a completely unknown life.

It took time, but the paradigm shift did occur. I moved from old, ingrained thinking to action. As I took more revolutionary actions, I created new affirming beliefs from those actions. My life would be about doing rather than theorizing. Heart over mind, feel over feeling, today over yesterday. I needed to believe that actions taken today were equal to the ones from my past. My yesterdays had to lose their exaggerated place in my psyche.

I would build my redemption on this principle from the ancient mystical Hindu text, the Brihadaranyaka Upanishad. I needed to believe in the core of my soul that, "...*as is your deed is, so is your destiny.*"

I would have to stop thinking myself to death.

Resurrection | Chapter 4

Everyone was hugging and laughing after the meeting, while I watched from across the street. I had left right before the end and walked back to the corner across from the Agricultural Museum to wait for Bud. I would see them next week. I couldn't wait to get to the next meeting.

Wow, next week....

I hadn't thought in terms of weeks in a long time. Bud pulled up and opened the car door. His car was big and comfortable, like riding on a couch, and we headed for home. I looked over at him. I loved the way he gripped the wheel. His fingers were strong, the kind that could hold you while you were hanging off a cliff. He was a very handsome man with a full head of silver hair that gave him a distinguished look.

Bud drove his big cranberry sedan with such easy confidence that from the outside people would have thought he was a movie star. But up close, he had his smokes rolled in his sleeve and was driving the Jag simply because he thought it was a great car to drive.

As far as I knew, Bud Powers came out of the womb not caring what anyone thought of him. My step-dad lived in the perpetual *now* and from the moment he came into our lives, he loved us as his own. I felt tremendous comfort in his company and he never let on that he had no experience with addiction or mental illness before me. All that mattered was that I had it and it was killing me and he was going fight like hell to save me from me.

We started for home and he asked about the meeting and listened for an answer. I had plenty of feelings but not much experience elucidating them, so I kept the answers short. After a few minutes he turned to me and said, "You gotta keep going, Eric. You are going die at this rate if something doesn't change."

Done and done.

I closed my eyes and listened to the English engine purr. He let me put the window down a little and we drove down a road I have been down a thousand times. We passed St. Bartholomew's on our left, the Catholic school where my father tried to end my life. This time it was different. This time I could see tomorrow. I might make it. I might not have to die.

I had been afraid to admit it until that moment, but I wanted live. I just didn't know how.

Resurrection | Chapter 5

The first few months of my recovery were difficult. Every time I felt hopeful, my past would pop up and overwhelm my thoughts. I had done a tremendous amount of damage to my family and had held them hostage with my actions. The *undertow* of my yesterdays was relentless. Merciless. It took the collective strength of my new support group to keep me from drowning in the guilt and shame of my past.

I was a huge open wound, so I tried to go to meetings every day. Two a day if I had rides. I was doing everything I could to fight the pull back into the nightmarish safety of the ward, but I was equally afraid of life outside. The *undertow* kept pulling at me like a tidal wave of despair. I did not actually see how I could build a life back from the hospitals.

My most hopeless moments were when I was alone. When my mind was allowed to run free, it always took me to the worst possible outcomes. It was constantly telling me I was a failure and that there was no way back for me. My mind was a collection of yesterdays and it did everything it could to recreate the failures of the past.

The meetings allowed me to see daily examples of how people like me had come back from terrible places. Each story led me a little farther from the ward, but when I left the group, when I got home, I would instantly revert back to the hopeless thinking. The key was being around people who were succeeding. My mind could destroy me when I was alone, but it could not argue away these new people.

I needed to change the way I thought. I needed to begin to live life from the inside instead of constantly judging myself by what I thought everyone else was thinking. If you looked at me, I would find ten ways to prove to myself that you were looking down on me. I believed others saw me as a monster, an outcast, a heretic. I had to define what I was. I had to re-write the story of Eric Arauz and it needed to be an autobiography with no ghost writer.

In order to address the wreckage of my failed life, I needed to begin in the most authentic place I knew—my family. They took the absolute worst of my disease and made Herculean attempts to save me from me. I needed to sit down with my mother and let her unload on me. I needed to fully expose myself to the disaster I had caused and see the hurt. I would need to learn how to divorce myself from my perspective and stand in the shoes of each of my family members. To try to see my life experience from their point of view and how it affected them. I knew what it felt like to be the driver of the car in a major accident; I didn't know what it felt like to helplessly witness it from the outside.

I had been compliant on my meds since release, and I had been sober a few months by the time I approached my mother and asked about the hospital and what the doctors told her I had done. A Virgil in my support network promised he would be there to pick up the pieces of me when the discussion was over.

We sat down and she started slowly, but then quickly gained momentum. Her voice flooded with emotion, and I could see the pain and shame on her face. She asked if I could imagine what it felt like to be a mother and to listen to such horrible things about her son. It was more lament than castigation. She was venting, decompressing, healing.

For my journey to resurrection to succeed, I would have to take my family along. I knew that I had to start building new experiences to create a new life, and that would require not just novel changes, but huge, revolutionary changes. I would have to keep stepping off the cliff of my known experiences into the darkness of the unknown manifestations of these new actions and hope I would find new footing in the free-fall.

My mother needed to understand that I was not going to fight her. She needed to understand that for the first time in my life I was not making excuses, not shunning responsibility. In order to turn my life around, I needed to know who and what I had become. If I was to know the "other" I turned into when my delusions claimed my consciousness, I would need first-hand reports. I needed to journey down into the circles of my hell, go past the comfortable sins, and get to the bottom of my burning soul.

My actions against my family had to be addressed, or my attempt to live would never get my full effort. Many people with serious mental illness and addiction give up because they feel they can never fix their family situation. The stories of infidelity and violence are common in my population. They are told in the maximum-security hospitals, therapist's rooms and various recovery meetings around the world. Our families are the last line of defense for most of us before we begin the death cycle. Most of us focus our most vicious attacks on our families, on the people closest to us. In my case, my Mom.

My biological father had no one. Once he tried to harm us and was thrown out into the streets, he was totally alone in the United States. He had no one fighting for him and the disease took its natural course unchecked.

My family had already gone down that path, and they risked their psychological lives to stop my descent. But it was still up to me to fix this. I needed a real change, no quick fix. I had tried before with dramatic pleas of change. When I'd get out of the hospitals, I lived in words and not actions. I would tell my family how it would be different this time. I would explain how I would *fix everything*. While they patiently stared at me, I would list the jobs I would get, the degrees I would earn and the money that I would accumulate. Depending on how bad the last episode was I would create a false future to match the hell I just came from. While the rest of my family was hoping I would just take my Lithium and get a part-time job, I would reassure them with plans of ascending to positions of power and prestige. The dream had to be grand enough to offset the shame and guilt. The dreams got bigger as I got sicker. Coming out of the VA there was no dream big enough to counterbalance the damage.

My mother was finishing her catharsis while I just sat and listened. I watched her face as she spoke. I looked at her eyes and mouth and saw her as a person, not a mother. She had beaten Stage 4 cancer and escaped an abusive, mentally ill husband. She was a strong, proud woman who fought and fought and who continued to fight for me since high school, and now I could see it was taking its toll on her. As she was talking to me, at the end of our discussion, I was certain that I was killing her. It was only a thought before, but this discussion made it clear the damage I was doing to my mother and my family.

The discussion was like a B-52 bomber pilot walking the grounds of a foreign land she had just bombed. From ten thousand feet, the little specks are not people and they do not suffer. But once on the ground, the suffering is real and grotesque. Death is not as clear-cut and sterile as it sounds in the war room. I was walking the landscape of years of bombing runs targeted at my family, on my mother. I saw and *felt* the damage. When I first got home, I hadn't been able to look at it, but I had to now. I was ready.

My family did not live on the *Burn Unit*; each family member needed to let his or her wounds close. Their pain had been caused by an outside source. They needed me to acknowledge my wrongs and through my actions they could let their wounds heal and smooth over. My self-inflicted wounds needed to burn forever, not theirs.

Mental illness and addiction have very strong societal stigmas but they are nothing compared to the stigma that I held against myself. My life was a story of atrocity narrated in the language of abomination embedded from the complex trauma of my childhood and the secondary trauma from my extended time in restraints. I had been telling and re-telling the story of me to myself for so long it had become fact.

My story went like this: I was the victim of a mentally ill father who tried to murder me; I lost the only thing I ever really loved when I gave up my step-daughter; I finish nothing and failed at everything; I am a mentally ill alcoholic and there's no way I'll make it in this life; I am a dead man walking, just waiting to be wrapped in my burial shroud.

The chapters read: I was different. You—i.e., everyone else—had it all figured out. I am an outcast and you are living the high life with no problems. If you really knew me, you would hate me. If I ever tried to be myself, I would be considered a freak. I lived my entire life trying to fit into your story. If you had it, I wanted it. I needed it. The sheer fact that you would desire something made it desirous to me. Then when I got it, it sucked. Up close it looked cheap and worn, and I instantly moved on to the next thing that I had to have, but that I knew was out of my reach.

I was so emotionally and spiritually bankrupt that I would let outside entities dictate the very idea of who I was. I was living from the outside in and it was killing me. I was a pariah. I would die like my dad ... like my dad. Just like Einar. Seriously mentally ill ... just like my dad. That label stuck and overruled them all.

I remember being elated to sit in a room and just call myself an alcoholic. It sounded like music to my ears compared to mental patient, consumer or whatever the medical community had come up with to define me as having bipolar disorder. I have seen others fight the "alcoholic" label in relation to their drinking, but I welcomed it. I had no self-stigma about my drinking; I knew it had been a problem since I was fifteen. In the Navy, I had women from all around the world tell me to come back the next day for a date, but only if I was sober. Once I was in Israel with a brown-haired knockout who was tending bar. We talked for two hours straight, and it felt really good, really honest. But I was drunk and she recognized I would be a better man if I wasn't hammered on tequila. We made a date for the next night—contingent, she said, on me showing up sober. The next day around noon, she found me laughing on a public bathroom floor with my shipmates, oblivious to who she was. Popeye the Douchbag.

Alcoholism was easy. The label of "mentally ill" was harder to accept. My family always told me I could live with the disease and succeed with it. My peers in the recovery program told me the same thing. But none of them had what I had. I could see they believed what they were saying, *but I didn't believe them.* I wanted some kind of proof, I wanted to see it lived, a stereotype of success to link to and follow.

My therapists were also great. They worked with me as long as I worked with them. They told me to take it one day at a time, and to take my medications the same way. One day at a time, over time, and I would eventually get better. It was good advice, but I didn't trust them. They were asking me to believe in an idea, an assumption, and it's hard to risk your life on a theory.

Some in the recovery program made negative comments about me taking Lithium and others taking their psych drugs. But let me say this clearly: It is absolutely none of anyone else's business when it comes to meds and recovering alcoholics. Some in recovery have even advised others to come off meds. I consider that tantamount to being an accomplice to murder. These people are not doctors, and even if they are doctors, they are not that individual's doctor. Many have died because someone else has decided that a few years of experience in recovery can take the place of eight years of medical school and residency.

Let me be clear on this point: *Do not tell anyone to come off his or her medications unless you are willing to sit with his or her parents at the funeral and tell them about your role in their child's death.*

It is completely irresponsible, and it is not your place. Two years into sobriety, I swallowed that bullshit and paid a heavy price. Because of my self-stigma about mental illness, I listened to people telling me to get off my meds, and after four years of being sober, I ended up back in a mental hospital. It was a much more sedate episode because there was no alcohol or drugs involved, but all of us—including my new wife—had to suffer anyway.

Resurrection | Chapter 6

Slowly, I was beginning to understand that my self-limiting beliefs and biases were controlling my life. I needed to take new actions to prove to myself that my mind was wrong, that the story of my yesterdays did not foreshadow the story of my tomorrows. I needed action. Then two things happened that changed everything: First, I was accepted into Rutgers University, and second, my true Virgil, Bud, was stricken with terminal cancer.

Most idols, when you get close to them, are just people like everyone else—flawed, less magnificent. They are not grand, powerful wizards, but are instead simple, everyday people just like the man behind the curtain pulling the levers and calling himself the Wizard of Oz. But this was not true of my step-father; he was stronger, more brilliant, and more deserving of my praise, admiration, and love when I saw him up close in the fight for his life.

I had been out of the hospital a couple of years before I allowed myself to really think about a future. I was working part-time jobs and going to Middlesex County College. I had to lie on all my job applications to explain the large gaps in my work history due to psychiatric hospital stays and was less than enthusiastic to be back at the same community college I attended before I joined the Navy. I felt better than I had in years, but I also felt alone. I had spent the last year trying to find someone with chronic addiction who had gone deep into the mental hospital system and who had made it back out again. But I found no one. I did find some hope around the recovering alcoholics I knew, but it wasn't the same. If they remained abstinent, then they would never get drunk or high again. But with my bipolar disorder, I was born with the alcohol/drug in my system. I didn't need to drink or smoke bipolar disorder into my bloodstream. It was lurking beneath my skin, with its hand grenades ready, since I took my first breath.

I could take my medicine religiously and the disease could still break through if my biochemistry changed. State hospitals are filled with patients taking all their medications and not getting better. I didn't tell anyone I was afraid of my own blood, afraid of my own biochemistry, but I was and it made acceptance of my situation nearly impossible. I lived in constant fear wondering when would I attack me again.

I was unsure of my moods. Was I happy or manic? Is this a sound, original idea or am I sick again? My particular mental illness has no signs for me to read before I am lost in delusion. I can be here one minute and gone the next. Like Icarus, when the wax started to melt on my wings, the freefall had already begun.

Rutgers University (RU) was a dream school for me. When I was in Egypt in Operation Desert Shield, I promised myself that if I could get out of my enlistment in one piece, I would enroll in RU and be the happiest person in the world. The university is adjacent to my hometown and I could get a great education and stay connected to my family.

As I started to think about getting my transcripts together and writing the entrance essay, Bud's cancer took a turn for the worse and he needed to get treatment in New York City. My education would run hand in hand with Bud's disease until both my Bachelor's degree and Bud's life would reach completion the same year. I wasn't sure if I could be man enough to accomplish either of my goals: to get a degree from Rutgers University and to escort Bud to the bitter end. I would be forced to confront my deepest fears from the very beginning of my collegiate career.

Resurrection | Chapter 7

When I got ready to apply to Rutgers University, I was terrified. I was sure Rutgers would reject me and I was prepared for the worst. I had the grades and the military experience to be a desirable candidate on paper, but my mind was telling me to quit. My self-defeating biases were deeply ingrained, and it was difficult to keep them at bay. But I knew I couldn't hide my wounds.

I had a terrible inferiority complex, and I was sure everyone was better than me—especially Rutgers' students. But I decided I needed to learn once and for all what I was all about. I needed to apply and let the world tell me yes or no. I couldn't keep creating a life on my assumed no's. But I also had to be careful to not let whether I was accepted to RU determine whether or not I could be a success. Because I still had so many doubts about my future and such a limited view of my potential, I had to work closely with friends and therapists to make sure the lies I told myself about my own failings did not make it onto my application.

I decided I needed to complete the application as an outside marker that my life was really changing. When I wrote the admission essay, I wanted to tell my whole life story. I didn't want to try and cut and paste my transcripts, military service and life to fit their expectations. I wanted to lay it all out on the table for them. If they let me into their school, they would be letting all of me in. They would be letting in a person with serious mental illness and addiction who would not be hiding and slithering around campus, waiting to be found out. I needed my present—and my future—to be authentic.

This idea met with brutal resistance from my support group. Everyone told me I was sabotaging myself. I weighed their advice and still did it my way. I am sure the essay is on file somewhere in the RU archives. The words painted a full and dynamic picture of the honors and horrors of Eric Arauz. It was my first real-world effort to match my reality to the reality of the world around me.

Ephesians 5:13 NIV says, "But everything exposed by the light becomes visible—and everything that is illuminated becomes a light." I had to bring the horror of who I had been to the light of day. It was time to take some chances. I put the admissions letter in the mail with a note at the bottom saying that whether they let me in or not, I was a success.

I believed it when I wrote it. I still do.

And God bless the staff of the Rutgers University Admissions Office for believing that someone as damaged as I was could not only learn at their institution, but could contribute to it.

There was no one program or person to turn to show me how to survive my co-occurring disorders. Instead, Rutgers University, a twelve-step program, a large support network and numerous therapists came together to try and save me. It was the concerted efforts of those around me that produced the life I lead today. I am one man, a man with no real reason to believe I would make it and a lifetime of reasons to believe I would not. But so many amazing people kept on top of me. They coached me. They fought for me. They believed in me before I ever could believe in myself.

They never stopped reaching into the ice to save me no matter how many times I went under.

Resurrection | Chapter 8

I entered Rutgers University the spring semester of 1998 as a Biochemistry major. I lasted in that major for about eight minutes, then I switched to Natural Resources Management, and finally I found my focus—American Studies. It was the perfect fit at the perfect time. I had registered late and couldn't get into the forestry classes I needed, but I had a few prerequisites to fill so I signed up for some random courses. I took American Government and Agricultural Economics. I had an early class on South Asian Anthropology and one other course. It was an American Studies course. It was on the women's campus, Douglass, and I walked in hyper-aware of my gender and unsure of my choice. The course was called Folk Songs and Ballads and the professor introduced himself and dove right into the curriculum.

I loved the class.

I loved the professor, Angus Gillespie, a son and grandson of sailors, and, through him, and other professors, I discovered I loved the major. It was interdisciplinary and allowed students to take classes across the spectrum of majors as long as they had a certain percentage of American focus. I could take American History and American Political Science, American Literature and American Intellectual History and, eventually, I could develop a full picture of our country as it grew and became aware of itself, just like I was doing on Rutgers campus.

Focusing on American Studies was the first decision I made in a long time that was authentic, and it was a turning point in my life. I was already involved in a twelve-step spiritual program centered on a main text, and I was living the difference that applying lessons from a book could make in my life. I was excited to start my college career with that same mindset. While delving deeper into the main text of my recovery program, I would read Emerson, Melville, Crane and Whitman and apply them as life directives.

Oh beautiful, beautiful Walt Whitman, my Jersey brother buried in Camden. When I read *Song of Myself* and saw the verse, "Do I contradict myself? Very well then I contradict myself, (I am large, I contain multitudes,)" I recognized a mantra to live by. What multitudes did I contain? What parts of my life needed to be discarded as remnants of the past? I began to see that I could dictate my future and that these great men were just men—men like me.

It did not diminish their accomplishments; instead, it made them more praiseworthy. They were not gods but humans who achieved great things with the same finite limits all others possess. What kind of life could I create if I listened to the existential directions of the greatest minds in history? Would that be enough to fight my dual diagnosis and childhood horrors? Would that be enough to create the full life I dreamed of each night as I drifted to sleep?

Many nights I would put myself to bed with dreams of a wife, kids, a great job and numerous degrees only to wake up single, in my parents' house, with thirty college credits, and a job as a security guard. As grandiose as my late evenings were, my mornings were equally brutal as the sun slapped me in the face and reality set in when my painful toes hit the floor.

I decided I would begin to dream with my eyes wide open.

I would use the books I encountered in my studies as *Existential Cookbooks* for the life I wanted to create, the living dream life. But first I had to clean up the wreckage of my past and that required work. I did not want to build on a false foundation. I needed to address the deepest and darkest parts of my past. I needed to address my biological father and our history. I had to see that situation clearly and find a way to ensure that it no longer determined the rest of my life.

To successfully face my past without getting drawn back into it, I relied on the team of angels I met through Rutgers—professors, students, thinkers, and long-dead authors who equipped me with the spiritual courage and the intellectual fortitude to actively move away from the darkness of my hellish past.

I wasn't getting a degree in American Studies as much as I was getting one in what I refer to as *Applied Existentialism*. I was determined to follow the instructions laid out in works from Goethe to Conrad to Fitzhugh to Kipling to W.E.B. Du Bois. Reading Du Bois and discovering the slave narrative, I heard the voice of suffering and isolation with which I could finally truly connect. I found salvation in Du Bois and the slave spirituals. The isolation he described in these narratives resonated in my physical, spiritual, and psychic wounds.

Theirs, ours, mine, was not just an isolation from others, but an isolation from a self-determined identity. The brutality inflicted upon them was not just physical but spiritual. The American slave looked outward at a world that hated them and looked inward at a soul prescribed and circumscribed by their masters. This population had wallowed in hell for centuries and their voice pierced my shell. My suffering did not equal the suffering of an entire people, but I could truly relate and would use *The Souls of Black Folk* by W.E.B. Du Bois and its discussion of the veil and of the slaves' double consciousness as a metaphor to finally break free from my oldest and staunchest self-stigmas. I would learn to live with the deepest lacerations from the "whippings" of self-hate embedded in my spiritual skin.

Resurrection | Chapter 9

To build a new life, I needed to go back and examine the problems and sorrow I had caused others. It was at that point that I was introduced to the process of "amends." Amends is an age-old act of contrition common to every spiritual tradition and spanning every religion. The idea is to go back through your life and determine whom you have wronged, see where and how you played a part in your resentments, and ask how to fix them. The phrase that sold me on the process was, "to clear the wreckage of my past." I was determined and inspired to begin to build a new life on a clean and clear foundation. This new foundation, without my old fears and internal biases, could withstand whatever was built on its back.

Compiling the list of people to whom I needed to make amends made me sick to my stomach. The thought of going back to some of these people and putting myself at their mercy made me cringe. But I knew I had to do it, and I had already worked through to see where I had created the most mayhem in my life. I always put too much of a burden on those around me, and, if someone failed me, I wrecked as much of his or her life as I could. I was unbelievably selfish and I only saw others as they related to my life. I never saw others' suffering, their heartaches, and problems. Everything was always about me. I used people the way I used alcohol and drugs. They had to fill a role in my life or give me the feeling I was yearning for or they were out. It never dawned on me that others had feelings—or were suffering—too.

The amends process started slowly but gained momentum. I was told that with each amends I would become freer. I liked actually "doing" something. The beginning process of the spiritual journey is between you and yourself. You have not yet taken the step out into the real world. But with each amends, I began to see my life in a new way. Like most people, I started with my family.

I told each individual what I wanted to do. If he or she wanted, I would set a date. I told them ahead of time that I would be telling them what I thought I had done to them. If it were left there, at that point, it would still be a selfish process just dressed up in another disguise. I would just be re-traumatizing them to make myself feel better. The full amends also entailed me asking: "What else I have done that I didn't know about?" and "What can I do to fix it?"

Each family member made an appointment with me and the reception was universally warm. I had no idea how to fix my relationships, but now I didn't need to guess. They would tell me. My mom and sisters told me what I had put them through with my lying and active addiction. They wanted me to stop bullshitting and start building a real life. They wanted me to stop lying and take my medications. They said they thought I would die if I didn't do these things and that they wanted me to live. They said they wanted me to shut up and listen to them, to stop constantly making excuses. My brother-in-law told me not to lie to him anymore, that it was disrespectful. My grandma cried and told me she loved me and that I never did anything to her. I told Grandma Joanie how much I loved her and, finally, I went down to Bud.

Bud listened. He didn't add anything. He sat in his brown leather recliner with his leg tucked underneath himself. When I finished, he said he loved me, that he loved all the kids as his own. He told me to keep doing what I was doing and that was that.

I now had a real world template on how to fix my family. I also had a true idea of the damage I had caused and didn't cause in my home. A new sense of ease washed over me as years of tension and shame seemed to vanish immediately. I could feel the sacred nature of true repentance and contrition and was "on fire" to move through the list of *over 150 people*. I had tried starting over many times, but each time I had quit because of my self-limiting belief that the wreckage I caused was beyond fixing. Now, I could see the situation clearly and had the roadmap to get to a new place, a revolutionary place. I wasn't bullshitting; I was honest. I wasn't groveling; I was rectifying. My life was beyond novel tweaks to the process. The whole system of living had to change. Amends was the beginning of that change, and I was beginning to take real world action to bring my life back to me: creating a destiny out of today's deeds.

The list included childhood friends, ex-wives, teachers, shipmates and institutions. I burned through the list. I was getting more and more comfortable exposing my wounded-ness to the world. The reception was almost universally positive and those who wanted no part of me were justified. I had hurt them terribly, and if they did not want to open old wounds that was their right and their prerogative. My burns had to stay fresh, but my victims needed to heal. In my effort to start over, I had to make sure I did not add to the damage I had already inflicted. The amends process was not an Eric Victory Tour, but rather a sacred process designed to create a positive space where a sense of "wholeness" and "realness" in my life could take root.

Each time I hesitated to look at another part of my life, an opportunity would arise to find light in the darkness. I was turning to face myself again and this time it was not horrifying. I was not evil. I was sick. I had two chronic and lethal diseases interwoven with severe trauma, and my thinking was killing me and destroying my relationships. Even my ex-wife was positive in our last discussion. In a letter, I took full responsibility for the divorce. I ruined a good thing and I thanked her for the time with my step-daughter. She did not offer to allow me back into their lives and that was the right thing. I had to learn that the world was not contingent on my participation and happiness. They were happy and better off without me. It hurt, but it was one of the greatest lessons of my life: *You are not mandatory; you are not god.*

I had made almost all the amends on my list and was coming down to the couple that were either hard to find or set up for a later date. One name sat on the list and the thought of that amends ever happening seemed more like fantasy than reality. That name was Einar Arauz. My biological father was dead. He had terrorized me my entire childhood. He deserved my scorn. I didn't understand how I could do the amends or why I had to do it. Why for him? Fuck him.

But the fact was that it was my resentment toward him that was killing me. I wallowed in the anger and hate. I was not his son, I was Bud's. Einar didn't matter. I had gone back to my childhood and fixed all I could. I recognized that my childhood was happy, and that only some extreme parts centered on his actions. He didn't deserve to be let off the hook. I felt very strongly about making sure that he was not exonerated for his role in my life, but the twelve-step Virgils who were leading me back into my hell explained how it was not him I was letting off the hook; it was me … it was *me*.

They asked me how free I wanted to be—only partly free or fully free? That was the right way to motivate a man who has been held in four-point restraints for over twenty-four hours.

FREEDOM!

Real freedom was a dream for me. Could I be free to exist in my own skin without the dark parts of my own life popping up to trap and control me? My life story had become hyper-dramatic and I needed to normalize it. I had to be able to walk through the landscape of my own mind and safely and sanely see my past. Einar's role was too pronounced to go unaddressed.

I finally relented. I recognized that I needed to make amends to him, but how? He had been dead for five years. Buried in a grave I never saw, in a cemetery I had never visited. Then it came to me. If I had to die to myself to be truly reborn, I would have to give myself over to the freeing process and revisit the exact spot where I had descended to the ninth circle of hell. I had to go back to the VA, to Building 53, second floor on the west wing.

I had to go back into the Ice.

I had to go back to the Restraining Room.

Resurrection | Chapter 10

During my second semester at Rutgers, Bud was scheduled to start chemo at a hospital in New York City. It was an hour drive from East Brunswick and the treatments would last for six hours. He would not be able to drive himself. He needed help. He needed my help.

Wednesday was chemo day. I always picked him up at 6:00 a.m. and we made our way into Manhattan and across midtown to the East Side. He was always ready and we were always on time. He was a man of action and to be able to drive him, to be able to actively demonstrate how much he meant to me, was an honor.

My routine at school was starting to follow the pattern of his visits. Early Tuesday morning I would start to get a little down and by Tuesday night my emotions had shut off. By the time I picked him up, I was already exhausted by the process. He was the one getting chemo and I was the one who looked wiped out. But I was determined to be strong for him.

As the chemo progressed, we spoke more and more about life. These were the talks you always dream of having. Each moment I spent with him, I felt my past reality begin to fade and my present become clearer. His strength gave me the courage to confront my diseases. He had saved my life and now he was giving me a future.

One day we were coming down 42nd Street after his treatment. We stopped at the traffic light. We were the first in line with our front tires in the crosswalk. The pedestrians were swarming our car, entombing us front and back. I always stopped with the nose of the car in the crosswalk and Bud always told me I would get a ticket. He was tired from another round and had his eyes closed. I was watching the people walk by and enjoyed the spectacle. Bud was breathing heavily, and I assumed he was sleeping. Each week the news was getting worse and the rides home seemed longer with the weight of the situation. But still, I loved sitting next to him in these quiet moments.

No doctors, no nurses, no chemo suites, and no prognosis. I could observe my hero without having to avert my gaze. I loved to stare at him and paint the portrait that would hang forever in my mind. His skin was ashen from the chemo and his thick silver mane was thinning but his eyes were very alive. But now they were hidden as he rested from the flood of chemicals flushed into his veins for hours.

His hands were still strong from years of work with metal and tools. His khaki jacket was stretched tight across his cancer-swollen belly. There at the corner of 42nd and 5th, I stared at him in the late afternoon light and tried to absorb him into my memory. With each one of his finite breaths, I loved him more.

Cancer painted the inside of our home; it lived with us like an unwelcome boarder who constantly reminded us that our Captain was sick and would not get better. When Bud and I got home, he made his way inside and settled in on the couch. Bud had given up his favorite chair—his recliner—to sit on the couch because it allowed him the space to lie down.

I wanted to do something for him to relieve his pain, but I didn't know what would help. I went to the living room to get myself together. I wasn't sure what I was going to do, but it would be for him—not for me, not to make me feel better. I got on my knees and prayed to a higher power of my understanding, a personal God, a personal guide. I asked for strength, just strength to tap into.

I needed an *Occupational Divinity*, a god with utility, a god of action, one that could give me the power to go in there with Bud and transgress my fears and do something for him. I had lost the god of my youth to my mental disease. In my acute stages of bipolar disorder, I had turned into the deities of my childhood devotion and the trauma of my incarceration and delusions stole my Christianity. I could not and would not allow myself the luxury of venturing that direction again. Instead, I looked to other avenues of transcendence. The divine I prayed to emerged from a connection more cosmic, more universal. Discussing the evolution of devotion and god, Einstein spoke of a "cosmic religious feeling." This was safer for me and allowed for transcendence without fear. One thing I found was the Hindu philosophy of Vedanta and its teachers: Krishnamurti, Ramakrishna, Romain Rolland and others. With Vedanta, I was not promised salvation or eternal life, but I could see past the opaque cloud of my past and listen to the songs of the present universe and act in accordance to its reality, a reality of love. Without the bias and translation of a thousand yesterdays, I could stop living in reaction. Quiet, in the ever-birthing moment, I knew existence was all God, all-inclusive and that Bud might have been in the process of departing physically, but that he was spiritually expanding into that consciousness. He would never not be present; we would—we will—always be one. I got off my knees, strong and determined, charged with the pulsing currents of the river of creation, and walked back to my father.

He was sitting up on the couch, and I sat down next to him. Without his glasses you could see the way his face had changed from the disease. His cheekbones were sharp and jagged and his eyes sunken. The TV was on but he wasn't watching. He had his head in his hands and was taking deep, painful breaths. The days in Manhattan always wiped him out and it took a while for him to recuperate. He was still determined to make my second wedding, to my dream girl, but it was months off. If he made it, it would be by days.

I wanted to be shoulder to shoulder with my hero, and I was willing to take the chance. I sat down next to him and he turned to look at me over his left shoulder. Besides the day of my release, the day he took me in his arms and embraced me with love and acceptance, we had never been so close outside of a car. His crystal blue eyes locked in on mine and we sat there. There was no *thought*, it was all *feel*. The life in his eyes dazzled from their sickened host, and we stared at each other for a few minutes. It was a beautiful, quiet forever. He had shown me that love is more real than any blood bond and at that moment—*eye to eye, father and son*—I felt like a man.

I let the moment unfold second by second, and my desire to touch him overcame me. I reached my right hand over his frail shoulder and put it on his back. He kept looking at me as I began to rub his fragile torso from side to side. I could feel his ribs; I could feel his death. I was trying with all my heart to make him feel my gratitude. I wanted him to know I would never leave our family. He had given me everything and I wanted to give everything—my all—back to him.

I stopped thinking all together and just *felt* my fingers tips on the skin and bones of my father. His eyes left mine and he put his head back in hands. I was here for him. He knew that. I was becoming the man I always wanted to be, the man he always wanted me to be, the son of Bud and Nadine Powers. I was proud of myself for the first time in a long time. He leaned back to go to sleep and I got up. I went back to the living room and sat on my mom's couch. The same couch I had been removed from by police years earlier in my first manic episode.

I looked around this room of Christmases and Thanksgivings, arrests and prayers and saw myself as I was in the moment. I saw that I could dictate my life, that yes, all those good and bad things had happened but they were no more important than today, than what had just happened on the other couch in the other room. I realized my perspective was in my control. My future was an empty canvas and I was allowed to paint and live in them both as I chose.

This realization moved me profoundly. I knew Bud would be gone soon, but I would walk with him to the other side just as he had walked with me to the door at the VA mental ward. I wouldn't waiver; we would go together. I thought of his blue eyes and closed my own. And there, in the living room of Bud and Nadine's house, I wept with the knowledge that even in his dying, my father was teaching me how to live.

I had always tried to find ways to make up for yesterday with delusions of grandeur for tomorrow. In that moment in my parents' home, I felt like a true part of the family—neither its pariah nor its superman, but simply a man, a son, a brother. I was actively living my amends to Bud and it was changing my life. Now, it was time to make a formal amends to Einar.

Resurrection | Chapter 11

Rutgers University, and college in general, is a great place to rebuild your life, to become self-aware and to break free of your subjective, *existential illiteracy*. You can learn how to read *yourself*, while you learn to read the *world*. At Rutgers, the structure of the grading system allows for growth each semester and as my grades came back I began to see myself in a different light. I made the Dean's list the first semester and bringing that news home felt great. The new grades were juxtaposed against the mediocre grades of my past and gave me a real world example of what could change with effort. I saw A's compared to C's and tried hard to believe that the A's were just as real.

Campus life is perfect for a man in metamorphosis. Each time you walk into a class you are anonymous. You get a fresh start four or five times a semester as you enter each class. At first, I couldn't be just one among many, so somehow I worked in the fact that I had been in the Navy into every conversation. Someone would ask when the next test was, and I would say, "Gee, in the Navy we always knew when the test was." Or someone would wonder when the next paper was due, and I would say, "The great part about the Navy was that there were no papers." No matter what the conversation, I was in the Navy. It was a big part of my defense mechanism when I felt insecure or vulnerable. The Navy moniker created the picture of me I wanted everyone to see. Before you could get your own read on me, I put up the "Navy Eric" *billboard* and advertised the version of me I wanted recognized. I wasn't strong enough yet to exist in the evolving now. That insecurity would eventually diminish, but I needed time to get myself grounded in reality.

My undergraduate journey was always about getting that first foot firmly out of my hell and removing the masks I wore to my true self and the world so I could start my true life. But I wasn't ready to spread my wings and fly off into the world to claim my spiritual riches yet. I was truly damaged and needed time to heal and gain my strength to learn to live. Whereas my twelve-step program was my spiritual *Burn Unit*, Rutgers was my intellectual *Burn Unit*. It was a place I could recover and learn to exist each day with my wounds until I could walk freely among the world.

College is also a great place to be wrestling with your identity because so is everyone else. When I would walk down the center of the main campus up College Avenue toward the Rutgers Club for the Thursday buffet, I would see the frat houses lining the side streets, next to the churches and across from the Seminary. I watched 18-22 year olds attempt to look different while all doing the same thing. The search for who you are is a prerequisite on all campuses and the whole student body is searching for answers. I never felt alone in that quest at school.

I enjoyed the environment, and it helped me to prepare for what was coming next for Bud. I could sit in class and listen to professors discuss Twain or Faulkner and release what I had once *known* and replace it with what I was now *learning*. Rutgers has a terrific academic community and the life of the mind was very enticing—and also very dangerous. I was not stable enough to be mindful of trying to create another self instead of just being myself. I teetered on the precipice of trying to replace "mentally ill" Eric with "academic" Eric and with each success the line got blurrier. It was a dangerous time for me as I was still not able to understand the full power of my need for outside validation.

To fully live, one must validate oneself from the inside, like the Buddha said, "... be a lamp unto yourself, a light unto yourself." I still needed more help, encouragement, and validation from the outside than was good for me. My therapist could see I was in trouble and she approached me with an entirely different technique. She helped me feel that I was perfect as is, born perfect. No more becoming, no more next thing. Like the Kabbalist sage Michael Berg teaches, "We can never damage our soul; it remains pure always. We can veil its light with negative actions; but we remain perfect always."

That stopped me in my tracks. During each visit with my therapist, she would center me. Let me see that I was "pure always." It was not about constructing a stronger mind and a better identity, but rather about letting the moment happen and letting my actions dictate the outcomes. It wasn't about more mind, it was about *no* mind. It was about *feeling* the truth of reality and existence instead of interpreting, characterizing, and judging myself and others against a "should be" world.

On a college campus fighting to have no mind was a unique battle. It may sound strange, but I believe it made me a better student. I walked into each class, sat down, and opened myself to a fifty-five minute baptism into a new intellectual conversion experience. I tried very hard to wait to the end of the class to judge the intellectual exposure. I tried to separate my opinions from my identity. I tried to be continuously aware, to let go and flow with the river of learning without holding onto rocks of ignorance or grasping for branches of bias or prejudice. I made it my goal to never go into a class intent on proving a preconceived point; I was open and receptive and, consequently, blessed. Academically, I evolved. I gained insight and foreswore pre-ordained conclusions. Besides, I had already lost my mind before. Losing it had never been the problem; keeping it lost would be the mission now.

Resurrection | Chapter 12

No book has affected my life like *The Souls of Black Folk* by W.E.B. Du Bois. I first read Du Bois at Rutgers in the class American Literature Post-1865. I had already been introduced to the music of the blues in American Studies and was reading more deeply into the slave narratives. I immediately connected to the crying laments of the blues singer and the abject hopelessness of the American slave. The vernacular of slavery and freedom spoke to my disconnected and shackled soul. Slaves were stolen from their African homelands and forced into lives of servitude to their masters while my bipolar disorder stole a life of normalcy from my father and me and forced me into a life of servitude to my disease, imprisoned on the plantation of my mind.

Even though I had no real life examples to turn to for my dual diagnosis, I listened to the "Sorrow Songs" and bridged the gap between me and the soul-striving singers. I found strength in their laments and promise in their overcoming. I began to move toward a more outwardly focused, global compassion and from *I* to *We*. And I began to believe *We* could triumph over our indentured servitude.

The American slave found freedom through knowledge, through self-knowledge. Because many were unable to read, they had their outer and inner worlds dictated to them by their captors. Being unable to read either books or their interior selves, they were viscerally illiterate to the language of their own souls. Their primary source of spirituality, the Bible, was translated by their captors into a language designed to continue to enslave them spiritually, physically and mentally. The masters knew that when the American slave could read and see the truths of the world they could never be controlled again. I related to that. The twelve-steps and the journey inward taught me how to read myself, how to translate my own soul.

I had been *existentially illiterate* my whole life and had mistranslated the story of my existence.

What was unique about Du Bois was that he didn't only speak of the horrors of the physical torment of the American slave but also the spiritual and mental devastation. W.E.B. didn't just list the brutal atrocities of the flesh; he included the degradation and theft of an entire culture's identity/essence. The freed slaves were no longer able to define their own identities. They viewed themselves through the eyes of their masters. Blind to their own spirits, they used the hateful scorn of their captors to define themselves spiritually. They were "others" to themselves just as they were "others" to the white man, and Du Bois gave voice to their "otherness" in a way that allowed me to see that I, too, viewed myself as an "other" to the world, as well as an "other" to myself.

Du Bois was no longer speaking to me, he was speaking *for* me.

Du Bois was speaking directly to my identity problem in his famously quoted passage:

> After the Egyptian and Indian, the Greek and Roman, the Teuton and Mongolian, the Negro is a sort of seventh son, born with a veil, and gifted with second-sight in this American world,—a world which yields him no self-consciousness, but only lets him see himself through the revelation of the other world. It is a peculiar sensation, this double-consciousness, this sense of always looking at one's self through the eyes of others, of measuring one's soul by the tape of a world that looks on in amused contempt and pity. One feels his two-ness,—an American, a Negro; two souls, two thoughts, two unreconciled strivings; two warring ideals in one dark body, whose dogged strength alone keeps it from being torn asunder.

The freed slave saw himself through this veil and everything in his vision was poisoned by it. Nothing made its way past the veil, not in and not out. They were effectively blind to society and to themselves, as I was in my last moments of torment in the hospital bed in the VA and again after I returned to society. This enforced blindness created what Du Bois called a double consciousness. The slaves' double consciousness arose because they had no common and intact identity to stand against the broken sense of self-identity thrust upon them by their masters.

Slaves were told by society that they were worthless, less than human, and ignorant. With no other source from which to find their identities, they imbibed their master's poison and accepted it as their being. Even after they were released from their physical shackles and freed from the institution of slavery, they remained enslaved on the plantations of their own minds. Like them, I needed a psychic emancipation proclamation.

I saw my entire life's problem in Du Bois's book and his description of the veil and double consciousness. I had never heard it put so clearly and concisely. I was not a freed slave and do not in any way compare my suffering to theirs in magnitude, but my problems of identity and self-stigma were the same.

Again, I could never "equate" the scope of the atrocity, but I could "relate" to it. I could not control what the world thought of people with mental illness, but I could become aware of the veil and double consciousness in my own accepted identity and then learn to control what I thought of myself.

The two-ness the freed slave suffered was how I saw my fractured self. Just as many slaves could not reconcile their identity as an "American" and a "Negro," I could not piece together my identity as an "American" and a "Recovering Mental Patient."

I also had a third identity that needed to also be addressed. Who did I become in my manic episodes? Who was the person I never got to meet but who destroyed my life? My identity was suffering from a three-ness that threatened to tear me "asunder" by "warring ideals." Du Bois gave voice to a problem I could not identify, let alone address. He gave me the vernacular of dissociation-disconnection that allowed me to attack the root of the problem. Just like the slave of the 19th century, I would have to see above and through the veil. There was no way to remove it, but it could be identified and transgressed.

I recognized how strong my own stigma against mental illness was because of my experiences with Einar, as well as my own experiences in the psychiatric hospitals. I had found a spiritual community in the twelve-step meetings that gave voice to the rupture of a certain part of my self-consciousness. Now, Du Bois could lead me deeper into myself and my issues with bipolar disorder. He gave me a map to my true problem: Me. I didn't know myself and had failed to truly define myself. I was letting a world I thought hated me determine my *Is-ness*. I would have to create a new way to validate myself by creating a life evolving in the present that would enable me to look over the veil.

Malcolm X asked in a famous speech, "Who taught you to hate yourself from the top of your head to the soles of your feet?" I knew that I had taught myself to hate myself. And no matter what my father did to me, no matter what I experienced while hospitalized, I would never be free until I took control of my own life's narrative.

Armed with Du Bois' insights, the purpose of attending college changed. I was no longer simply working toward a degree that would signal my worth to the world. I would no longer be caught in that cycle of academic inferiority that breeds itself from a life of outside grading. I saw my answer. It was written in a book over one hundred years old for a group of people that had nothing and everything to do with me. I had to drop the veil. Both veils—the one going in and the one going out. It was easier to see how I could drop the veil I held between me and society but I wasn't totally sure how to completely drop the veil that hid me from myself. I was doing a lot of spiritual work in an attempt to get to that place and I was making real progress, but I needed a little push, one more tool.

I had to find another *The Souls of Black Folk,* another spiritually revolutionary book to aid in the inner battle. I didn't know where it would come from, but I was sure I would find it. With my burgeoning insights, each day of classes seemed like an exciting adventure, one where I could gain wisdom from each class, where I understood that each class directly pertained to me and my world. I related as well to the Intellectual American History class, The Fictions of Modernization, with its stories of Goethe's Mephistopheles and Conrad's Marlow, as I could in American Political Thought Post-1865 and Agricultural Economics. No matter what I was taught I saw the humanity and the universality behind the author or the researcher or the musician. I was no longer in an academic institution but in an interconnected, interdependent dream factory.

Resurrection | Chapter 13

Killing time in a campus bookstore one morning while sipping a six dollar cup of coffee and nibbling on a muffin made with three types of berries from three different continents, I noticed a book by Rudyard Kipling, the English poet and novelist who won the Nobel Prize for literature in 1907. It was called *Kim*.

I had read his poem "If," but I didn't know much of his longer works. I checked the back cover of *Kim* and read about a boy, born in India but of English heritage, who became a spy for his country (England), and the tortuous duality of self he suffered as a traitor to his land of physical birth (India), his culture, and himself. The back copy said the book was brilliant not simply because of its discussion of masks worn to the world but of visceral masks to oneself: "Who was Kim? Was he English? Was he Indian? Was he both? Was he neither? What makes an identity, a persona?"

I put the book down and took in the moment. Behind the counter, the milk steamer gargled. Students came and went, covered in red and black, talking, laughing. The smell of parchment, new books and old, filled my senses. This was what I had been looking for. The metaphor was perfect: masks. Kim could be my guide as I explored the masks I wore on the journey to discover my true self.

In *Kim*, the protagonist has a battle between himself and his dual identities of being British and being Indian. As he fights to rectify this issue, Kipling shows that what Kim really needs is to find a singular essence devoid of label, neither English nor Indian, above the veil. To become aware of the permanent, eternal mirror to the universe that sits behind his eyes. The "is," the affirming "I-am," that defines Kim is beyond any 'warring' preconception of his identity. Kipling also paints a clear and painful picture of the existential turmoil that the journey entails, a Dante's *Divine Comedy* set on the smoldering ground of Imperial India.

I still saw myself as two people: Eric, the mentally ill man, son of a mentally ill man destined to die like my father Einar, and Eric, son of Nadine and George Powers, college student with a bright future, from a comfy Jersey suburb. This duality hinged on my feelings about my biological father. My own self-stigma of not wanting to be bipolar was blinding even though I outwardly acted like I accepted it. At that point, I had not taken my Lithium in over a year and no one, including my fiancé, knew.

Taking the medication every day may have helped my biochemistry, but it felt like it damaged my soul. It reminded me of my otherness, of my father, the altar, the restraints and my shame. I could taste the VA hospital in each dose. It didn't taste like recovery; it tasted like suicide, like death, like hell itself. At my deepest level, I had not accepted my disease as something to live with, and I was creating a new life based on half-truths. I couldn't accept my disease because I couldn't see the word "bipolar" without feelings of hate and hopelessness, without Einar's eyes looking straight through me in the rain-soaked parking lot of St. Bartholomew's parochial school.

I had been terrified of mental illness and people with mental illness since I was a kid visiting my dad at the Marlboro Psychiatric Hospital for Father's day, watching patients leer at my pre-pubescent sisters and exposing themselves to me while we waited for Daddy in the yard. I had never overcome that terror. The memory would strike and freeze me in a wordless horror. The feel of it, eternal, exactly like the first time it ripped through my stomach on the grounds of the state hospital waiting for Daddy. This wordless terror still happened daily, with memories of my twenty-four hours in restraints. Standing in a convenience store, I would wake up with tears in my eyes, with no memory of how I got there. I could leave reality at anytime and relive my greatest torments. I was never safe from my memories. My life was lived in a perpetual game of Russian roulette with the gun being fired from behind my eyes every five minutes.

To erase my own self-stigma I knew I had to face how I felt about Einar and mental illness, and overcome the perpetual dread sewn into my daily existence.

Resurrection | Chapter 14

There had been a brief hiatus in Bud's cancer treatments, but the chemo therapy was scheduled to begin again in a few weeks. I used this time to set up a date to make amends to my biological father prior to the beginning of Bud's next round. Rudyard and I had work to do and W.E.B. was willing to help. I had found two true literary Virgils to help me navigate my way out of the hell of my own existential blindness.

But Kipling and Du Bois were not my only literary guides. Each day I began to chip away at the wall between me and all the authors I met at Rutgers. I understood these great writers were human and they were writing for me. No longer was I learning their works simply to achieve an academic grade. I was reading their works as sacred testimonies, as guidance, as maps to the heart of life.

Libraries and bookstores seemed different than when I first started school at Rutgers. When I entered Alexander Library on College Avenue, I didn't just see stacks of books anymore; I saw the authors behind all these great works sitting at their writing tables, walking through fields, pondering and debating life's greatest questions, and conversing with each other through time and space. Each looking forward to engaging me in the conversations I had yearned for since my youth.

I, too, looked forward to the conversations. The Hasidic Revivalist, Martin Buber, believed you found G-d in true, open, "naked" discussion with another. In a linguistic *divinity by association*, you connected to something greater in your shared dialogue, your shared experience, with souls exposed as a conversational communion.

I decided I could use Sigmund Freud and Carl Jung as my psychiatrists to work with my current recovery team. I found direction and guidance in Walt

Whitman's hopeful catalogues of the American experience and his delicate whispers for connection in the Calamus section of *Leaves of Grass*. Whitman was my new life coach. Ralph Waldo Emerson spoke directly to me in his essays on *Self Reliance* and the *American Scholar*. Emerson was my academic advisor. And as a Jersey boy, I loved his "Jersey" insolence in his Harvard Divinity School Address.

William James showed me how to follow my passion and not discount the mystic in religious experience. Randolph Bourne urged me to stand up to my teachers and not let government silence my words in times of war. Joseph Conrad told me to journey deep into the dark places and that the heart of man is, concurrently, both brilliant and horrible. Goethe revealed the devastation of a life lived in perpetual motion without rumination, and Icarus seemed more human as he started to resemble a winged Faust.

Hemingway was sadder and Melville more brilliant as the curtain dropped between me and the creators of these texts. I had no need for any more "Wizards of Oz." I could not relate to the idea of great men or women. I wanted to be face to face with my heroes, observe the cracks in the mirror, the cracks in their own souls that made them real, that made them human. No more idols, only equals.

The best books have the best introductions. It is in the introduction that you meet the author separately from the work. It tells the back-story of the writer and the story. It is here, I found the humanness of Cather and Crane. The introductions gave a true starting point and context for the works and brought to life the passions and follies of the very mortal writer.

While I sat in the classroom desks in the basement of the River dorms of Rutgers University, I dreamed of my next step and my own eventual fulfillment. Before, I had always dreamt in the novel, imagined myself part of the action but never the introduction. With the insights from Du Bois and the sewing together of all these other works, I was now excited about becoming the *introduction*: the real person, not the "perfectly penned" novel. I was losing my fear and loathing of myself because I saw these great academics and philosophers as flawed humans as well. The humanness of these touted gods made my goals more right-sized and immediate.

Friedrich Nietzsche, the German philosopher and cultural critic, wrote in the third essay of his book, *On The Genealogy of Morals*, of the basic problem of artists. Nietzsche makes the point that Richard Wagner, the 19th century composer and librettist, the *person* would never be as great as the music he created. That the artist is the "pregnant mother" who suffers the disfiguring pangs of creation and is not to be confused with her offspring: the beautiful, perfect infant. Artists throughout history fall into misery and suicidal depression when they realize they will never be as great a person as the work their talent produces.

In their misery and depression, what they fail to realize is that they cannot and should not compete with the product of their genius—the novel—and that by giving birth to their creations they have validated their worth to themselves as humans. But, most importantly, that by being alive, by being human and by being themselves, they become the introduction to the truth and to the art.

I, too, needed to realize that I was worthy on my own merits, and that I should not judge nor care if the outside world judged me by my grades or by what I produced in the world. Just being alive, being honest, true, generous, authentic, and loving was merit enough. But in order to see through the final masks to accept my true self, I would have to meet Einar one last time. I would have to pry this last mask to my self off my burned face. It was welded on by decades of shame and would take tremendous effort, but there was no other way. I would never fully take the final steps out of hell without this act.

Resurrection | Chapter 15

The spring of my senior year at Rutgers University I turned thirty years old, married the girl of my dreams, and found out I had been awarded a partial scholarship to a law school in northern New Jersey.

Before Bud's illness, I planned to work toward a doctorate in American Studies and examine the degradation of hell, and/or any other historic religious depiction of a penal afterlife and its role as a deterrent in the moral choices in modern American society. But I discovered I would have had to leave the state for the program I wanted. That was unacceptable as Bud's condition continued to deteriorate. Law school was a viable option because I could commute and still take Bud for his chemo. So law school it was.

I had two wonderful mentors in my undergraduate years at Rutgers and they both wrote recommendations for my law school application. One was more like my mother and the other was, well, hard to explain. The mother mentor was a devoutly religious person with a Ph.D. from an Ivy League school, and, although she was brutally honest with me, she was also caring and very generous with her time. She accepted me as I was and worked to make me a better student and a better person. She was excited about my law school decision.

My other mentor was unique. He also held a doctorate from an Ivy League school. He had been a Naval officer. He had stayed at Rutgers even when offered a full professorship at an Ivy League institution. He was my instructor in Intellectual American History and the Fictions of Modernization and he gave me the tools to attack the best of the World's cultural thinkers from H. L. Mencken to J. M. Coetzee. When I asked him about writing a recommendation for law school he said he would write it, but that law school was "the death of all original thought."

I love that guy.

I love them both.

With my Sanghra, my spiritual community, getting stronger each week, I was ready to tackle the final, deepest level in my process of making amends—making amends for my murderous lifetime resentment against Einar Gasper Arauz, the sins that froze me in my hell. This would be a turning point, where I would be eye to eye for the final time with Einar, in the fullness of all my resentments. The nature of the word resentment is to re-sentimentalize, to bring the full pain back and live in it. My identity, my life, was constructed around my feelings for my father and to get beyond the past and move toward a healthy future, I had to confront the part I had played in the emotion.

It was easy to see what he had done to me. He tried to kill me. He punched me in the face in public. He beat me with belts and abducted me to Jersey City whenever he wanted. He dropped me off in cities I had never been to and made me walk until he eventually came back for me—maybe in five minutes, maybe in five hours. He abandoned my family and caused us to move from a beautiful home in the Jersey suburbs to a two-bedroom apartment. He terrorized us. We never knew when or where he would appear. With my shame and misery on public display, I became a pariah in my hometown. My friends' parents would get calls from him or see him and start hunting for me to protect me. I imbibed the anguish in my mom's face and felt useless because he had taken my manhood from me.

Einar took everything: my ambition, my security, my home, my youth, my anonymity. My life first became an embarrassment, then an excuse, and finally a lie. My name had no roots and no validity. I am an Irish/German looking man with a Basque/Spanish last name. People would ask me about the name Arauz and the door was open for all the pain and secrecy to emerge again. My father was gone or he was dead or he abandoned us, pick your poison. The fact was my own name caused me injury. He did this; he created this.

Other fathers tried to step in, but they could never be what I needed. I was a problem fathered by a bigger problem. I looked nothing like him physically and felt sick whenever I saw pictures of him. We had that box of random dead pictures from our family's youth, and from the outside we looked as happy and unhappy as any family. Oddly, as a family we called him Daddy but that word meant nothing to me. I had defined him as sick and evil for so long the label was burned into my memory. Now I was sick. Now perhaps others called me evil. If I didn't find a way to accept and forgive him, I could never truly forgive myself.

I knew I had to drop this resentment as it was the cornerstone of my old, fixed identity. I was sure that the key to my recovery was living without a static identity, evolving moment to moment in real time with the universe. I saw the weakness in holding on to other titles: liberal, conservative, winner, loser, popular, fighter, lover, whatever. These constructs limited growth and stagnated awareness, but this one label or identity seemed unchangeable. I feared an existence beyond this resentment, but living life walking backwards, blaming my dad was killing me.

I was very secure in my relationship with Bud. With the specter of his illness, I thought often of death and the finite nature of life. But the fear of letting go of the hate, of breaking through the final walls that "protected" my damaged life, was paralyzing to even think about.

At the time, I had been fighting in judo tournaments for several years. I rarely won in practice, and had been pummeled numerous times in tournaments in high school and college gyms across the Garden State. I wasn't fighting to gain belts; I was fighting to physically overcome fears. I knew there was no way to think myself into being a spiritual warrior so I tried to fight myself into spiritual shape. One year, I fought in the East Coast Championships and should have won an award for most unprepared fighter. I was like the Big Lebowski in a Judo gi.

During weigh-ins, as I stepped on the scale, the official looked at me with disgust and asked if he smelled smoke. I said, "No," but in reality I had been drinking coffee and smoking Camel Lights on the turnpike on the way to the tournament. There were fighters there from Olympic training facilities all over the country, and then there was me. No training in months due to a back injury. Instead of losing ten pounds to fight guys my size, I gained twelve on a strict diet of HoHo's and lethargy. Net result: In a double elimination tournament where if you lose twice you are eliminated, I somehow lost three times in three fights.

Perfect.

What I did learn was to step into the fight even if you are scared. Even if the opponent is 6' 4" with a shaved head and weighs three hundred and thirty pounds, step in. Fight the fight. Fear is fine, quitting isn't. Step in. Engage. Live.

In life, I had the greatest corner a fighter could have as I prepared to step in against my fears and my past. I had Bud, my sisters, my fiancé, my Rutgers mentors, and Virgils in my twelve-step program. They couldn't fight my fight, but they could—and did—pick me up after the battle and celebrate the bloody effort.

Resurrection | Chapter 16

I had returned to the VA hospital once before to make amends to the hospital staff for whatever I had put them through. When I had walked up to the ward door on the second floor of Building 53, they were all so happy to see me. While I was waiting for the staff to come out, something amazing happened.

When the head nurse saw me standing in the main hallway she came out of the nurse's station to the exit door of the ward to greet me. She called down the hall to the other staff to say I was there and came out of the ward to hug me. As she embraced me, the phone rang at her station. Without hesitation, she pulled away from me and asked if I would hold the ward door open until the others came to say "Hi."

This door, the door I had bounced against mindlessly for hours, days, months, dreaming of what was on the other side was now in my hand. I squeezed hard around the door and tried to really feel it in my grasp to prove to myself it was all really happening. It was smooth to the touch and weighed almost nothing in my grip. I was lost staring at the tan wood peeking out between my fingertips when the other nurses all rushed out to greet me.

I thanked each one of them for saving my life and apologized for everything I did and didn't know about doing. I asked them how to fix my transgressions and they all said to stay out of the hospital. Even the head orderly was there. He still didn't like me and that was fine. I made amends to him the same way I had done to the nurses, and he told me "to fuck off." But that was OK; I wasn't there for him.

I was there for me.

The doctor who I thought had done nothing for me turned out to have been taking great care of my mom and family. Through my non-manic eyes, I saw how human and frail she was. I saw the compassion she had for me. I was convinced in my mania that this psychiatrist was trying to kill me and now I saw that she cared for me and wanted me to succeed, to survive.

Since then, I have visited every psychiatric hospital in which I have ever been a patient to make them less terrifying in my memories, to normalize my journey. And after every visit, I come back to the same thought: Thank you to the entire world's psychiatric nurses and psychiatrists, you are soul-workers and angels.

My life was saved by your loving efforts.

Resurrection | Chapter 17

On the morning I went to make amends to Einar, I parked in front of Building 53 and made the familiar walk down the sidewalk to the front steps. There were veterans in the smoke shacks and, as usual, I gave them some cigarettes. Sometimes I would go in and share a smoke with them, just to experience that familiar closeness. But on that day, I had other things to accomplish.

I reached into my pocket for the letter I had written Einar, to make sure it was still there, and sat on the bench situated directly under the window of the seclusion room in which my spirit had finally been broken. I really wasn't sure what was going to happen. The self-centered fear in my gut made me nauseous, stiff. I dry-heaved a few times and tried to hide the violent jerks from anyone observing me. The fear was pulsing in my blood, flowing throughout my body. I couldn't concentrate. The voice in my head begged me to go home, said that I had gone far enough. The voice of defeat said that if I flew too high, too close to the sun, I would burn my wings. I would fall. I would fail. I would die.

I forced myself to look up at the window above me and remembered the hell I went through as I lay strapped to that bed. I remembered my screams for absolution and mercy. I remembered getting no reply. I knew I could end up in there again if I didn't go through with this last step. A veteran could be in the bed at that very moment facing the same miseries, imprisoned within a room all the stronger from devouring my pain and the pain of countless others like me.

No, I no longer feared burning. I needed to do it. I wanted to live in the sun. If I could free myself from this last shackle, I could try to burn as brightly as possible for others whose lives were still consumed by the flames of disease and shame.

I could show them that it is not the fire that is the problem; it is what kindles the flames and fuels the inferno. I would show my fellow sufferers that they didn't need false remedies to put the fire out. That the burns made you beautiful.

I unfolded the letter.

Most people told me to have it completed, but I didn't do that. I wasn't sure what to write and felt that I would put the day off forever if I waited to construct the perfect letter. I had two lines on the paper and that was it. It was judo all over again. I was even drinking black coffee and smoking Camel Lights.

I looked down at what I wrote and knew that once I started talking, the process would take on a life of its own. I just needed to bow in and engage. I put my smokes in my front pants pocket and placed my coffee on the table. I let my weight slowly sink into the cement bench.

I turned to face Building 53. The window hovered in the air above me, between my damnation and my salvation. I whispered Reinhold Neibhur's "Serenity Prayer," and I stepped in for the fight of my life.

As the process began, I started to think about Einar.

My friends grew up with, learning from, and even fighting with their fathers while I watched and hoped for news of the end of Einar's existence. If my last name was mentioned, my thoughts turned to the delight I would know on the day he was finally dead and gone. As I grew older and my strength and anger matured, I wanted to kill him myself. I wanted to mete out his punishment with my own hands. I wanted to hold him down and choke the life out of him.

Eye to eye, father and son.

When the call finally came that he was dead, I had cried briefly for what was lost, for what might have been. But my tears were mostly from the sheer exhaustion and outpouring of the anonymous emotion of waiting so long for the anticipated and inevitable news. I stopped crying almost immediately. Then smiled. He was gone. Good. Fuck him. He deserved much worse.

The deepest, darkest circle of hell in my dead soul was saved for the son who dreamed and delighted in his sick and helpless father's death—the father who had given him life, who had tried so hard to succeed and provide and create a new life for a beloved family in a new and hopeful country. The man who provided a connection to all that was terrible and holy in the son's life. The man who died broken and alone, estranged from the son who both loved him and wanted him dead.

My hate was so strong that after Einar died, it would not dissipate. It turned inward into suicidal guilt. I should have tried to find him. I should have tried to help him. He shouldn't have died alone. It was all my fault. Once I was diagnosed and suffered the same pain he must have suffered, I hated myself even more for failing him. I was at once the little boy who loved his daddy so much he chased him across a rain-slick parking lot and the grown man who despised his father so much he had wanted to kill him with his bare hands.

The son who knew that everything he had become—both the good and the bad—had been forged in his father's shadow. I was guilty of the ultimate betrayal. I was guilty of patricide—even if I hadn't killed him myself, I was guilty of wanting him dead, guilty of abandoning him, guilty of hating him. And in my guilt, I made his suffering my own. I bore the anguish of two generations of Arauz men on my shoulders and in my heart. In that moment of realization, I thought I would die of shame and regret.

But I had to continue. To travel this far without completion was out of the question. I had to start reading the letter and trust I had been trained and guided by enough Virgils that I would survive the flames and find my way back to the surface of my existence. If I was unprepared, if I failed, I knew I was literally facing my future—buried alive again in Building 53.

Resurrection | Chapter 18

The letter read: "Daddy, I am sorry for not seeing you as a person, especially a person with mental illness. I have hated your guts my entire life and prayed for your death."

That's it.

Two sentences.

That's where the letter ended.

I took a deep breath. Paused. And looked down at the ground between my feet. Ants were furiously tunneling passageways in and out of newly constructed brown dusty mounds.

I took another deep breath and started talking again.

"I have bad mouthed and cursed you to everyone I know. I refused to see your suffering. I now know you did not want this life for me, for your children. I do remember, I do remember going to all the Yankee games and you coaching my soccer teams. I remember the pride you had in introducing me to people and calling me 'son.'

"I could not help you when you were the sickest and I hate myself for that. I know you were homeless and in shelters getting beaten. I know you ended up in jail and probably had no idea what was happening to you. Daddy, I am so, so sorry for your life. God ... if I just could have done something for you. But, I didn't, Daddy.

"I haven't even gone to your grave.

"I have no pictures of you hanging in my home.

"I have hinged my life, my story, on hating and neglecting you and I am sorry. Forgive me, Daddy! Please, please forgive me, Daddy! I wish we could have known each other, you were a veteran with an MBA and I am a veteran, and I am getting degrees. I bet we would have been good together.

"I wonder if you were funny, witty, athletic, compassionate ... I know absolutely nothing about you. Yet, I know your suffering, Daddy. I have been diagnosed with mental illness, too. I have bipolar disorder and it terrifies me. I have been in the same hospitals and tasted the same deaths, Daddy. We are sitting under the window of the room in which I experienced the worst moments of my life. I have felt the pains you must have dreamed and hoped I would never feel.

"I'm so scared, Daddy, so scared of myself ... I don't know a future for someone like me, I don't want to die your death, I don't want to fucking die like you, Daddy. I don't want to be 'like father, like son.'

"I have felt so much guilt for loving Bud and hating you. I don't know if I can love you, Daddy. I just don't know ... Were you a great man who just got sick? Who are you? Who were you?

"I am getting married, Daddy, and she is so beautiful. She accepts me as I am. Her name is Cheryl and she is kind, noble. I was afraid to love her, Daddy, because nothing seems to ever work out for me, but she has stayed, she makes me believe I am not meant to die your death, she makes me believe in miracles, you would have liked her, you would have ....

"I apologize again, Daddy, I am truly sorry for your life and I can thank you now for the example.

"But ... but ....

"Did you ever think of me while you were gone, Daddy?

"Did you love me, Daddy? Did you love me?

"Did you really want to kill me, Daddy?

"Did you really want to kill me? Did you?

"Did you really want to drive your car over my body? Did you hate me that much, Daddy?

"I don't hate you, Daddy, I don't hate you.

"God, I don't hate you, Daddy. I don't hate you.

"I forgive you, Daddy, and I do love you.

"I love you.

"I love you, Daddy, and hope on your fourteen Father's Days without me you found a way to have fun ... I truly forgive you.

"I have just one wish, Daddy, and I mean this: I hope my memory caused you no pain, I hope this vicious disease took enough of you that I stopped existing for you.

"You didn't deserve this death and as a man I can live with being forgotten by my father.

"I hope you never sat on your deathbed and knew what you did to me, to all of us. I hope in your last moments you found solace, Einar.

"You suffered enough.

"I love you, Daddy, and I miss you. I have missed you for 20 years.

"Goodbye, Daddy. I am truly sorry and will love you forever ...."

I wiped my eyes, leaned back on the bench, lit a cigarette and sipped my cold, black coffee. I was drained. I felt empty, but there was no need to replace the emptiness with anything. I didn't need to fill this unknown with a known. This was revolutionary, beyond my past experiences. On this new deed, I could build a destiny.

Awake to the moment, I listened to the day breathe in and out in a tranquil symphony with no separation, no need for translation. The sun warmed my back, as the cigarette crackled and burned in my fingers. I looked out from behind my eyes and the veil seemed gone. I felt a clean and direct connection between what I saw and what I was. I was here. Free.

Unified.

I had burned through to *Now*, above the veil of yesterday and tomorrow. I was free from my past and was no longer dictating my future from my lifelong story of atrocity.

I had forgiven my father.

I was sure that my father had forgiven me.

God had forgiven me.

And finally, after a lifetime of hating him, I forgave God.

Resurrection | Chapter 19

The next page in the story of my life was now blank, unwritten. I had taken responsibility for my hate and accepted my biological father for who he was. I no longer held any resentment towards him. Instead, I felt a deep compassion for Einar G. Arauz, the human being. I loved him and saw how helpful his example would be for me in my recovery. It also made me realize that I was being a true son to my father, Bud Powers. I didn't see that my love for Bud in any way negated that Einar Arauz was my biological father. In my own way, with my service to Bud, I was making amends to two fathers at once. My journey with Bud was sacred, and I wished I could have done it for Einar. Bud raised me and sacrificed for me. He was the best father a guy could have had and an unbelievable role model. Perhaps, had mental illness not intervened, Einar would have been the same type of father, the same type of man.

But I do know that all men have fathers, but very few have Bud's.

Bud and I would make the journey together to the end of his life. His death terrified me, but I knew I would stand up to it for him. I had learned that life is not about stopping in front of fears; it is about finding out who you are on the other side of them. With the redefinition of my biological father, I could allow my mental disorder to be something to live with and not try to overcome. I saw that bipolar disorder was a disease just like any other.

But I was still not taking my Lithium.

I was actually no longer afraid of Lithium or holding a bias against it, but the side effect of not taking it for so long was that I really believed I didn't need it. I accepted what I had now. My disease did not represent the fear and shame that kept me from medication compliance. I really thought it was a simple byproduct of not taking it for so long that I could just use the twelve-step program for my mental illness as well.

I was wrong and I would find that out in my third and last, to date, maximum-security psychiatric hospital ward.

It is said that people can never know themselves totally, but they can reveal themselves. I kept the fact that I was off my meds a secret to everyone; therefore, no one could help me with the decision. Some masks are welded on so deeply that you don't know they are there until it is too late.

Resurrection | Chapter 20

My final semester at Rutgers was nearing completion, and I filled out paperwork to get my Bachelor's degree in American Studies. It didn't seem real that so much had happened in the short time I was at Rutgers, but it was time to move on.

My plans for law school and for taking Bud to his treatments for next year were in place. After the trip to the VA and the amends to my biological father, the last few classes at Rutgers were totally different. I didn't see any division between me and other students or me and the instructor. Before that moment, I had often researched where my instructors got their degrees and erected a pedestal high enough for me to see them, but so far above me that I could never dream of being equal to them. Now as I sat in the rows facing them, I saw that they were human, that they had once been on my side of the desk and that some day, if I chose, I could sit on theirs.

By redefining my father and, therefore, my disease, I could exist without any particular definition of myself. I was organic and evolving in each hour-long block of classes.

I had recently started to read some of the Hindu mystical texts, the Upanishads and the Bhagavad Gita, and had found a voice that resonated with my spiritual journey. In the introduction of the version of the Bhagavad Gita I was reading, the editor said that a few thousand years ago human cultures had developed a schism in the way that they viewed and related to the world. The Greeks and Europeans believed that the world was meant to be discovered and interpreted, using the mind with its subjective and fragmenting bias as the tool of discovery. Reason was born and the search was on to develop more and more static knowledge. On the South Asian continent in the Indus Valley, the quest was different. The goal was to discover the Self and the nature of universal existence, and with those piercing insights, one could know this world. I believed in the South Asian approach and the teachings that followed. I believed and adhered more to Hermann Hesse's idea about man's vocation:

> Each man had only one genuine vocation—to find the way to himself [...] His task was to discover his own destiny—not an arbitrary one—and to live it out wholly and resolutely within himself. Everything else was only a would-be existence, an attempt at evasion, a flight back to the ideals of the masses, conformity and fear of one's own inwardness.

I had been locked away from society before and when I was released nothing in the outside world had changed. But when I dug into my core, negating the fixed and false non-reality of my identity, I was able to see above and then through the veil between my biased self and the indestructible and forever Self.

With this last mask to my authenticity removed, my world looked completely different. I found nuance and freedom in activities I had done a thousand times. Like William Blake said, I could experience "heaven in a wild flower ... and eternity in an hour."

Classes were not about learning to be tested and to create a future profession. They were self-help sessions to help me live life. I looked around the classrooms and loved my fellow journeymen and journeywomen. But I could also clearly see the masks the students wore. I watched them piling up, one after another, often perpetuated by parents who could have still been wearing masks from their childhoods and years in school.

I saw the unity of the Galaxy of Rutgers University and all its colleges. The different departments, majors, and minors were just various solar systems in the integrated intellectual experience of a Universal Cosmic Education. Only the fallacy of separation created a division between Political Science and Physics, Music Appreciation and Linguistics. It was all one; no major a discipline in itself, nothing mutually exclusive. In the Jersey-based Einstein, I found the human desire to connect to the ethos through mathematics and become one with the heart and mind of our universe. In the poetry of Rainer Maria Rilke, I found a congruent yearning for a personal connection with God that sang in the soul of a 19th century German existentialist who sought to become one with his own heart.

If I wanted to have a group discussion at home, I could bring Jung, Thatcher, Lincoln, Roosevelt (Both), Robeson, Whitman, Dickinson, Twain, Anthony, Spinoza and Hawkins into my study and converse. From the introductions of all their works and their personal journals, I could get to know them as humans and see how their personal stories motivated their work. I knew from Emerson's journal that he never knew he would be "Emerson" while an undergrad at Harvard, and in Goethe's discussions with Eckermann, I learned of his reticence to give advice in ventures in which he had no stake, " A person should only give advice in matters where he will co-operate. If anybody asks me for good advice, I say I am ready to give it, but only on the condition that he will promise not to use it." I learned about Hemingway's mental illness and Twain's failed business deals. My heroes were humans and I was comfortable exposing my humanness and ideas to them.

I felt connected to the authors through their books, but now the books were secondary to my experience. I yearned for the days before book-centered instruction, before teaching was focused on the mind of the students and instead was focused on the essence of the soul, the feel of life. I was drawn to the imagined scene, twenty-five hundred years ago in the forests of the Indus Valley, when knowledge of the Vedas and the Upanishads was spoken to the students, when the teacher had to have lived the lesson to be able to teach it.

The 9th century Buddhist master Lin Chi famously proclaimed, "If you meet the Buddha on the road, kill him." He didn't want anyone to look for gurus or spiritual teachers. People themselves were not the goal of enlightenment, they only carried the message. Two thousand years ago when Jesus of Nazareth walked the earth, he taught his students, his disciples, to worship and maintain the inner church housed in their hearts, the church with the lower case "c." He railed against false teachers and the evils of large spiritual institutions that corrupt the basic message of humanity. From the teachings of Hinduism, Judaism, Islam, Buddhism, Christianity and others, we have been warned for years to not create false gods, images, or prophets to separate us from the world and ourselves.

We have failed and the wall between student and actualization thickens daily. I saw an alternative to this deadening experience and was fighting for my own perspective in the thousands of streams of thought rushing through and around the Rutgers campus. The way learning is conveyed in the modern classroom only serves to enhance students' dissociation from themselves. Many of my classmates never imbibed the greatest works.

They crammed for tests and then forgot all about the great works. Pedantically, they understood from *Moby Dick* that Ahab chased a whale and that fixation could be dangerous. But what they needed to understand was their own role as Ishmael the observer, participant and sinner and Queequeg the savage, tattooed pagan, and honorable warrior. They needed to feel as heavily laden as the ship burdened by two separate whale heads on port and starboard side, each head representing the overarching philosophies of positivistic thought and the weight it adds to the life journey. In the text of *Moby Dick*, Melville beseeches them to, "Throw all these thunderheads overboard, and then you will float light and right." Free to captain yourself in the sea of existence.

Freedom.

Freedom from label, freedom from preconceived conclusions about the world or about yourself, freedom from the known to sail on the waves of what is and what could be. Existential evolution. Vedanta. The absence of psychological knowledge. Real freedom without parameter, *to truly be*.

I came to believe concentrating on the book and the test blocked the growth of the soul/spirit, and I wanted nothing more than to sit with my fellow students on the shores of the mighty Raritan and discuss their dreams, their fears, their loves and hates while we washed our feet and hearts in the ever-changing river.

I saw through the greatest lie ever told: that we are separate and individual, and I wanted to help pull down their veils by exposing my journey to them. I was on fire to be an example for them, to help my fellow travelers narrate their insular journeys, but I did not see a way to burn for my fellow students.

I was graduating soon, but it was the journey that mattered to me. It was not the degree that counted so much as the tools to existence that I acquired; these tools were eternal. I had to apply these life tools in my own life, my own situation before I would be able to show others how to apply them in theirs. I could not give what I did not have. But I finally saw a way back to me through the universal teachings of history's greatest thinkers and in my last moments of undergraduate study in New Brunswick, NJ, I knew I had finally found myself. I now had an inner church to call my own and I would be my own avatar.

The Dean of the University of Me.

I had no role models of success for my serious mental illness, PTSD, and addiction, so I looked to others who were forced to go beyond themselves and their known limits. I studied test pilots, astrophysicists, single mothers, Olympic bi-athletes and Special Forces operators. I used my academic skills to make a patchwork of guides that would give me the courage to live in the ambiguity of existence.

Rutgers University gave me hope and acceptance, and, along the way, RU helped to save my life.

Walking down College Avenue days before graduation, I looked into the faces of my anonymous collegiate support network as they hurried place to place. For the first time ever, I was simply a part of the larger whole of humanity. The next day I had to take Bud for his treatment, but I was not sad or drained. I was eager to be of service to my father. I didn't think about my degree or my wedding in two months. I only thought of him and his pain. It was to be our last trip into the city and the greatest lesson of my life.

Resurrection | Chapter 21

The trip to the cancer hospital with Bud was always the same: morning talk radio, strong coffee and a crumbling breakfast bar. That particular morning, Bud looked very weak and his stomach was really distended and hard from the tumor. But he never complained. He always adapted like a good Marine and we made our way up the Jersey turnpike, through the Lincoln tunnel and across midtown to the hospital. I dropped him off as close to the door as I could and then parked on my own and ran back. He was waiting at the elevator when I realized we hadn't spoken the entire trip.

I was always a little scared entering the hospital. People just like Bud and I came from around the world seeking miracles. Cancer had ravaged many of the patients and the place reeked of desperation, of hope teetering on the edge of the abyss. It wasn't uncommon to see very sick children walking the halls with their devastated parents. Nothing can break your heart like seeing a bald four-year-old girl in a pink Cinderella bandana and Winnie the Pooh eye patch.

The normal procedure was that Bud would go to a chemo suite with four or five other patients. The process took five to seven hours as the IV flooded his veins with life-saving poisons and then we were gone until the following week. Once in a while we would have to meet his doctor and discuss the treatment and the fluid nature of his disease. It was a doctor day so we went to the waiting room to sit down. Bud was quiet and I was perched next to him like a Secret Service Agent. I kept asking him if he needed anything and he would say "No" until I asked again ten minutes later. The feel and smells of the waiting room seemed to saturate my skin. I drank coffee after free coffee and counted my breaths to center myself, to calm myself so I could concentrate on Bud.

During the last several visits, I had noticed that Bud was letting me do more. I would open more doors and get him more drinks. Our conversations were longer and more personal on the way home while he shared his life with me. I was so thirsty for these moments that I felt guilty enjoying them.

Bud was giving me the space—and the responsibility—to be a man. I had let myself be a young boy with him, always leaning on him, even in my late twenties, but that time was coming to an end. The transition was happening and I could see him very clearly. He wasn't the kind of man that sat you down and had a heart-to-heart talk. He was the kind of man that demonstrated—through his daily actions—how a man should behave, how a man should be. Of course, he had been teaching me how to be a man since the day he met me, but I didn't see it. I was so used to words and mind that I was missing the actions of a great man passing on his intelligence, his honor, his respect. I was closed off to these lessons until they fit my expectations. But in those last weeks, I came to recognize his wisdom and his calm assurance, and in the waiting room that day, I could feel the canon of his teachings flowing through me.

Sitting next to him waiting for our turn with the doctor, I wanted to feel his physical connection. He was already leaning in my direction and I gingerly pressed myself against my Virgil. He didn't react or move away. With a shock, I realized how much bigger I was than him. My power was young and healthy and next to him, I looked massive. Once again, I swore to myself that I would take care of this man, my true father, no matter what happened next.

We sat welded together until our names were called.

I always went in with my father to see the oncologist. I don't know if they minded, but I wouldn't have cared. The doctor made a few notes in Bud's chart and Bud made small talk with the nurse. As was his habit, Bud always called everyone by his or her first name and that day was no exception.

The doctor turned and stood in front of Bud. The man looked tall, sterile, imposing while Bud looked withered, weak, nervous. The doctor looked at me and then at my dad and he began to speak.

"Mr. Powers, we have tried numerous rounds of chemo and the tumors are not reducing in size at all. They are actually growing. We have exhausted every avenue possible this hospital has to offer. I am sorry, Mr. Powers, but your treatment with us is over."

It was like being kicked in the throat. The doctor was kind and thorough, but it didn't matter. He mentioned some experimental studies or trials at other hospitals, but I couldn't concentrate on his words.

The doctor had just read my dad's death sentence.

Bud's chin dropped and hit his chest.

He had stood tall and strong during my mom's cancer, my numerous hospitalizations, and anything and everything else his family threw at him. But now he faced the ground while the doctor looked at me. I hated the doctor, but it wasn't his fault. He was just the messenger. Like all those involved with the cancer of others, he worked in death and made this brutal battle his life's mission. He was a good man and all the oncology nurses on this earth are angels of mercy fighting daily for their patients in the soulful practice of their divine occupation.

My heart pounded. I wanted to scream. I didn't know what to do. I thought about myself, my wedding, my family. I didn't think of Bud. I was spinning out of control because, even though I knew the cancer was terminal, I had never really faced the prospect of life without Bud.

What would I do without him?

I fought to regain my composure. I looked over and tried to focus on my dad. He was gray from the chemicals and his muscle mass so diminished, his clothes hung off him—except for where his severely distended, cancer-bloated belly pulled at his shirt. He was breathing deeply, his face buried in his hands, and I knew I'd have to get a wheelchair to help him out the hospital.

I stared at my fallen hero and wondered what he was thinking. I saw the defeat in his body and knew it was over, the good fight fought. But as I watched, he began to bend his neck back slightly. Slowly but surely, he started to pull himself up to face the doctor. It took over a minute, but he was now more erect than before he got the news. He was eye to eye with the doctor and he started to ask questions about his situation.

I was completely frozen. I had never seen anything like it in my life. I saw, in that moment, the embodiment of the greatest lesson Bud would ever teach me: *Life is a choice.* Your actions are your future. That no one is programmed for a good or bad life, but through heroic measures in the worst of situations, it is up to you to decide how you face the next moment. Life can throw all kinds of terrible things at you, but only you can react to them. And your reaction, your choices, determine who you are.

Somehow, I had believed that the heroes of Bud's generation had been given a set of tools I didn't have. I thought men like Bud just knew what to do from one moment to the next, that there was no sacrifice, only surety, that it was something magical in their DNA. But in that moment, I saw that Bud was consciously making decisions, consciously choosing actions, consciously becoming the man he was.

The magic was that it was not magic.

It was choice. It was freedom. In that moment, my hero stepped out from behind the curtain and proved to me he was , in fact, the Wizard.

We made our way out of the hospital for our two-hour ride home in rush hour. This ride was different than all the others. Bud said he would do any experimental treatment they could find. He said he would continue to fight. He wanted to live. He told me he wanted to make it to my wedding. He told me he always knew I would be okay and that he loved me, but why the hell was I going to law school? I did not tell him it was for him, for time with him during the rides to and from the hospital. I did not tell him I intended to walk with him every step of the way, just as he had walked with me. He didn't need to hear that.

We made good time and he continued to talk as the Empire State Building faded in my rear view mirror. My Virgil was now Dante and we would guide each other as we journeyed together into his dark fears, passing exit after exit. We left the turnpike and turned for home. The news would be a serious blow to the family; this was real and life would change. I no longer had any thoughts of myself or my own hell.

I cut through town using miles of side roads just to keep moving. I couldn't feel the ground beneath the tires. I felt like I was on a sacred journey and I wanted my dad to be at peace. I needed to be strong for him and for my mom. She had been through so much and I needed to be there for her. I didn't know what the future held.

Overwhelmed, I wanted to direct the conversation away from the cancer, away from what came next. But for Bud I was determined to ride the thing right off the cliff. I would walk side by side with my hero until he took his first step into the unknown. I would not fail him. He deserved all of me. This was a Kamikaze mission; I didn't need to survive.

We pulled up to a light near the house and waited for the green left-turn-only signal to wave us on. The radio had been off the entire ride and the blinker thundered throughout the car. He had stopped talking and we were breathing together. Deep breathing. Ward breathing. He said my name and I looked over at him. We stared at each other for a second and he touched my arm and said, "Thank you."

I was stunned.

He stopped for a second, gathered himself, and continued. He said he didn't know what he would have done without me. He said he wanted me to know how much this meant to him and he thanked me again.

Eric C. Arauz

How could this man thank me for anything? He saved my life, righted the course of my family, and gave me the strength to walk back from hell. I couldn't process a moment this big. I was beyond crying. My heart ripped in two and the emotions of a lifetime poured into my body.

He loved me.

I knew he needed me, but he loved me.

He said one last thing before the light changed.

He said, "Thank you … son."

He called me "son" for the first time in my life.

I was his son. Bud's son.

Now he was Dante and I was his Virgil, standing by his side as he faced the last few months of his life. Sailor and Marine, for years we had been marching shoulder to shoulder teaching each other how to live and now, together, we would learn how to die.

We entered the house, and I helped him off with his coat. We would have to break the news to the family. Eventually, hospice would have to be arranged. A lot of talk of death would fill the living room in the near future, but not now. Bud got comfortable on the couch and situated his cancer-bloated stomach. I got him ice water and put CNN on the TV. I sat with him until he slept and then tucked a blanket around him to keep him warm. Gingerly, I ran my hand through his thinning gray and white mane and let the hair fall lovingly between my fingers.

He slept and I caressed him, *like father and son.*

Resurrection | Chapter 22

Imarried my beautiful wife Cheryl two months before Bud died. My father was too sick to make it to my college graduation, but he did make it to my wedding. We weren't sure he would be able to attend, but at the last minute, when we knew he would make the event, I called the tuxedo store and told them the situation. I told the clerk about my dad's cancer-bloated stomach and they told me they had stretch pants that would work.

The following day, the whole wedding party walked in to get our tuxedos with my dad, and I hurried to intercept the store attendant to remind him not to bring up the cancer.

Bud walked in behind me and in pure Bud fashion said, "Hi, Bud Powers here. I need some tuxedo pants for my son's wedding and they have to stretch in the front. Goddamn cancer is killing me, and my gut is all distended."

My best man, groomsmen and I all watched in disbelief and then just smiled. Of course, a life lived in the light stays lit and authentic. He was not ashamed of his disease or his situation; it just was. This man from Newark, a Marine, a boiler technician and international steel salesman was my Jersey Zen master and he did it without ever over-analyzing life. He did it by *living* life. A suburban Samurai living in constant reality, operating in the space without mind, the ancient mind of Mushin.

Our family came together and enveloped Bud in love up to the last moment. My father showed courage and dignity as he made the last few steps of his journey, and my mother never wavered in her love and honor of this great man.

I had many Virgils at this time of my life and they sacrificed for me so I could be there to serve Bud. Different people from all the various parts of my life told me how they got through the loss of a loved one. Many told me the things they did to make the passing easier for the family member.

What was amazing and truly sacred were the Virgils who let me into their hell and told me what they wished they had done. They did not hide their wounds and showed me the true sorrow they felt for amends not made, forgiveness not granted or simply time not given. One by one they would find me and trust me to listen and then act on their greatest failings. My actions with Bud were the collective best practices of my support group in attempting to ease the pain of a truly good man.

It was in these discussions that touch was again discussed for its healing power. I remembered how that soulful, wet-nosed, VA dog soothed my pain on that linoleum floor as I curled my fingers into her golden fur and drew comfort. Letting my spirit rest in her steady gaze. With the passing of my father imminent, many in my various support groups urged me to keep using my hands to give comfort to him.

Examples of the healing, connecting power of touch in literary works can be found everywhere, from the Grand Inquisitor section and Christ's kiss to the Cardinal's forehead in Dostoevsky's *The Brothers Karamazov* to Hesse's final kiss in *Siddhartha*.

In those last weeks, my whole family embraced Bud and, through touch, we made sure he knew how much he meant to us, how much we loved him, how much he would be missed. I held his hand while he slept and ran my fingers through his hair while he moaned in a painless morphine-soaked confusion in his last days and hours in our living room hospice. But he knew I was there, and he knew he was not alone. As he faced the final frontier and eased ever so closely to release, my fingers massaged his scalp and I gave him all I had to give.

I saw in the power of touch a language to understand the passionate soul of the universe. Touch gives comfort and without it, bodies shrivel and spirits die. It is the inverse of mathematics, which is the operational, technical language of the mind of the universe.

While mathematics allows us to describe connections in distant galaxies or in the microcosms of quantum physics, touch allows us to *feel* those connections—whether we are looking for a spiritual connection within ourselves or reaching beyond ourselves. Touch is a panacea for the most basic and tragic of human conditions: Disconnection from self and others. In touch, in feel, you transgress mind and move to intuition, to unity. The perennial fallacy of spiritual independence ceases to entrap the mind as the interdependence of all things is revealed in the tides rushing through our veins.

You become a "Child who Knows," as quoted in *The Tao of Pooh*, and with this new language you can receive Pooh's wonderful "...wisdom of the Great Nothing, the Way of the Universe."

My body and soul remembered the nurse's hands as she wiped the cool cloth on my head and neck while I was in the seclusion room. I remembered the connection of the freely-given touch of my grandma and mother. Touch that allowed me to believe I was not the animal my double consciousness told me I was. Touch that offered small moments of peace in an otherwise living hell.

I had lived disconnected from society since the day my biological father's mental illness came to light and exposed itself to the neighborhood. I hid from my neighbors, my friends and myself. There would always be a piece of me that no one else could ever know and as that place grew I became more disconnected from myself. But touch transgresses the lines we draw and the walls we build outside and inside ourselves. Touch is beyond doctrine, beyond creed and its texts are written in the eternal ink of enlightenment, tattooed on the soulskin of its followers.

I would honor my dad with the gift of touch one last time—on the day he died.

Resurrection | Chapter 23

When the call came that Bud had passed away, my body switched on to autopilot. It took about fifteen minutes to get from New Brunswick to my mom's, and I had made the drive hundreds of times. That day I drove it without thinking. I had prepared for Bud's death. I had been all that I could be for my dad, and I knew I had to do the same for my mom. Bud had been the calm and consistent hand we needed to get through our troubles as a family and his presence allowed us to better relate to each other. His loss would be tragic to our little network, but we would work together and pull through. That was what we did.

I counted my breaths and thought about my few judo fights as I reached my Mom's front door. I had studied martial arts to confront my fears and now it was time to bow in and fight again. Like any real match, each moment is important and builds on the next. I wanted to be aware, I wanted to be present, but I had wanted more time with Bud.

I felt weak. My mind was not quieting but racing. Over and over again I kept screaming in my head that he was dead. Bud was dead! I can't do this! I can't go inside. I can't deal with any more pain. No more pain … *no more fucking pain!*

I couldn't control myself. I had feared this day since I learned of the cancer four years earlier. I had known it was coming. What was happening to me? Get a grip, Eric, get a grip!

And then I felt her hand, the hand of the kind and loving soul that saw in me what I could not see in myself. A woman of feelings and action, not words and thought. The beautiful person who made me believe I could leave my personal hell of mental illness and addiction behind and live in a place of clarity and love.

My wife took my hand in hers and her firm touch transgressed and calmed the tumult growing in my mind. Her tactile interruption brought me back to myself, to her—and back to Bud.

As we walked inside, the hospice nurse greeted us and offered us her condolences. The dining room looked empty and sterile and I could hear people in the kitchen. Everything was playing out in slow motion. I turned the corner into the kitchen and glanced toward Bud's hospice bed in the background of the family room. I had not seen his body yet, but the sense of death in the house was tangible.

I let go of my wife's hand when I saw his naked back facing me. A strength came over me when he was visible. Bud would never have made this situation about him. He was always *in service* to another. It was the way he talked about the military. He rarely mentioned his particular branch and never said "HOOAH" to show his colors. He merely said he'd been in The Service. He looked at it as an honor to serve your country and to serve your fellow man.

The phone rang and it was our family's oncologist in New Jersey. He was the same doctor that treated my mom ten years earlier and saved her life when she had Stage Four cancer. He was calling on the other end of the disease this time. I heard my mother crying. It was me and the hospice nurse alone in the family room now. Bud's body was on his left side as if he was trying to grab something on the floor with his outstretched right hand. Just by looking at his body, I could see that whatever it was that made him my dad was gone. His essence had left. His soul was no longer contained within the physical vessel of Bud Powers.

He had disavowed his religious convictions long before I met him and did not start seeking religious counseling as he readied himself to die.

One time in the hospital a few months earlier, a priest or some sort of clergyman came into my dad's room and asked him if there was anything he wanted to discuss or get off his chest.

Bud looked him right in the eye and said, "No Padre, I'm good."

When the clergyman left, he turned to me and said, "I did the right things in my life, Eric, because they were right."

That was it; he turned over and went to sleep.

Bud Powers: Rock fucking solid.

While I studied my father's body, the hospice nurse asked if I would pick him up and turn him over. She thought it would help the rest of the family to see him laying on his back for our last good-byes.

It would be my final act for this man, and I was honored to be of service to him. I bent forward and placed my arms under his shoulders and lifted with my legs. I pressed my chest to his chest and felt all of him as I slowly moved him back to the bed. To not drop him, I had to lean all the way over the mattress.

I was face to face with Bud.

Eye to eye, father and son.

Everything came back to me. The talks on the way to the city. The way he had driven me to the VA hospital and then driven me home again. The way he had wanted to fly out to Memphis to do what he could to help fix my first marriage. The way he had stood on the pier with my mother when I returned home from Operation Desert Shield. How he had proudly given me his blessing the day I married Cheryl. How he had loved my mother so completely, and had taken on her troubled family without any regrets. The way he gave away my big sister at her wedding, and how he fulfilled his role as a true father to my younger sister. Every role he had undertaken—from his time in the service, to his career, to his role as a husband and father—he had undertaken with honor and commitment.

I loved the way he felt in my arms. I placed my lips to his forehead as I lowered him onto the pillow. For just a moment more, I remained wrapped around his body. Then I gave him one last hug farewell and tucked him into his final bed, to sleep forever.

Semper Fidelis, my Marine Corps Virgil, Semper Fidelis.

Resurrection | Chapter 24

In 2000, after burying Bud and starting law school, I entered my third and last maximum-security mental hospital. At that point, I had not taken Lithium in over two years. I thought being a member of a twelve-step program and remaining clean and sober would be enough to hold my bipolar disorder at bay.

I was wrong.

It was a hard lesson to learn. I was blind to the stigma I had against compliance to my medication. I was lying to all my doctors and constantly switching from one therapist to another. As the first semester of law school was coming to an end, I began to slip into a manic episode. As is the case with my particular form of the disease, I had no idea it was happening. The delusions started and I believed them as if they were 100% real. Even though I had been sober for four years and had been through the twelve steps numerous times, my episode was every bit as textbook as before.

I stopped sleeping; I had the delusions of grandeur and eventually the terrifying paranoia. Psychotic, I walked through my old Catholic school and entered the church in which I last saw Einar at the altar. The statue of the Virgin Mary watched over me as I lit candles for all the souls I would save in my coming showdown with the legions of evil. I was escorted out by the school staff, just as Einar had been sixteen years earlier.

Back in my car and heading south on Route 1, the radio played songs specifically for me. With my mania reawakened, I barreled down to Princeton University for my final showdown with the angels of Satan on the streets of the Theological Seminary.

Later, while sitting in my study in New Brunswick and staring at the simple, wood front doors of the Hungarian Rectory next to my home, I composed my Manic Opus for the world and sent it via e-mail to my two mentors at Rutgers and an Israeli doctoral student.

I ended up walking through the aisles of a Home Depot playing a fantasy spy game where everyone with a name tag was an assassin. While I outwitted my would-be attackers, my two mentors got together and agreed they had to save me. As late afternoon made its way into night, Prof. Jackson Lears and Prof. Leslie Fishbein talked and decided it would be better if Prof. Lears called my wife.

Prof. Lears made the call and told her what he feared was happening to me. They discussed the situation, and he said that he would like to talk to me "when" I returned.

No one used the word "if."

My friends in the twelve-step program knew something was wrong. My support group was in emergency mode. I had developed a network that loved me, and they were flying around Central New Jersey trying to find me, to rescue me. My mother and sisters got to sit this one out while my beautiful bride was exposed to the reality of my disease. She was anointed into the panic and suffering associated with loving someone out of control and beyond reason. She took on the burden and responsibility of saving me from me. She knew how I feared the hospitals. She had seen me weep when speaking of how I had suffered while in restraints, and now she had to prepare herself for the worst thing she thought she could do to me—put me back in the hospital.

It had only been four months since Bud's death and my disease and my actions were about to tax my family further. The only one not suffering was me. I was lost in the Land of Make Believe of my mania.

When I returned home invigorated from my day of chasing serotonin-soaked windmills, my wife told me about the call from my mentor. It all made sense. This noted academic had read my manifesto and had recognized my brilliance. He had circulated it around Yale, and I was to be recognized as a living Buddha.

Of course he had.

I called him and he said he wanted to meet the next day in his office. He had a few people he wanted me to meet. It was even better than I expected. I was to be introduced to the world with him at my side. We spoke for a few more minutes and hung up.

I was hospitalized that night.

Prof. Lears and Prof. Fishbein took immediate action. Officially, they were no longer my professors as I was no longer attending Rutgers University, but they had not stopped being my teachers. They stepped in to join the other angels in my life who were doing the hard work of trying to stop a simple boy fighting to die because he still couldn't understand how to live.

Later, they would both write the recommendations for my Master's degree and for my eventual admittance into a doctoral program at Rutgers in the Social and Philosophical Foundations of Education. I deferred the doctorate to write the book you are holding. Both Rutgers and these professors knew my life story. My professors witnessed my disease in full force and each of them judged me on my merits and not my disease. They accepted me before I could do the same for myself. Rutgers University accepted me by letter and spirit years before I ever could. I love both professors as friends, mentors and saviors, and I have thanked them face to face.

In these pages, I now thank the full university.

Resurrection | Chapter 25

My last institutional stay was much less fantastic than the previous two. Although my concept of reality was stilled skewed, I "knew" not to get strapped down. I was in the same private hospital from my first episode and they used Haldol immediately. I got out in thirteen days. Instead of being shoeless and limping for months in a ward meant for the sickest in the state, I was wearing my best man's black penny loafers and plaid sweater vests. Back in the hospital, I started to smoke again and became a master birdhouse painter. I kept completely to myself until I was released right before Christmas.

A few days before I was discharged, I called my best man, Steve, and rambled with frantic delusion. My Taurian brother listened patiently and asked me if I was doing OK. In the background his girlfriend was listening to our phone call. She was a close friend of Cheryl's and mine and had even helped to pick our wedding song. At a lull in the conversation she yelled, "We love you, Eric!"

I thought about that as I made my way back onto the locked ward. This time in the hospital I didn't feel alone. I didn't feel hopeless. I had built something real, and it had been working for me. Although I wasn't perfect in my recovery to that point and had still lied to myself about some things, I had taken real and revolutionary actions, actions that in their manifestations would keep the momentum moving forward toward my destiny.

I had built a strong support group of people who accepted my disorder as part of me and didn't shun me when I was back in its throes. The manic episode was my fault due to my non-compliance, but I was not judged. I was accepted. I even ran into people I knew at a twelve-step meeting held in the hospital. While others in my ward, the acute ward, had no one, I was hugging my friends in the hallway.

Maryellen, thank you for that yell into the darkness of my disease. You will never know what your voice and your words meant to me as I cycled deeper into my mania looking for a way out

The actual and metaphorical wards of the world would be better places with millions of Maryellen's screaming heartfelt encouragement into their frozen halls.

Resurrection | Chapter 26

I was discharged from the psychiatric hospital just before Christmas in 2000. My release from the third and so far final maximum-security mental ward marks the end of the introduction to the book of my life. I fully accepted I had Bipolar Disorder 1 and that I had to abstain from alcohol and drugs for the rest of my life to fully recover. Although the symptoms of my PTSD would go undiagnosed for another seven years.

Recovery from mental illness, trauma and addiction is not always linear. It ebbs and it flows; it is marked by stability and relapse for many. Recovery must be looked at in the gestalt, not the minutiae—as a trajectory, not a static destination.

Going into the last hospital I was in law school on scholarship and held a degree from Rutgers University with High Honors. After I got out, I answered phones in a warehouse on a temp job where I couldn't go the bathroom without asking. Strangely, I didn't feel bad about my life or my situation. For the first time, I fully accepted my disorders and was finally free from my self-stigma. I saw the bipolar disorder differently and wanted to live authentically in my own skin. I did not see a monster or a killer or an outcast in the mirror. I saw a man who had risked everything trying to overcome the story of himself and had made it to the other side.

However, it was also clear that I had to treat my mental illness equally or even more seriously than my addiction. I had spent the last two years compliant to my recovery program and it did not do a thing to stop the manic episode. I am Bipolar 1 first and foremost and the abstinence from alcohol and drugs is a mandatory part of my treatment. The twelve-step program is one part of my treatment protocol for my mental disorder in conjunction with working with a treatment team centered on my recovery, an educated and dedicated social network, diet and exercise, my own constant vigilance for the symptoms of my PTSD, such as the dread of intrusion or the "absolute passivity" of constriction, and a diversified and personal/universal spiritual program.

Since that Christmas, I have started a new life based on today with hope for tomorrow because I no longer fear yesterday. I recognized that I have the power to redefine the realities of my life. Lithium is a blessing now and not a curse. I know bipolar disorder is a part of me, not an outside condition, and I take full ownership for the actions and ramifications of my mania.

I am able to look back at all the parts of my life and see them clearly without fear. I can face the five-year-old Eric playing innocently on the backyard swingset and the ten-year-old Eric noticing his dad's quirks and starting to fear Einar. I see the twelve-year-old Eric weeping while running after his murderous father in the St. Bartholomew's parking lot, and I can step forward and embrace them all to my chest as the man I had always wanted to become—a father to the lost and frightened children of my own youth.

I can now face the paralyzing memories of my childhood. I cannot stop the suffering of those little boys, but I can reach back over the timeworn memories and let us know we would make it. That it was not our fault. We would survive. Hold on, I am coming.

And I can finally face the manic Eric, the Eric dying in his car heading west out of Memphis crushed by the loss of his step-daughter, and the Eric strapped down and screaming in the VA bed begging for his death. I can wrap my arms around these young men and absorb our pain. I can wipe away all our tears and mercifully kiss our cheeks.

It took a long time, but finally all the Erics of my past would turn to face me looking for salvation and *eye to eye* we would hug and become one. I knew I could be a Virgil for myself, my own guide out of the fiery hells of my traumatized mind. The schism to my many tortured selves was healed. I could offer the Erics in my frozen memories the solace of knowing *We lived!* It was over. We had found the shore after a lifetime lost at sea. Free, safe, whole: *one*.

As an *applied existentialist*, I found a vein of works to guide me, a "Literature of the Spirit" as described by Joseph Campbell, a literature from the soul that continued to lead me further down the inward path of self awareness.

In Jiddu Krishnamurti, the twentieth-century Indian philosopher, I found clarity and the absence of non-reality. I saw the fallacy of image, my image, and how my biases and preconceptions can create a feigned reality. That the observer and her memories, her remembered experiences are sewn into all she observes making the observed and the observer one.

I had no guides on how to live a successful life with such serious mental illness and severe addiction and I was done looking for something that didn't exist. In Krishnamurti's cookbooks for life, I read existential recipes to bring me to *Now*, without illusion. Krishnamurti offered me an end to psychological time and my slavery to yesterday. He is a mandatory key to a universe of divine loving intelligence and "freedom from the known."

I fully understood the Zen phrase, "Be the uncorrupted mirror." I could reflect life back to itself without personal bias when mindful and could fight back to that state when cluttered. I had eliminated the veil of my self-stigma and could see that there is no story of Eric that could ever "fix" my past. I understood I had to live in the absolute moment and author my life step by step. I looked forward at a blank page and I knew that the text was mine to write.

Scared and excited, I had been looking for people to lead me my entire life, but now I saw that dependence on others was a recipe for spiritual death. In the addiction communities, people are not equipped to deal with serious mental illness, and in the mental health communities, treatment providers don't see many get better with severe addiction. And the fact is that severe trauma and its symptoms are not understood and often go unaddressed in both communities.

Discussions of G-d, spirit and soul and something greater are cornerstones of addiction recovery, but mental health treatment providers shied away from such discussions as it mimics symptoms of hyper-religiosity common to psychosis. But I needed all of it for my recovery, my salvation: the addiction treatment, the mental illness treatment, the trauma treatment and the ability to link to something greater outside and inside myself.

So I would have to create my own *existential recovery plan*. In the end, I would have to save myself. Without known paths to lead me to my salvation, I would have to become the savage intellectual.

I decided I would become a bipolar test pilot. I would push Lithium, sobriety, and recovery to the far reaches of known experience and past, guided by the mantra: *It's My Life, My Limits.*

I have no idea if some day my meds will fail and I will be hospitalized again. That fear is only present in conjecture, and I refuse to live in the future. I must author the novel of my life now or die trying.

I am a *man on fire* and my goal is to burn brightly enough to lead others into the dark places of themselves. I have seen the pits of hell in my disease and do not fear the landscape of suffering and degradation. If you are traveling the same paths I have traveled, know that I have been there, too. Know that I am by your side.

Feel my hand in yours. You are never alone.

The trick for me was to learn to live above ground, out of hell, and I did that by finding spiritual lessons in the glow of awareness and connection. Roadmaps for a life lived in the Sun.

I was guided by Thich Nhat Hahn and his Mindfulness teachings from Plum Village; the Bhagavad Gita and its non-attachment to outcomes, Yoga and selfless service; Rumi, the 13th century Sufi mystic and his unmatched beauty and mystical caress (Sufism being the mystical arm of Islam); Martin Buber; Lao Tzu and the Tao; Meister Eckhart; Amma, the hugging saint of India; Tolstoy; Emerson; the drunkards and diviners, Mr. Wilson and Dr. Smith; and many others who sat at my elbow and, through their words and lived experiences showed me how to build my own bridge to a personal divine connection to eternity.

I found in this language of connection and resurrection a common theme. These many named spiritual tributaries to the nameless, universal flow of the eternal energy of existence all showed me that the mind was the weakest and most fragmented of constructs as it can only know yesterday. I saw how the mind was constructed layer by layer by subjective biases and conditioned childhood reactions laid on top of each other creating suffocating, fixed adult identities. Veil upon veil of non-reality. The mind is always working back to a "was," a "should be" existence.

The language of connection and resurrection is a language of *feel*. A language of now attempting to translate the felt experience of our interaction and intertwining with the larger evolving Self, samadhi, heaven, soul, nirvana, reality, the breath of God and beyond.

Into the wind of the universe, I could release myself, my limited identity, my ego, my static story of self to live in the real time of Now and its wonderful impermanence and changelessness.

These guides for a life on fire gave me a language to *feel* the heartbeat of the universe inside my own chest, to *feel* my life as it happens.

I found strength in the beauty and insight of such global existential understanding. I saw the commonalities in the collective work of thinkers and mystics writing across every age and across all cultural traditions. In this way of understanding, I came to know that I am an equal to the world and always will be. That the connection to that thing that is looking out from behind your eyes to this page is the exact same, divine and timeless essence looking down at my fingers as I typed it for you.

We are conduits to the universal ground of existence; billions of outlets for the pulsing power of God in his many names. We are not independent and unique entities but interconnected and divine.

All of us made of stardust and dinosaur shit.

Disconnection and isolation are the forever lies that have birthed all the misery of the world. It is disconnection and isolation that offers the physical and spiritual space for murder and rape in the Congo and seclusion and restraint in the United States. It was Adam's and Lucifer's original punishment, a perennial disconnection and cemented entrapment in oneself. It took three mental hospitals and all the suffering of my existence to burn off the fallacy of this delusion and to see, finally, my communion with all.

I realized that my destiny was to stand at the door of the *Burn Units* of the world to show others how to stay alight, to remain sensitive to living life.

It is painful to expose our sensitive soulskin to the sunlight of awareness and public scrutiny. So we wince and shield ourselves in many ways. We buy larger cars, more jewelry, we lie and cheat, we steal and kill, and we rape and pillage, either metaphorically or actually. We all have the same internal scars but fear their exposure. In our isolation and loneliness, we die cut off from our source.

I was willing to die alone in a hospital bed rather than expose my wounds to myself and then the world, but, mercifully, I had many, many hands reaching in to grasp my frozen soul and pull me back to safety.

I had psychiatrists, psychiatric nurses and social workers in their existential firefighting gear weathering the flames of my degradations and keeping a firm grip on me. I had other sufferers and Virgils walking the landscapes of their own hells while trying to lead me to salvation. Professors, friends, police officers and other soul-workers all tried to help me escape the suffering of disconnection. Most importantly, I had the strongest family in the world, pulled into the inferno with nothing to protect them, scorched by my disease yet fighting to keep me alive. And I had the love and maternal fury of my mother, willing to fight into the gates of hell to pull me back into her embrace.

I realized I was ready, finally, to be a Virgil to others and to myself. I had been out of hell long enough to start fighting back into the wards of the world to help save others from isolation, despair and disconnection.

I was comfortable walking into my own hell and navigating my way out. I could freely expose my deepest burns to help another. My wounds would not be allowed to heal; it was through them that I discovered the divinity in all of us.

Lost in their suburban psych wards and inner city cells, I could help lead fellow sufferers out of their own isolated hells. I could show others the cookbooks to living that the universe has left for us since the dawn of time. I could expose those in pain and those searching for answers to an *Applied Existentialist Curriculum* that could help bridge the gap of self-actualization ever widening in their hearts and reconnect them with their lives.

I would never forget Mike, Lee and Rich—those young men with whom I worked in the Navy—and their fears and questions about life after a mentally ill discharge. I knew I would never be unable to answer those questions again.

"Petty Officer Arauz, what do you do with a mentally ill discharge?" Well, you change the world, my sailor saviors ... you change the world.

I promised myself I would go back for my three Virgils of the VA hospital and countless others like them. I would drop my mask to society and expose my mental illness and addiction to the world to serve as a lighthouse for sufferers adrift in the sea of disease. Those with mental illness and other behavioral health issues and their families needed to see that a man as damaged as I was could succeed in the world.

I had been dying in public since I was ten years old, and now it was time to resurrect in public.

The problem was that although I was on fire to begin my role as a Virgil to others in need, I had no idea how to start. Even though I had built a nice life and earned a professional Master's degree, I knew my life and my dreams were not congruent. I was dreaming at night of helping others, of doing great things, but would wake to find, as Lawrence of Arabia says in his famous quote about the dreamers of the day, "It was vanity."

I wanted to heed the advice of this great Desert Virgil and dream with my eyes wide open, but I still didn't know how to begin. I needed another Virgil, another example, powerful enough to help me make this last blind leap into the unknowns of mental health and human rights advocacy and inspirational speaking.

To try to actually change the world.

But where and how could I find my next guide for a leap this large?

I would finally find it on the Rutgers Campus and the event would be nationally televised on ESPN. Chris Fowler would narrate my resurrection and this Virgil experience would be a team effort.

Resurrection Day

November 9, 2006
Piscataway, New Jersey

If I am only for myself, what am I? And if not now, when?

*~ Quote from Jewish philosopher Hillel. The quote came to mind as
Rutgers graduate First Lieutenant Jack H. Jacobs, U.S. Army, took the actions
that earned him the Medal of Honor during the Vietnam War ... a Rutgers Virgil*

Don't give up ... Don't ever give up!

*~ Jim Valvano, 1967 Senior Athlete of the Year at Rutgers University and
Head Coach of the 1983 National Championship men's basketball team
from North Carolina State University ... a Rutgers Virgil*

Resurrection | Chapter 27

Along with a few friends, Cheryl and I had season tickets for the Rutgers football team, the Scarlet Knights. RU had a new coach who had finally had a winning season in 2005. He was still new to head coaching and Rutgers was still new to winning. The football team was 8-0 to start the 2006 season and ranked 15th in the nation and tonight's game was against the number 3 team in the country, the Louisville Cardinals.

On the undiluted hopes of a true fan, our buddy Chris "College" had gotten a few extra tickets—just in case it meant anything for bowl game consideration. My father-in-law, a Rutgers alumnus from the early sixties and a diehard fan, went with us to cheer on his Knights.

The school had gone all out to promote the sixty-minute war. National radio personalities, Mike and the Mad Dog, were doing their pre-game show from the parking lot in front of a huge crowd at the stadium. The game was being broadcast on ESPN as the featured, stand-alone Thursday night game and the Empire State Building was ablaze in Scarlet Red.

Grandparents, parents and their young children were piling into the stadium to excitedly wait for the opening kickoff. Thousands of students were covered in Rutgers' red and their energy level crackled like late-summer lightning striking all around us.

I watched the evening unfold and felt overwhelming pride in my alma mater. She had given me a chance when no one else would. She did not offer me acceptance or my degrees with caveats geared to my disorder. She accepted me fully, tested me equally, and I built my life anew with her certifications. I knew Rutgers University was not ashamed of me, and I was proud to be there to stand with her in her battle.

Rutgers is the eighth oldest college in the country and only one of two colonial colleges that would later go from private to public. She allowed acceptance to students from all walks of life and with varying skills.

At Rutgers you can sit with students fresh out of high school with perfect SATs, foreign students with English as their second language, inner-city students from the vivacious and vicious streets of Camden, Newark and Irvington, suburban pot heads, returning vets, mothers back to finish their degrees after their kids were grown, newly sober students in the school's nationally award winning Recovery Housing program, and dual-diagnosed disabled vets with PTSD fighting for their lives.

At Rutgers we walked College Avenue, circled Passion Puddle, and trekked from Livingston campus to the Cook Farms to pet the horses. Rutgers had changed its identity once to stand freely from the private institutions to create a more inclusive student body and alumni population. Could they usurp a fixed identity again? Could they remove the mask of their failed football past as one of the worst college football programs in the country?

The buildup swept the Northeast and my friends from around the country were calling me as they settled in to watch the battle on their TVs in living rooms from Jupiter, FL to Dallas, TX. The fans were willing to suspend belief, were willing to hope that on this one night, the collective history of our record would not predetermine this outcome. As a Rutgers fan you were used to losing, it stopped hurting as bad after a while. You can get used to tremendous amounts of degradation, especially with people available to share your pain. But winning, success, that would be new for us.

Both Rutgers and I were used to the dark but could we get used to the light? Could we step from our known hells to an unknown heaven?

On that night the fans were being asked to hope for something communally we couldn't believe in individually. We would support our family of fighters on the field and suffer or exalt as they fared. We would push past our fears together and believe.

Rutgers was down big early, 25 to 7, and the stadium was tense. The electricity was still there, but clearly the game was not going the way any of us had hoped. But, the sea of red was still swirling and the din of cheering still filled the night. This was Jersey and it takes a lot to keep us down; we are born insolent and we know how to keep fighting to find a way to win.

The game began to turn and the defense started to overwhelm Louisville's offensive line. Rutgers was finally playing to win and not just to avoid losing. The defensive line and linebackers were blitzing with reckless abandon. The young men flew at the Louisville quarterback in their situational kamikaze missions and the stadium roared as momentum shifted to the Scarlet Knights. The energy of the seething stadium pulsed through everyone in RU red. With each Rutgers score and each Louisville punt we edged closer. By the fourth quarter the game was tied and Rutgers was deep in her own territory with one last chance as the clock was running out.

Our tickets had us directly in front of the pass that landed in Brian Leonard's hands as he caught the ball on a screen pass and ran up field to put us in field goal position. The rapture of the moment engulfed the stadium as screams mixed with high fives and hugs.

This was happening, it was real.

Real.

Sports at its worst is defined by steroids, cheating, rapes, and demigod building. Sports at its best is defined by community and personal enlightenment, it is the "real" replacing conjecture and bias. It is the manifestation of miracles of effort and accomplishment. It is the human spirit personified and celebrated. It can show anyone, anywhere, that the impossible is possible, that action will trump thought and preconception every time.

It is deed determining destiny.

Tens of thousands of Rutgers fans believed, but we could not make it real with just our thoughts or hopes. The unthinkable had to happen, the revolutionary had to manifest. We were broadcasting a miracle to the world from Piscataway, NJ. When Jeremy Ito kicked the winning field goal and the clock ran out, we knew it was real.

They had done it! Oh my God, they had done it!

They had transgressed themselves and transcended the veil of our losing history.

The fans rushed the field and so did I. I told my wife to stay in the seats so she wouldn't get hurt and I made my way down to the field. I slowly eased over the wall with my bad knees and weak toes and I found myself on the field cheering alone. I wanted Cheryl to come down and looked up in the stands and saw her and her father. I waved to her to come and she ran down the concrete steps to me. Her father was standing with his head high looking over the school that had given him his degree in 1962 and sent him into the military as an officer. Another veteran father figure for me, another great man. My Air Force Virgil.

Cheryl and I made our way through the crowd to the large R in the middle of the field. The fans and the players were laughing and crying together. Everywhere you saw and felt the power of this win. Rutgers' motto on its seal reads, "Sun of righteousness, shine upon the West also," and that night the bright lights in Central Jersey were shining for the world.

We got to the R at midfield and held each other. I wanted to kiss my wife on that spot, on that field, at that time. Rutgers had given us everything. It gave her father and grandfather degrees. It was where we got engaged (at Passion Puddle on the Douglass Campus), and where we met some of the best friends of our lives. It was where I first attended the twelve-step meeting (founded by a Rutgers professor) that started my journey to the light. Rutgers had accepted me into its community and then awarded me the degrees that go with completion of those studies, with full knowledge of my disease, and lastly Rutgers gave me Professors Jackson Lears and Professor Leslie Fishbein who stepped in as true savior-teachers when I had my last manic episode. Rutgers University saved my life and that night it gave me my destiny.

As I watched my wife's face, it radiated in the moment. She smiled the full and selfless smile that makes every woman beautiful as she reveals her true nature. Free. Feminine. Fierce.

I turned to watch the crowd. In a sea of red, I was surrounded by different and unique individuals, each with a past, each with a story, but still there together, part of the oneness of the moment. To many, the win that night was more than just a game, it was proof that they could change their destinies, that yesterday did not determine tomorrow.

The world needed more public stories of redemption and resurrection. The world needed stories like mine.

The late Colonel Lawrence Sullivan once told me I owed society, that I had been freed from a prison from which many do not escape. I enlisted in the US Navy in 1990, and I have never de-enlisted. I wanted to serve again.

As the moment and the epiphany were setting in, I felt lightheaded, not manic but clear, clearer than I had ever been. *Un-Restrained.*

I grabbed my wife and let my consciousness expand horizontally across the field and then vertically straight up from my core. Like a 13th century Iranian Sufi mystic, *a man of light*, I was connecting from my heart to the north and into the heavens. The light in my stomach filled my senses, and with my wife as my ground, I released completely to the universe. Opened to receive, the universe poured into my vessel. I felt absolute connection to the source of all things.

I saw what I thought was wrong with the painting in the Sistine Chapel when I was there in the Navy in 1992 looking up like the rest of the crowd in Rome. I had no use for any higher power or super image that I could not touch and I stared at that sacred inch of distance between Man and God and would not accept it. Now I saw the two, God and Man in full embrace. No thing mutually exclusive—it was all God.

I wanted to be all light from the inside out. My entire life I had been seeking a source that had always been deep inside me, but that remained hidden. Now it was clear. I could see the truth, my truth, the *Ubermensch*—the power and possibility of the inward transcendence to the human spirit. Standing on the Piscataway field I fully embraced myself: mind, body, and spirit with no division.

As the energy of the moment burned the haze off my existential vision, I patiently watched the movement of the universe. I saw forever. I was what I had dreamed about since my youth and in the restraints in VA hospital. I was free. Truly free. Unburdened by non-reality. And from that place came my answer to every question I have ever asked. From the soulful beseeching of thirty years of heartbreak came pure love to sooth my queries.

I was completely awake and knew as the fire burned in my veins that I must step forward and give back to the world what was given to me in its writings and teachings. I would speak anywhere and everywhere that would have me. I would be a beacon to the suffering in all walks of life. With the love of wife and family, I was sure of my mission. Joseph Campbell said in the *Power of Myth*, that it is not heroic to journey through hell and survive, it is heroic to share your knowledge so others do not have to suffer the same journey.

Resurrection | Chapter 28

Iwrote this book as an amends to society, to Rutgers University, and the world. You have given me everything when for so long all I could ever do was take. Now, I am here to right the balance.

I will serve the spiritually dislocated and disconnected. I will find the children beaten and maimed by their parents and forever cut off from the safety of existence. I will find "my poor," the traumatized, the forgotten, the persons with mental illness and addiction and show them recovery is possible. I will go to the therapists, psychiatric nurses, and doctors and give voice to their sickest patients and revitalize them to keep fighting. I will go to the families of the people with mental illness and tell them I have been on both sides and that they must take care of themselves first, and remind them to forgive themselves.

I will go to the veterans returning from war and those who have been back for years, suffering alone and afraid. Many of these veterans have never returned mentally from the wars that ended decades ago; they are still *Domestic POW's*, homeless, injured, and bleeding on the national battlefields of our urban streets. I will extend my hand back into the hells of their torments and pull them into the light.

Lastly, I will go to the high school and college students on our nation's campuses. I will light myself on fire and expose my wounds to keep them connected to themselves, just as Dale did for me on the ward. I need to show them they do not walk alone.

In that moment on the football field, hand in hand with my wife, I knew my life was about to change. I would quit my current jobs and move into advocacy. I would use my story and voice to sound my Whitmanian "barbaric yawp" from the rooftops of Jersey and then the world, spreading the message that sufferers everywhere must understand: *Resurrection is possible.*

What I understood in that moment standing on the Rutger's field can be summed up in one statement. It is the answer to every existential question ever posed in the dark recesses of your soul, and if lived, it would end war and violence forever. It has been told by many better women and men than I and written in a thousand books. But if it is believed and lived, it is heaven on earth and the holy grail of understanding.

That statement is: *I am you and you are me, and together, we are One.*

What is behind your eyes is the exact same as mine and all the inhabitants ever on this earth. There is no division between anyone of us. There is no existence in isolation. *There is only Us.*

I look out through my eyes in communion with Einar, Bud, and now, my beloved, deceased Grandma Joanie. I see out from the same source as my sisters and wife. Light recognizing light, earthbound stars forever dancing to the song of the universe.

And in the ultimate miracle, I see you behind the eyes of my baby daughter as I hold her in my hands, my baby Olivia. She is still more soul than ego, and I will fight myself to keep her that way. She is a dream that for too long I would not let myself dare dream. She is hope manifested. She is beauty.

She is my Salvation.

Sitting on my lap and running her porcelain palms gently over my face, she does not look at me as a monster. She looks at me as Daddy. Her Daddy.

Eye to eye, father and daughter.

As Rumi said, "I have lived on the lip of insanity, wanting to know reasons, knocking on a door it opens. I have been knocking from the inside."

Your Resurrection is knocking … answer the door.

Arauzian Original Concepts

Applied Existentialism: Is an active philosophy of life. The goal of Applied Existentialism is to build your own meaning of existence and then take the daily actions to fulfill your self-created destiny. This applied philosophy is built by searching for lessons of living left for us across time in disciplines such as literature, art, music, science, psychology, religion, astrophysics etc. and actively applying those lessons in your daily life.

Applied Existentialist: A person that follows their own Applied Existentialism: An individual that lives with a purpose and dream created by themselves.

Billboarding: When a person tells a person unsolicited information about themselves to create an image of themselves to the other person. Also, in social media, creating an image of yourself for others that is meant to advertise one's self to others in an exaggerated or overly dynamic fashion. One would rather have someone read their 'Billboard' rather than others see them clearly without hyperbole.

Burn Units: Are the recovery programs for addicts and alcoholics. The Burn Unit is a safe place for the participants to heal while their wounds are still fresh from a life lived in active addiction. The participants learn how to live with their emotional 'burns' by the other recovering addict/alcoholics(burn victims).

Dante/Virgil Support Model: A model created out of the *Divine Comedy* by Dante Alighieri. In this work, Dante journeys through Hell and is able to observe the damnation and find his way out because the great poet Virgil is there with him. Virgil lives in the underworld and, therefore, does not fear the journey. In this model, two people journey together through the pain, shame and suffering of recovery. They support each other and stay connected throughout the journey. It is not a therapist/client model like the therapeutic process or the sponsor/sponsee model from the twelve-step programs. The participants are equals and the roles interchangeable.

Domestic POW: Veterans of the United States armed services that served their country, and are now prisoners of the acute symptoms of their behavioral health issues (Post-Traumatic Stress Disorder, any mental health issue, addiction, Traumatic Brain Injury etc.) on the streets of their homeland.

Either during active duty or after discharge, the stress of service has triggered a behavioral health issue. These veterans have returned home to now wander homeless on the streets of the country they love. Domestic POWs are imprisoned in their minds by their symptoms.

Divinity by Association: A connection one can feel to something 'greater than themselves' that is accomplished through real, true communication with another person or persons. Many experiences are beyond words, and to stare into such an 'unknowable' abyss alone makes many give up the search and lose hope as they try to describe linguistically that which can only be felt. It is the shared experience created by the energies of two or more individuals/seekers letting the force of the universe manifest when they drop their egos/biases/knowns and stand together in direct relation to the unknowns of an ever-evolving universe.

Existential Cookbook: The manner in which an Applied Existentialist uses any type of existential tool (song, poem, painting, movie, book, speech, documentary, play, sporting event, concert, funeral, wedding, birth etc.) For example: the applied existentialist will read sacred texts and follow their directions to create the life they want (or) the applied existentialist will go to a movie and live out the message (or) listen to a song and take the advice freely given by the singer. Lyrics, aphorisms, ritual dances, speeches, tweets etc. become real directions to create the life you desire.

Existential Illiteracy: The inability to understand your own life experience. You cannot articulate to yourself what happened to you and this lack of literacy to your lived experience will have many negative ramifications (dissociation, shame, constriction, anxiety, intrusions, self-doubt, anger etc.). In trauma the symptom of Intrusion is defined as a wordless terror where the sufferer relives the traumatic memory and is attacked by the vision without the narrative ability to cognitively restructure the event. You are a prisoner in your own mind, burning alive in your own skin.

Occupational Divinity: Is a concept of 'something greater, God, G-d, Universal Spirit' that focuses on the mystical side of the great religions that deal with the 'feel' of the divine. Occupational is used the way it is in Occupational Therapy, a divinity to aid one to participate in their daily life.

Suicide by Omission: Not actively living your life. Making decisions and taking actions that stand in direct contrast to elongating and improving your life. Living life as if you were dead already.

Treatment Provider to Torturer Paradigm Shift: While being housed as an in-patient in a psychiatric treatment facility this shift occurs when your treatment team takes actions that cause you extreme suffering. For example: When the nurse that oversees your treatment is part of the team that forces you into restraints. When the hand that is expected to help you then hurts you, you will not look to that source for aid again. Unsure when the attack will come again, the person that is inpatient will fear the provider of their treatment.

Undertow: The pull back to known experiences even after you have taken real actions to change your behavior. Managing the Undertow is the key to effective change of human behavior. Many programs designed to aid people to change their behavior fail because they only discuss the positive change. An effective program of change will identify the past behaviors and beliefs that will continue to try and 'pull' a person back into failing actions.

Glossary of Medical Terms

Absolute Passivity: A state of existence when a prisoner loses the will to live. "Losing the will to live...represents the final stage of the process...adopting an 'attitude of absolute passivity'...They were regarded as the living dead."

> Herman, J., "Chapter 4-Captivity," *Trauma and Recovery*. New York: Basic Books, 1997, 86.

ADHD - Attention-Deficit/Hyperactivity Disorder: When problems with attention, hyperactivity, and impulsiveness develop in childhood and persist, in some cases into adulthood, this mental disorder may be diagnosed.

> Behavenet.com - Diagnostic and Statistical Manual of Mental Disorders, Fourth Edition, Text Revision

Antidepressant: The term antidepressant describes the category of drug whose original or most common use and intended therapeutic effect is to control or prevent the psychiatric symptom depression or mental disorders whose primary feature is depressed mood.

> Behavenet.com - Diagnostic and Statistical Manual of Mental Disorders, Fourth Edition, Text Revision

Antipsychotic: The term antipsychotic describes the category of drug whose original or most common use and intended therapeutic effect is to control or prevent psychiatric symptoms of psychosis or to treat mental disorders whose features include psychotic symptoms such as hallucinations and delusions.

> Behavenet.com - Diagnostic and Statistical Manual of Mental Disorders, Fourth Edition, Text Revision

Biogenic Disease: A disease resulting from the activity of living organisms, as fermentation.

> Dictionary.com http://dictionary.reference.com/browse/biogenic

Bipolar Disorder: Manic-depressive or Bipolar Mood Disorders are character-ized by dramatic "mood swings" or episodes of Mania, Hypomania, or Major Depression.

> Behavenet.com- Diagnostic and Statistical Manual of Mental Disorders, Fourth Edition, Text Revision

Bipolar Disorder 1: For a diagnosis of Bipolar I disorder, a person must have at least one manic episode. Mania is sometimes referred to as the other extreme to depression. Mania is an intense high where the person feels euphoric, almost indestructible in areas such as personal finances, business dealings, or relationships. They may have an elevated self-esteem, be more talkative than usual, have flight of ideas, a reduced need for sleep, and be easily distracted. The high, although it may sound appealing, will often lead to severe difficulties in these areas, such as spending much more money than intended, making extremely rash business and personal decisions, involvement in dangerous sexual behavior, and/or the use of drugs or alcohol. Depression is often experienced as the high quickly fades and as the consequences of their activities becomes apparent, the depressive episode can be exacerbated.

> Behavenet.com - Diagnostic and Statistical Manual of Mental Disorders, Fourth Edition, Text Revision

Bipolar Disorder 2: Similar to Bipolar I Disorder, there are periods of highs as described above and often followed by periods of depression. Bipolar II Disorder, however, is different in that the highs are hypomanic, rather than manic. In other words, they have similar symptoms but they are not severe enough to cause marked impairment in social or occupational functioning and typically do not require hospitalization in order to assure the safety of the person.

> Behavenet.com - Diagnostic and Statistical Manual of Mental Disorders, Fourth Edition, Text Revision

Complex Trauma: The term complex trauma describes the problem of children's exposure to multiple or prolonged traumatic events and the impact of this exposure on their development. Typically, complex trauma exposure involves the simultaneous or sequential occurrence of child maltreatment—including psychological maltreatment, neglect, physical and sexual abuse, and domestic violence—that is chronic, begins in early childhood, and occurs within the primary care giving system. Exposure to these initial traumatic experiences—and the resulting emotional dysregulation and the loss of safety, direction, and the ability to detect or respond to danger cues—often sets off a chain of events leading to subsequent or repeated trauma exposure in adolescence and adulthood.

> National Child Traumatic Stress Network - http://www.nctsn.org/trauma-types/complex-trauma

Co-Occurring disorder: (Dual Diagnosis) Coexistence of a Substance Use Disorder with any other mental disorder; coexistence of a developmental disorder with a mental disorder.

"… the terms suggest that there are only two disorders occurring at the same time, when in fact there may be more. Clients with co-occurring disorders (COD) have one or more disorders relating to the use of alcohol and/or other drugs of abuse as well as one or more mental disorders. A diagnosis of co-occurring disorders occurs when at least one disorder of each type can be established independent of the other and is not simply a cluster of symptoms resulting from the one disorder."

> Psychology Today website - http://www.psychologytoday.com/conditions/co-occurring-disorders

Death Imprint: The image some survivors held about themselves after the traumatic events of Hiroshima. How they described the event embedding in the their memory.

> Herman, J., "Chapter 2-Terror," *Trauma and Recovery.* New York: Basic Books, 1997, 38.

Delusions: Commonly defined in behavioral health care as a fixed false belief (excluding beliefs that are part of a religious movement) this psychotic symptom is present in a variety of serious mental disorders.

Erotomanic Type: delusions that another person, usually of higher status, is in love with the individual

Grandiose Type: delusions of inflated worth, power, knowledge, identity, or special relationship to a deity or famous person

Jealous Type: delusions that the individual's sexual partner is unfaithful

Persecutory Type: delusions that the person (or someone to whom the person is close) is being malevolently treated in some way

Somatic Type: delusions that the person has some physical defect or general medical condition

Mixed Type: delusions characteristic of more than one of the above types but no one theme predominates

Non-Bizarre Type: (i.e., involving situations that occur in real life, such as being followed, poisoned, infected, loved at a distance, or deceived by spouse or lover, or having a disease) of at least one month's duration

> Behavenet.com- Diagnostic and Statistical Manual of Mental Disorders, Fourth Edition, Text Revision

Depression: We often compare the psychiatric symptom depression or depressed mood to sadness or grief in response to a loss, but one of the essential features is loss of interest in life activities. The term is used interchangeably to refer to a mental disorder or to a mood state or symptom. A Major Depressive episode is marked by some of the following and more:

1. depressed mood most of the day, nearly every day, as indicated by either subjective report (e.g., feels sad or empty) or observation made by others (e.g., appears tearful). Note: In children and adolescents, can be irritable mood
2. markedly diminished interest or pleasure in all, or almost all, activities most of the day, nearly every day (as indicated by either subjective account or observation made by others)
3. significant weight loss when not dieting or weight gain (e.g., a change of more than 5% of body weight in a month), or decrease or increase in appetite nearly every day. Note: In children, consider failure to make expected weight gains
4. insomnia or hypersomnia nearly every day
5. psychomotor agitation or retardation nearly every day (observable by others, not merely subjective feelings of restlessness or being slowed down)
6. fatigue or loss of energy nearly every day
7. feelings of worthlessness or excessive or inappropriate guilt (which may be delusional) nearly every day (not merely self-reproach or guilt about being sick)
8. diminished ability to think or concentrate, or indecisiveness, nearly every day (either by subjective account or as observed by others)
9. recurrent thoughts of death (not just fear of dying), recurrent suicidal ideation without a specific plan, or a suicide attempt or a specific plan for committing suicide

> Behavenet.com - Diagnostic and Statistical Manual of Mental Disorders, Fourth Edition, Text Revision

Endless Present: When life is so painful for prisoners that they cannot bear thinking about their past or the hope of the future. "The past like the future, becomes too painful to bear, for memory, like hope brings back the yearning for all that has been lost. Thus, prisoners are reduced to living in an endless present."

> Herman, J., "Chapter 4-Captivity," *Trauma and Recovery*. New York: Basic Books, 1997, 89.

Haldol (Haloperidol): Used to treat psychotic disorders (conditions that cause difficulty telling the difference between things or ideas that are real and things or ideas that are not real) ... Haloperidol is in a group of medications called conventional antipsychotics. It works by decreasing abnormal excitement in the brain.
> US National Library of Medicine - http://www.ncbi.nlm.nih.gov/pubmedhealth/PMH0000604/

Hallucination: This psychotic symptom found in a variety of serious mental disorders involves sensory perceptual distortions, for example seeing (visual), hearing (auditory), smelling (olfactory), feeling (haptic, tactile), or tasting (gustatory) sensations that others would not sense and do not exist outside one's perception.
> Behavenet.com - Diagnostic and Statistical Manual of Mental Disorders, Fourth Edition, Text Revision

Hypersexuality: Exhibiting unusual or excessive concern with or indulgence in sexual activity.
> Merriam-Webster http://www.merriam-webster.com/medical/hypersexual)

Hypomania: Hypomania is a mood state which like mania is characterized by persistent and pervasive elated or irritable mood, and behaviors and thoughts that are consistent with such a mood state. It is distinguished from mania by the absence of psychotic symptoms and less impact of functioning.
> Behavenet.com - Diagnostic and Statistical Manual of Mental Disorders, Fourth Edition, Text Revision

Ideas of Reference: This form of thought disorder is characterized by a delusional belief that media content, e.g. television or radio broadcast, refers to oneself, or that others are talking or thinking about oneself.
> Behavenet.com - Diagnostic and Statistical Manual of Mental Disorders, Fourth Edition, Text Revision

Librium (Chlordiazepoxide): Chlordiazepoxide is in a group of drugs called benzodiazepines (ben-zoe-dye-AZE-eh-peens). Chlordiazepoxide affects chemicals in the brain that may become unbalanced and cause anxiety. Chlordiazepoxide is used to treat anxiety disorders or alcohol withdrawal.

Chlordiazepoxide may also be used for other purposes not listed in this medication guide.

> E Medicine Health - http://www.emedicinehealth.com/drug-chlordiaz-epoxide/article_em.htm#whatis

Language of Abomination: The language a trauma victim uses to describe themselves in self-narrative creating deeply embedded self-hate and mistakenly assumes responsibility for the atrocities inflicted upon them. "The language of the self becomes the language of abomination."

> Herman, J., "Chapter 5-Child Abuse," *Trauma and Recovery.* New York: Basic Books, 1997, 105.

Lithium: Lithium is used to treat and prevent episodes of mania (frenzied, abnormally excited mood) in people with bipolar disorder (manic-depressive disorder; a disease that causes episodes of depression, episodes of mania, and other abnormal moods). Lithium is in a class of medications called antimanic agents. It works by decreasing abnormal activity in the brain.

> US National Library of Medicine - http://www.ncbi.nlm.nih.gov/pubmedhealth/PMH0000531/

Manic Episode: When an individual experiences a discrete period of persistent and pervasive manic (elated, irritable or euphoric) mood, this term may be applied. The individual may be diagnosed with one of the bipolar disorders.

> Behavenet.com- Diagnostic and Statistical Manual of Mental Disorders, Fourth Edition, Text Revision

Mania: Mania may be thought of loosely as the opposite of depression. It is characterized by elated, euphoric or irritable mood and increased energy. The term may refer to a mental disorder or to a mood state or symptom and is associated with Bipolar Disorder.

> Behavenet.com - Diagnostic and Statistical Manual of Mental Disorders, Fourth Edition, Text Revision

Poland Syndrome: Named after Sir Alfred Poland, Poland's Syndrome is described as an absence or underdevelopment of the chest muscle (pectoralis) on one side of the body and webbing of the fingers (cutaneous syndactyly) of the hand on the same side (ipsilateral hand). Sometimes referred to as

"Poland anomaly," it is a rare condition present at birth (congenital). For people born with Poland's Syndrome, the breastbone portion (sternal) of the pectoralis is also missing.

> http://www.polandsyndrome.com

Psychosocial Stress(or): Psychosocial stress is the result of a cognitive appraisal of what is at stake and what can be done about it. More simply put, psychosocial stress results when we look at a perceived threat in our lives (real or even imagined), and discern that it may require resources we don't have. Examples of psychosocial stress include things like a threat to our social status, social esteem, respect, and/or acceptance within a group; threat to our self-worth; or a threat that we feel we have no control over. All of these threats can lead to a stress response in the body.

> http://stress.about.com/od/stressmanagementglossary/g/What-Is-Psycho-social-Stress.htm

PTSD-Post-Tramatic Stress Disorder: When an individual who has been ex-posed to a traumatic event develops anxiety symptoms, re-experiencing of the event, and avoidance of stimuli related to the event lasting more than four weeks, they may be suffering from this Anxiety Disorder.

> Behavenet.com- Diagnostic and Statistical Manual of Mental Disorders, Fourth Edition, Text Revision

Retin-A (Tretinoin): The acid form of vitamin A and is also known as all-trans retinoic acid or ATRA. It is a drug commonly used to treatacne vulgaris and keratosis pilaris. It is available as a cream or gel (brand names Aberela, Airol, Renova, Atralin, Retin-A, Avita,Retacnyl, Refissa, or Stieva-A). It is also used to treat acute promyelocytic leukemia (APL), and is sold for this indication by Roche under the brand name Vesanoid.

> Wikipedia- http://en.wikipedia.org/wiki/Tretinoin

Schizophrenia: A term introduced by Eugene Bleuler, schizophrenia names a persistent, often chronic and usually serious mental disorder affecting a variety of aspects of behavior, thinking, and emotion. Patients with delusions or hallucinations may be described as psychotic. Thinking may be disconnected and illogical. Peculiar behaviors may be associated with social withdrawal and disinterest. The disorder can marked by some of the following symptoms:

A. *Characteristic symptoms*: two (or more) of the following characteristic symptoms, each present for a significant portion of time during a one-month period (or less if successfully treated):

1. delusions
2. hallucinations
3. disorganized speech (e.g., frequent derailment or incoherence)
4. grossly disorganized or catatonic behavior
5. negative symptoms, i.e., affective flattening, alogia, or avolition

Note: Only one Criterion A symptom is required if delusions are bizarre or hallucinations consist of a voice keeping up a running commentary on the person's behavior or thoughts, or two or more voices conversing with each other.

B. *Social/occupational dysfunction:* For a significant portion of the time since the onset of the disturbance, one or more major areas of functioning such as work, interpersonal relations, or self-care are markedly below the level achieved prior to the onset (or when the onset is in childhood or adolescence, failure to achieve expected level of interpersonal, academic, or occupational achievement).

C. *Duration:* Continuous signs of the disturbance persist for at least 6 months. This 6-month period must include at least 1 month of symptoms (or less if successfully treated) that meet Criterion A (i.e., active-phase symptoms) and may include periods of prodromal or residual symptoms. During these prodromal or residual periods, the signs of the disturbance may be manifested by only negative symptoms or two or more symptoms listed in Criterion A present in an attenuated form (e.g., odd beliefs, unusual perceptual experiences).

D. *Schizoaffective and Mood Disorder Exclusion:* Schizoaffective Disorder and Mood Disorder With Psychotic Features have been ruled out because either (1) no Major Depressive, Manic, or Mixed Episodes have occurred concurrently with the active-phase symptoms; or (2) if mood episodes have occurred during active-phase symptoms, their total duration has been brief relative to the duration of the active and residual periods.

E. *Substance/general Medical Condition Exclusion:* The disturbance is not due to the direct physiological effects of a substance (e.g., a drug of abuse, a medication) or a general medical condition.

F. *Relationship to a Pervasive Developmental Disorder:* If there is a history of Autistic or another Pervasive Developmental Disorder, the additional diagnosis of Schizophrenia is made only if prominent delusions or hallucinations are also present for at least a month (or less if successfully treated).

> Behavenet.com - Diagnostic and Statistical Manual of Mental Disorders, Fourth Edition, Text Revision

Self-referential Thinking: Thought process characterized by persistent tendency to relate material to one's self.

> Behavenet.com - Diagnostic and Statistical Manual of Mental Disorders, Fourth Edition, Text Revision

Serotonin: Serotonin is a naturally occurring chemical in the brain (a neurotransmitter) that is responsible, in part, for regulating brain functions such as mood, appetite, sleep, and memory. Problems with serotonin have been linked to mood disorders such as depression and to borderline personality disorder(BPD). Antidepressant medications that alter the availability of serotonin in the brain have been used to treat these conditions. "What is Serotonin? by Kristalyn Salters-Pedneault, PhD, http://bpd.about.com/od/glossary/g/serotonin.htm.

Story of Atrocity: The narrative a victim of trauma and captivity tells themselves about themselves. "To the released prisoner, there is only one story: the story of atrocity."

> Herman, J., "Chapter 4-Captivity," *Trauma and Recovery.* New York: Basic Books, 1997, 92.

Thorazine (Chlorpromazine): Thorazine is used to treat the symptoms of schizophrenia (a mental illness that causes disturbed or unusual thinking, loss of interest in life, and strong or inappropriate emotions) and other psychotic disorders (conditions that cause difficulty telling the difference between things or ideas that are real and things or ideas that are not real) and to treat the symptoms of mania (frenzied, abnormally excited mood) in people who have bipolar disorder (manic depressive disorder; a condition that causes episodes of mania, episodes of depression, and other abnormal moods) … Chlorpromazine is in a class of medications called conventional antipsychotics. It works by changing the activity of certain natural substances in the brain and other parts of the body.

> US National Library of Medicine-http://www.ncbi.nlm.nih.gov/pubmedhealth/PMH0000553/)

End Notes

Introduction

<u>"It is unbelievable…."</u>: Castaneda, C. *The Active Side of Infinity*. New York: Harper Collins, 1998, 182.

Book 1 | Life

<u>"God had one son…." St Augustine of Hippo</u>: Koessler, J. *God Our Father*. Chicago: Moody Publishers, 1999, 122.

<u>"As a single withered tree…." Chanakya</u>: Logan, C.B. *The Awakening: The Anthem of the Angels*. Authorhouse, ebook, 2011, 129.

<u>"Am I entitled to live…."</u>: From the work *The Second Coming*. Miller, John(ed). *On Suicide*. San Francisco: Chronicle, 1992, 106.

Life | Chapter 1 p. 6
<u>Bardo</u>: A term from *The Tibetan Book of the Dead*, Compiled and edited by W. Y. Evans-Wentz. *The Tibetan Book of the Dead or The After Death experiences on the Bardo Pane, according to Lama Kazi dawa-Samdup's English Rendering*. London: Oxford University Press, 1960. "It is highly sensible of the Bardo Thodol to make clear to the dead man the primacy of the soul, for that is the one thing which life does not make clear to us. We are so hemmed in by things which jostle and oppress that we never get a chance, in the midst of all these 'given' things, to wonder by whom they are 'given.'" - *Psychological Commentary* by Dr. Carl G. Jung pp. xxxix-xl of *The Tibetan book of the Dead*.
> *The bardo is the plane of existence between death and rebirth in certain schools of Buddhism. A plane I felt I fell into awakening in the restraints in the White room.*

Life | Chapter 2 p.10
"Adversity introduces a man to himself." Albert Einstein, Dalia Lama Study Circle Montreal. http://hhdlstudycirclemontreal.com/?s=adversity+introduces+a+man+to+himself.

"Service ghettoes": The term "service ghettoes" is from "Down and Out in Chicago," T. M. Luhrmann. *Raritan: A Quarterly Review,* Ed., Jackson Lears. Winter 2010, 146.

> *These are the places I have seen in my years doing trainings and speeches visiting partial care programs in the poorest and most violent cities of New Jersey and across the country. My population is virtually defenseless while living in sections of urban America where weakness is devoured and people get preyed upon.*

Life | Chapter 2 p.12

"People with serious mental illness (SMI) die, on average, 25 years earlier than the general population. State studies document recent increases in death rates over those previously reported.": *Morbidity and Mortality in People with Serious Mental Illness,* Ed., Joe Parks, MD; Dale Svendsen, MD; Patricia Singer, MD; Mary Ellen Foti, MD; Technical Writer Barbara Mauer, MSW, CMC; National Association of State Mental Health Program Directors (NASMHPD) Medical Directors Council, Executive Summary, 5.

> *NASMHPD is a wonderful organization of the mental health commissioners and state hospital CEOs from around the United States. It is headed by Dr. Bob Glover who has been a strong ally for the inclusion of people with a lived experience participating in the recovery models and movements in the US.*

Life | Chapter 7 p.29

Hesse, Hermann. *Siddhartha.* New York: Barnes and Noble Classics, 2007 (orig. 1922).

> "Govina bowed low; tears of which he knew nothing, ran down over his old face; the feeling of most intimate love. Of most humble reverence burned like fire in his heart." - 118.

> *At the conclusion of the story Siddhartha kisses his friend Govina of his forehead. Placing his lips on the skin of his friend, Siddhartha is showing the power of connection through the "feel" of another to overcome the wall Govina has built between himself and the experience of life with his accumulation of knowledge. Heart overcoming mind. Connection. Love. Soul-birth.*

The Fisher King: "The mysterious Fisher King is a character of the Arthurian tradition, and his story may sound familiar: suffering from wounds, the Fisher King depends for his healing on the successful completion of the hero's task. There are many different versions of the story of the Fisher King, and the character is not represented uniformly in every text." From the Camelot Project at the University of Rochester. http://www.lib.rochester.edu/camelot/Fisher-king/fkessay.htm#intro.

> *My father will forever be wounded and searching for his solace in his manic driven adventures in my memory. The pain of such a memory is never offset by his demise as he lives forever suffering in my heart, and it is a wound I will die with and live with as the son of the Fisher King trying to usurp the pass down of the poisoned crown.*

Life | Chapter 8 p. 36

Jung, C. G. *Synchronicity: An Acausal Connecting Principle.* Trans. R.F.C. Hull. Princeton, NJ: Princeton University Press, 1973.

> "The causality principle asserts that the connection between cause and effect is a necessary one. The synchronicity principle asserts that the terms of a meaningful coincidence are connected by simultaneity and meaning. So if we assume that the ESP experiments and numerous other observations are established facts, we must conclude that besides the con-

nection between cause and effect there is another factor in nature which expresses itself in the arrangement of events and appears to us as meaning." - 69.

Life | Chapter 8 p. 37

The Inferno: "Dante Alighieri, 1265-1321, Italian poet, author of *The Divine Comedy*. A Florentine patrician, he fought on the side of the Guelphs but later supported the Imperial party. In 1290, after the death of his exalted Beatrice (Beatrice Portinari, 1266-90), he plunged into the study of philosophy and Provençal poetry. Politically active in Florence from 1295, he was banished in 1302 and became a citizen of all Italy, dying in Ravenna.

The Divine Comedy, a vernacular poem in 100 cantos (more than 14,000 lines), was composed in exile. It is the tale of the poet's journey through Hell and Purgatory (guided by Vergil) and through Heaven (guided by Beatrice, to whom the poem is a memorial.) Written in a complex pentameter form, terza rima, it is a magnificent synthesis of the medieval outlook, picturing a changeless universe ordered by God. Through it Dante established Tuscan as the literary language of Italy and gave rise to a vast literature. His works also include La vita nuova (c.1292), a collection of prose and lyrics celebrating Beatrice and ideal love; treatises on language and politics; eclogues; and epistles." From The Concise Columbia Encyclopedia. Copyright © 1991 by Columbia University Press. - http://dante.ilt.columbia.edu/about/index.html.

> *I used the translation of "The Inferno" by Henry Wadsworth Longfellow, a Barnes and Nobles Classics, NY, NY. Original 1308-1321, Longfellow's translation -1867, Current Edition 2003.*

Life | Chapter 8 p. 38

Herman, J. *Trauma and Recovery*. New York: Basic Books, 1997.

> "Language of abomination": The language a trauma victim uses to describe themselves in self-narrative creating deeply embedded self-hate and mistakenly assuming responsibility for the atrocities inflicted upon them. "The language of the self becomes the language of abomination." - 105.

> "Story of atrocity": The narrative a victim of trauma and captivity tells themselves about themselves. "To the released prisoner, there is only one story: the story of atrocity." - 92.

Marcus Aurelius: "The second century CE Roman emperor Marcus Aurelius was also a Stoic philosopher, and his private Meditations, written in Greek, gives readers a unique opportunity to see how an ancient person (indeed an emperor) might try to live a Stoic life, according to which only virtue is good, only vice is bad, and the things which we busy ourselves with are all indifferent. The difficulties Marcus faces putting Stoicism into practice are philosophical as well as practical, and understanding his efforts increases our philosophical appreciation of Stoicism." From Stanford Encyclopedia of Philosophy - http://plato.stanford.edu/entries/marcus-aurelius/.

"How can our principles become dead, unless the impressions (thoughts) which correspond to them are extinguished? But it is in thy power continuously to fan these thoughts into a flame. I can have that opinion about anything, which I ought to have. If I can, why am I disturbed? The things which are external to my mind have no relation at all to my mind.- Let this be the state of thy affects, and thou standest erect. To recover thy life is in thy power. Look at things again as thou didst use to look at them; for in this consists the recovery of thy life." From Book 7 of *The Meditations* at The Internet Classics Archive at MIT - http://classics.mit.edu/Antoninus/meditations.7.seven.html.

End Notes

Life | Chapter 10 p. 43

Du Bois, W. E. B. *The Souls of Black Folk.* New York: Penguin, 1995 (orig. 1903).

> "veil": "Then it dawned upon me with a certain suddenness that I was different from the others; or like, mayhap, in heart and life and longing, but shut out from their world by a vast veil." - 44.

> "double consciousness": "It is a peculiar sensation, this double consciousness, this sense of always looking at one's self through the eye's of others, of measuring one's soul by the tape of a world that looks on in amused contempt and pity." - 45.

> *This quote describing double consciousness gave me a literary example to explain to myself the crushing self-stigma I felt upon release from the psychiatric hospitals.*

Life | Chapter 10 p. 44

Socrates: "Plato was credited with the quote, 'An unexamined life is not worth living,' in this column. It does, indeed, come from *Plato's Apology*, which is a recollection of the speech Socrates gave at his trial. Socrates is attributed with these words after choosing death rather than exile from Athens or a commitment to silence." From The Guardian OnLine, Culture Section-Books by Julian Baggini, writer and founding editor of *The Philosophers' Magazine.* His books include *The Ego Trick* (Granta), *Welcome to Everytown: A Journey into the English Mind* (Granta), *Atheism: A Very Short Introduction* (OUP) and, with Antonia Macaro, *The Shrink and The Sage* (Icon). http://www.guardian.co.uk/theguardian/2005/may/12/features11.g24.

> *I believe in the negation of one's identity to strip one's self to their essence and free themselves from the tradition and bias of past knowns, but it is a painful journey to become that sensitive to the song of the universe. One need not enter the journey if it will destroy them. It is important to have a Sanghra, spiritual community, around you when you question what IS to prevent from being lost in despair.*

Life | Chapter 10 p. 45

"Banality of evil": A term coined by Hannah Arendt. "At this historical juncture, for Arendt, it became necessary to conceptualise and prepare for crimes against humanity, and this implied an obligation to devise new structures of international law. So if a crime against humanity had become in some sense 'banal' it was precisely because it was committed in a daily way, systematically, without being adequately named and opposed. In a sense, by calling a crime against humanity 'banal', she was trying to point to the way in which the crime had become for the criminals accepted, routinised, and implemented without moral revulsion and political indignation and resistance." From The Big Ideas Series at The Guardian-OnLine, contributors: Judith Butler, the Maxine Elliot Professor in the Departments of Rhetoric and Comparative Literature at the University of California, Berkeley. http://www.guardian.co.uk/commentis-free/2011/aug/29/hannah-arendt-adolf-eichmann-banality-of-evil.

Life | Chapter 12 p. 52

Fieve, Ronald. *Moodswing: Dr. Fieve on Depression: The Eminent Psychiatrist Who Pioneered the Use of Lithium in America Reveals a Revolutionary New Way to Prevent Depression.* New York: Bantam,1989.

> *This was the first book my parents got for me after my first hospitalization and diagnosis.*

Jamison, Kay Redfield. *An Unquiet Mind: A Memoir of Moods and Madness.* New York: Alfred A. Knopf, 1995.

Jamison, Kay Redfield. *Touched with Fire: Manic-Depressive Illness and the Artistic Temperament.*

New York: Free Press, 1993.

> *I read these two books by Kay Redfield Jamison in my early recovery, and I loved Touched by Fire and its insights into some of the inherent creative genius of those with my diagnosis.*

Duke, Patty. *A Brilliant Madness: Living with Manic Depressive Illness.* New York: Bantam,1997.

> *I read this wonderful book in one sitting in the East Brunswick Library praying to find some answers in its pages.*

Life | Chapter 12 p. 53

Faustian: "Restless endeavor, incessant striving from lower spheres of life to higher ones, from the sensuous to the spiritual, from enjoyment to work, from creed to deed, from self to humanity—this is the moving thought of Goethe's completed *Faust*." From Lectures on the Harvard Classics. The Harvard Classics. 1909–14. Drama: IV. "The Faust Legend" by Professor Kuno Francke. Bartleby.com-http://www.bartleby.com/60/204.html.

> *Term referring to an endless, never ceasing journey emulating Faust's life after his wager with Mephistopheles for non-stop experience in Goethe's masterpiece, Faust, written in 1808.*

Charlie Rose: "Charlie Rose, acclaimed journalist and interviewer, engages America's best thinkers, writers, politicians, athletes, entertainers, business leaders, scientists and other newsmakers in one-on-one interviews and roundtable discussions." From http://www.charlierose.com/

> *The set for the Charlie Rose television show is just Charlie and the interviewee sitting in front of a black background. It feels like they are talking directly to the audience in an intimate one-on-one discussion that aided my delusions in their strength.*

Life | Chapter 13 p. 58

Ziggy Stardust: The fictional rock superstar from the album *The Rise and Fall of Ziggy Stardust and the Spiders from Mars* (1972) by David Bowie. According to Bowie, "Ziggy really set the pattern for my future work. Ziggy was my Martian messiah who twanged a guitar. He was a simplistic character. I saw him as very simple ... fairly like the character Newton I was to do in the film [The Man Who Fell to Earth] later on. Someone who was dropped down here, got brought down to our way of thinking and ended up destroying himself ... I fell for Ziggy too. It was quite easy to become obsessed night and day with the character. I became Ziggy Stardust. David Bowie went totally out the window. Everybody was convincing me that I was a Messiah, especially on that first American tour (late 1972). I got hopelessly lost in the fantasy." Bowie adopted Ziggy Stardust as his alter-ego and even, in 1972, began introducing himself and his band as Ziggy Stardust and The Spiders From Mars. From A David Bowie Companion website. http://www.5years.com/.

Life | Chapter 13 p. 59

Eli Siegel and Aesthetic Realism: "Eli Siegel (1902-1978), poet, critic, philosopher, educator, founder of Aesthetic Realism, was born August 16, 1902 in Dvinsk, Latvia, the son of Mendel and Sarah (Einhorn) Siegel. He was brought to the United States in 1905, and grew up in Baltimore, Maryland ... Aesthetic Realism, in keeping with its name, sees all reality including the reality that is oneself, as the aesthetic oneness of opposites. It is clear that reality is motion and rest at once, change and sameness at once. Are we ourselves change and sameness at once, motion and rest at once? If a person asks himself, is he in motion this morning at 11 o'clock, and also is he still as he was—the answer is: 'Certainly, John Bell is moving and still is John Bell at 11 o'clock of an American morning.' It happens that music is felt always as a oneness of motion and rest, or of difference and sameness. A person, like music, is an aesthetic reality; for every moment of his life, he is at once rest and motion, sameness and change." From The Aesthetic Realism Foundation. http://www.aestheticrealism.org/.

Life | Chapter 14 p. 63

"I think therefore I am:" "René Descartes (1596–1650) is widely regarded as the father of modern philosophy. His noteworthy contributions extend to mathematics and physics." From http://plato.stanford.edu/entries/descartes-epistemology/.

Life | Chapter 14 p. 64

Jim Carrey and _The Truman Show:_ "_The Truman Show_ is a 1998 American satirical comedy-drama film directed by Peter Weir and written by Andrew Niccol. The cast includes Jim Carrey as Truman Burbank, as well as Laura Linney, Noah Emmerich, Ed Harris and Natascha McElhone. The film chronicles the life of a man who is initially unaware that he is living in a constructed reality television show, broadcast around the clock to billions of people across the globe. Truman becomes suspicious of his perceived reality and embarks on a quest to discover the truth about his life." From Wikipedia - http://en.wikipedia.org/wiki/The_Truman_Show.
> _A manic episode can mimic this movie with the feel that the world focuses solely on your actions and every happenstance from Iceland to Indiana pertains to the sufferer of this acute mental state._

Life | Chapter 15 p. 66

"Carry On My Wayward Son": A song written by Kerry Livgren and recorded by Kansas for the Kirshner label,1976.

Life | Chapter 15 p. 67

Dostoevsky, Fyodor. _Notes from the Underground._ New York: Signet, 1961 (orig. 1864). "Many people would say that Dostoevsky's short novel _Notes from Underground_ marks the beginning of the modernist movement in literature. (Other candidates: Diderot's _Rameau's Nephew_, written in the seventeen-sixties but not widely read until the eighteen-twenties, and, of course, Flaubert's _Madame Bovary_, from 1856.) Certainly, Nietzsche's writings, Freud's theory of neurosis, Kafka's _Metamorphosis_, Bellow's _Herzog_, Philip Roth's _Portnoy's Complaint,_ perhaps Scorsese's _Taxi Driver_, and half of Woody Allen's work wouldn't have been the same without the existence of this ornery, unstable, unmanageable text—the fictional confession of a spiteful modern Hamlet, an inhabitant of St. Petersburg, 'that most abstract and pre-meditated city,' and a man unable to act and also unable to stop humiliating himself and embarrassing others. A self-regarding, truculent, miserable, paralyzed man." From a _The New Yorker_ blog post by David Denby. http://www.newyorker.com/online/blogs/books/2012/06/dostoevsky-notes-from-underground.html.

The Ancient Greek Myth of King Midas: "King Midas was a very kind man who ruled his kingdom fairly, but he was not one to think very deeply about what he said. One day, while walking in his garden, he saw an elderly satyr asleep in the flowers. Taking pity on the old fellow, King Midas let him go without punishment. When the god Dionysus heard about it, he rewarded King Midas by granting him one wish. The king thought for only a second and then said I wish for everything I touch to turn to gold. And so it was.

The beautiful flowers in his garden turned toward the sun for light, but when Midas approached and touched them, they stood rigid and gold. The king grew hungry and thin, for each time he tried to eat, he found that his meal had turned to gold. His lovely daughter, at his loving touch, turned hard and fast to gold. His water, his bed, his clothes, his friends, and eventually the whole palace was gold.

King Midas saw that soon his whole kingdom would turn to gold unless he did something right away. He asked Dionysus to turn everything back to the way it had been and take back his golden touch. Because the king was ashamed and very sad, Dionysus took pity on him and granted his request. Instantly, King Midas was poorer that he had been, but richer, he felt, in the things that really count." From An Introduction to Ancient Greece; Greek Mythology Homepage; Highland Park Elementary School; Austin, TX, http://www.hipark.austin.isd.tenet.edu/mythology/midas.html.

Life | Chapter 16 p. 70

"Sugar Magnolia": a song written by Bob Weir and Robert Hunter of the Grateful Dead and released in 1970 on the album *American Beauty* from Warner Bros. Records.

> *The Grateful Dead was my older sister's favorite band. She seemed to link to their compassionate consciousness and lived the kindness in all their songs. The car she drove me to the shore for my oceanic baptism had a Terrapin Station sticker in the back showing her allegiance to this traveling band of mystics and misanthropes.*

Life | Chapter 16 p. 71

"I am the silent watcher": Tolle, Eckhart. *The Power of Now.* San Franciso: New World Library, 2004.

Superman: "He celebrated the artistic heroism of Beethoven and Goethe; denigrated the "slave morality" of Christianity, which transfigured weakness into virtue and vital strength into sin; and called on the strong in spirit to bring about a 'transvaluation of all values.' The 'higher man' — or as Nietzsche sometimes called him, the 'overman' or 'Übermensch' — did not succumb to envy or long for the afterlife; rather he willed that his life on earth repeat itself over and over exactly as it was. In later works, Nietzsche wrote with continued brilliance and growing megalomania of his disdain for the common 'herd,' the dangers of nihilism and the possibility that the will to power is the 'Ur-fact of all history.' He spent his last stricken decade in the care of his mother and then his sister, a fervent anti-Semite who would put him in good standing with the German nationalists he despised." From "What Frederich Nietzsche Did to America" published in *The New York Times Book Review*, by Alexander Starr, January 13, 2012. http://www.nytimes.com/2012/01/15/books/review/american-nietzsche-by-jennifer-ratner-rosenhagen-book-review.html?pagewanted=all.

> *A limited translation for "Overman" from Friedrich Nietzsche's Thus Spake Zarathusthra. In Zarathusthra, he famously says "god is dead," showing that the modern man will journey inward to overcome himself...his biases and conditioning-Self Stigmas.*

Life | Chapter 18 p. 77

Meister Eckhart: "The goal of the rational form of life—of living in and with the spiritual perfections at the level of that transcendental being or being (esse, ens) convertible with the termini transcendentes (the one, the true, and the good)—is living in and from the absolute one (in and from the divine nature as presuppositionless unity). If the ground of the soul, as something uncreated and uncreatable—attributes which Meister Eckhart's contemporary Eckhart von Gründig explicitly ascribes to the ground or 'little spark' of the soul that Meister Eckhart often invokes (cf. Winkler, 1999), thus indicating that he in fact employed these attributes—if human reason—not as human, but as reason—is one with the divine nature or ground (Echardus, Predigt 5b; DW I, 90, 8: 'Hie ist gotes grunt mîn grunt und mîn grunt gotes grunt': 'Here, God's ground is my ground and my ground God's ground'), then man is no longer simply on the way towards unity (unio). Instead, unity is something that has always already been achieved. This being-unified is alone what matters (Echardus, Predigt 12; DW I, 197, 8–9; Predigt 39; DW II, 265, 6–266, 2), because man as reason has left behind everything that stands in the way of his living in and from unity, and because the ground of the soul is more interior in this unity than it is in itself (Mojsisch 1983a, 140–141; 2001, 163–165). This is true equanimity—letting-go (Gelâzenheit)—as the goal of human life." From The Stanford Encyclopedia of Philosophy: Meister Eckhart. http://plato.stanford.edu/entries/meister-eckhart/#7.

> *Meister Eckhart was a 13th century German theologian, member of the Dominican Order, philosopher and mystic. Meister Eckhart looked for the absolute unity with God. A god that waits to rush through you when she/he is acknowledged-wiping out all the divisions between You and the divine. One. This is how my mania presents and drowns me. It waits for it bio-chemical invite and takes all of me. Unifying me with the disease and its myriad of symptoms. One.*

Book 2 | Death

"Murder is abstract....": "Jean-Paul Sartre, (1905-1980) - Sartre is one of those writers for whom a determined philosophical position is the centre of their artistic being. Although drawn from many sources, for example, Husserl's idea of a free, fully intentional consciousness and Heidegger's existentialism, the existentialism Sartre formulated and popularized is profoundly original. Its popularity and that of its author reached a climax in the forties, and Sartre's theoretical writings as well as his novels and plays constitute one of the main inspirational sources of modern literature. In his philosophical view atheism is taken for granted; the 'loss of God' is not mourned. Man is condemned to freedom, a freedom from all authority, which he may seek to evade, distort, and deny but which he will have to face if he is to become a moral being. The meaning of man's life is not established before his existence. Once the terrible freedom is acknowledged, man has to make this meaning himself, has to commit himself to a role in this world, has to commit his freedom. And this attempt to make oneself is futile without the 'solidarity' of others." From NobelPrize.org: the official website of the Nobel prize. http://www.nobelprize.org/nobel_prizes/literature/laureates/1964/sartre-bio.html. Quote from http://www.iperceptive.com/authors/jean_paul_sartre_quotes.html.

"Tonight at the Magic Theater....": Hesse, Hermann. *Steppenwolf.* NY: Picador, 1961 (orig. Berlin, 1927).

> *A good warning as the reader enters Book 2 | Death. This part of the book is over one hundred pages chronicling my life inside a maximum-security VA psychiatric hospital while I*

drowned in madness lost from the world in the opaque construct of my mania. Your mind will not help you here … just let go and see where you are when we all walk out together at the end.

<u>"This place has only three exits, sir: Madness, and Death.":</u> Rene Dumaul was a 20th century French spiritual para-surrealist writer and poet. http://www.goodreads.com/author/quotes/4491402.Rene_ Daumal.

Death | Chapter 7 p. 109
<u>Bhagavad Gita, Kuruksetra, Arjuna:</u> "The Bhagavad Gita is a dialogue between Lord Krishna and Arjuna, narrated in the Bhishma-Parva of the Mahabharata. It comprises eighteen chapters of a total of 701 Sanskrit verses. Considerable matter has been condensed and compressed within these verses. On the battle-field of Kurukshetra, Lord Krishna, during the course of His most interesting and instructive talk with Arjuna, revealed the profound, sublime and soul-stirring spiritual truths, and expounded to him the rare secrets of Yoga, Vedanta, Bhakti and Karma. All the teachings of Lord Krishna were subsequently recorded as the Song Ce-lestial or the Bhagavad Gita by Sri Bhagavan Vyasa for the benefit of humanity at large. The world is under a great debt of gratitude to Sri Vyasa who has presented this Celestial Song to humanity for their daily conduct in life, spiritual uplift and Self-realisation. Only those who are self-controlled and are endowed with faith can reap the full benefit of the Gita, which is the Science of the Soul." From *The Bhagavad Gita* by Sri Swami Sivananda. http://www.dlshq. org/religions/gita.htm
> *I used the reference to the Kurukshetra as a metaphor for the battle that would be waged inside myself between my acute mental illness and my 'being.' I would have no Lord Krishna to lead me and guide me and the battle was fought with no regard for enlightenment but bitter, bloody survival.*

Death | Chapter 8 p. 111
<u>No more Untruth-No more Non-reality:</u> "Pai-chang Huai-hai (Hyakujo Ekai)." *The Enlight-ened Mind.* Ed., Mitchell, Stephen. New York: Harper Collins, 1993.
> "Pai-chang was a student of Ma-tsu and teacher of Huang-po (Obaku) and Kuei-shan. He is the subject of the second koan in the mumonkan (Hyakujo's Fox) Hyakujo's fox is considered to be one of the most complex of the koans containing several hua-tou (wato). Pai-chang was the founder of the Ch'an monastic tradition and established the rules for Ch'an monastic life and daily routines such as work practice, dining, zazen, etc. He was known to say, 'A day without work is a day without food.' He stressed the importance of combining Zazen with Daily Work Practice. He also stressed the importance of sutra study. Pai chang also wrote the Tun-wu ju-tao yao-men-lung which is a text on 'sudden enlighten-ment.'" *KaiHan Zen Magazine.* http://www.kaihan.com/.

Death | Chapter 9 p. 115
<u>According to the National Institute on Alcohol Abuse and Alcoholism (NIAAA), more than half of the people in treatment for addiction to alcohol will die due to tobacco:</u>
> National Institute on Alcohol Abuse and Alcoholism. http://pubs.niaaa.nih.gov/publica-tions/arh293/236-240.htm
> "Integrating Tobacco Dependence Treatment and Tobacco-Free Standards Into Addic-tion Treatment: New Jersey's Experience" by Jonathan Foulds, Ph.D.; Jill Williams, M.D.; Bernice Order-Connors, L.C.S.W.; Nancy Edwards, L.C.A.D.C.; Martha Dwyer; Anna

Kline, Ph.D.; and Douglas M. Ziedonis, M.D., M.P.H.

> 20% 90% 70% Smoke with mental illness: "Addressing Tobacco Addiction in Office-Based Management of Psychiatric Disorders: Practical Considerations." *Primary Psychiatry: The Largest Peer Reviewed Psychiatric Journal in the Nation.* Douglas Ziedonis, MD, MPH, Jill M. Williams, MD, Michael Steinberg, MD, and Jonathan Foulds, PhD. From http://www.primarypsychiatry.com/aspx/articledetail.aspx?articleid=853

> "Smoking and Mental Illness: A population-based prevalence study." JAMA (Journal American Medical Association). 2000 Nov 22-29;284(20):2606-10. Lasser K, Boyd JW, Woolhandler S, Himmelstein DU, McCormick D, Bor DH. Department of Medicine, Cambridge Hospital, Macht Bldg, 1493 Cambridge St, Cambridge, MA 02139, USA. http://www.ncbi.nlm.nih.gov/pubmed/11086367.

Death | Chapter 11 p. 126

"Cold Gin": A song written by Ace Frehley of the rock group KISS, from the album *KISS* on Casablanca Records and produced by Kenny Kemer and Richie Wise, 1974.

Death | Chapter 14 p. 140

"Abandon hope all ye who enter here,": Alighieri, Dante. "The Inferno," *The Divine Comedy* Trans. Henry Wadsworth Longfellow. Original 1321. Edition used 1867. Quote from Canto III-pg 14. In Canto III: "Dante, following Virgil, comes to the gate of Hell; where, after having read the dreadful words that are written thereon, they both enter. Here, as he understands Virgil, those were punished who had passed their time (for living it could not be called) in a state of atrophy and indifference both to good and evil...." Introduction p. XIII.

Death | Chapter 17 p. 149

Coetzee, J. M. *Life & Times of Michael K.* New York: Viking, 1983. "Conscience, insight, innocence: Michael K cannot aspire to such high recognitions - he is 'dull,' his mind is 'not quick.' He was born fatherless and with a disfigurement: a harelip that prevented him from being nourished at his mother's breast. When he needs some tools to make a cart to transport his dying mother, he breaks into a locked shed and takes them. The smallest transgression, undetected and unpunished, the single offense of life; yet nearly every moment of his life is judged as if he were guilty of some huge and undisclosed crime - not for nothing is his surname resonant with the Kafkan 'K.' His crime is his birth." From "A Tale of Heroic Anonymity," *The New York Times Book Review,* December 11, 1983 by Cynthia Ozick. http://www.nytimes.com/books/97/11/02/home/coetzee-michael.html.

Death | Chapter 20 p. 160

"endless present": Herman, Judith MD. "Endless Present" *Trauma and Recovery.* New York: Basic Books, 1997. "But as coercion becomes more extreme and resistance crumbles, prisoners lose the sense of continuity with their past. The past, like the future, becomes too painful to bear, for memory, like hope, brings back the yearning for all that has been lost. Thus, prisoners are reduced to living in an endless present." - 89.

Death | Chapter 23 p. 169

Camus, Albert. *The Fall.* New York: Vintage, 1991. Originally published as *La Chute* by Librairie Gallimard in France in 1956.

> *This novel's first sentence is the "judge-penitent" Jean-Baptiste Clamence, beginning a mono-*
logue/confession that illustrates his fall and the fall of man until the last sentence of the book.
Jean-Baptiste never stops talking. I liked it as a metaphor for the absolute torrent of feels,
emotions, thoughts and flashbacks that flooded me during my mania. I was effectively washed
away by the deluge of terrifying symptoms from my bipolar disorder and the complex trauma
of my youth. I would not answer until my screams from the restraining bed.

Death Chapter 24 p. 177

King Lear losing a thousand Cordelia's: "King Lear written by William Shakespeare between 1603-1606. King Lear is a tragedy by William Shakespeare. The title character descends into madness after foolishly disposing of his estate between two of his three daughters based on their flattery, bringing tragic consequences for all. The play is based on the legend of Leir of Britain, a mythological pre-Roman Celtic king. It has been widely adapted for the stage and motion pictures, and the role of Lear has been coveted and played by many of the world's most accomplished actors." Wikipedia: http://en.wikipedia.org/wiki/King_Lear.

> *In the play his one true and loyal daughter, Cordelia, comes back for him to try and save*
the King. This is the daughter the King had turned his back on and banished, yet she came for
him. In her efforts to save the King, Cordelia is captured and murdered for her efforts. King
Lear holds her dying body and screams to the world his lament. His anguish tears from his
soul as he realizes the love and loss of his beloved daughter and his madness envelops him in
his guilt. My scream in the bed when I gave up to the pain, anguish and torture of mania was
fueled by the thousand deaths my soul endured at the loss of my step-daughter. A pain I will
die with and have had to learn to live with for the remainder of this life. Like Lear, it was the
final call to the world before the forever night of Madness entombed me. Like Lear, I will be
forever guilty of this 'sin.'

Death | Chapter 26 p. 182

Rilke, Ranier Maria. "The Panther." The Selection of Poetry of Ranier Maria Rilke. Trans. by Stephen Mitchell. New York: Vintage, 1989, 25.

> *Rilke is everything. Mystic and Avatar. He found God dancing in the whispering waves of*
a city puddle and allowed you absolute access to his churches. A soul Virgil for the realms of
yearning and connection through which I could not walk alone.

Death | Chapter 26 p. 184

Shelley, Mary. Frankenstein. New York: Signet, 2000. Originally published anonymously by Mary Shelley in London in 1818.

> *In the film version (1931, Universal), the monster kills the young girl by mistake thinking*
she will float like all other beautiful things. In the novel, he saves her.

Book 3 | Resurrection

"The dead only know one thing—it's better to be alive.": *Full Metal Jacket*. Produced/directed/screenplay by Stanley Kubrick. Warner Brothers, 1987.

> *This line was spoken by the character played by Matthew Modine. The boot camp depiction*

is the best depiction of boot camp and the mental transformation that takes place under the constant pressure and patriotism. Like Private Joker, I stood outside the event and inside the event-committed to kill for my country. To kill for myself. I am not sure what parts of me are from my time in Orlando in 1990 doing push ups and praying to kill and what parts are authentically me. But I am sure of one thing ... I am a proud veteran that would serve again.

"Do not be conformed to this world, but be transformed by the renewal of your mind.": Romans 12:2, New International Version (©1984)
> *A quote given to me from Emma Shelby, my friend and one of the best trainers in the country. An appropriate start to the Resurrection section to show the enormity of the task ahead. To Change ... A Metamorphosis ... To die and be born again anew to the truth of existence.*

"there must be something greater than anything I've known": *From the song "Something Greater" written by Jason Schnatter of Mean Venus. Jason sang this song at my wedding in 2000 with Bud listening before he passed away. I love the song, and I love the man. My hub city hombre. www.meanvenus.com.*

Resurrection | Chapter 1 p. 202
St. John of the Cross. *The Dark Night of the Soul.* Trans. E. Allison Peers Trans. New York: Doubleday, 1990.
> *Enlightened-Spirituality.org. http://www.enlightened-spirituality.org/John_of_the_Cross.html.*
> *St. John of the Cross found his God in the 1500's when the tortures of his captors negate his physical constraints to expose him to a soul he knew was part God and therefore all divine. I did not find that. My beatings stole God from me. My childhood horrors moved G-d out of my reach and ended any comfort in this world. I knew god hated me and I hated him. It would take years of work to find solace in this world again-to feel a part of it and not scorned as a domestic demon meant to suffer.*

Resurrection | Chapter 1 p. 203
"Stereotypes of success": "How Stereotyping Yourself Contributes to Your Success (or Failure)", *American Scientific Mind.* S. Alexander Haslam, Jessica Salvatore, Thomas Kessler and Stephen D. Reicher. April 3, 2008.

Resurrection | Chapter 1 p. 204
"Death imprint,": Dr. Robert Lifton: Herman, Judith MD. *Trauma and Recovery.* New York; Basic Books, 1997, 38.
> *This image spoke to my lifelong feeling that I was meant to die or not fully live. A feeling I can still have today, but I can recognize it and live with the feel and re-interpret my life experience. The imprint stood between me and everything-like Du Bois' veil.*

Resurrection | Chapter 3 p. 210
"Language of the heart": *This is a phrase used in twelve-steps meetings across the globe and is also the name of a book put together with the various Grapevine writings of one of the founders of Alcoholics Anonymous, Bill Wilson. He wrote about many topics including his journey to help create this movement out of the temperance movement in the Oxford Group, his spirituality and his sobriety. The term means to speak directly to another's experience, their essence, their pain, their feel ... their heart. A place not dominated by the dualistic nature of mind, of like and dislike ... but of love ...*

of compassion ... or eternity.

<u>"Jamesian 'torn-to-pieces-hood'"</u>: Kurtz, Ernest and Katherine Ketcham. *The Spirituality of Imperfection: Storytelling and the Search for Meaning.* New York: Bantam, 1993, 2-3.
"This is not a spirituality for the saints or the gods, but for people who suffer from what the philosopher-psychologist William James called 'torn-to-pieces- hood' (his trenchant translation of the German Zerrissenheit). We have all known that experience, for to be human is to feel at times divided, fractured, pulled in a dozen directions ... and to yearn for serenity, for some healing of our 'torn-to-pieces-hood.'"

Resurrection | Chapter 3 p. 211
<u>"as is your deed, so is your destiny,"</u> Brihadaranyaka Upanishad: The full passage is: "You are what your deep, driving desire is. As your desire is, so is your will. As your will is, so is your deed. As your deed is, so is your destiny."
> *This quote gave me the ability to think I could build my life from actions taken today that did not need to be weighed against yesterday or measured against my failed life. A true fresh start ... every moment.*

Resurrection | Chapter 6 p. 220
<u>Icarus</u>: "Icarus was the son of the inventor Daedalus and a slave named Naucrate. King Minos of Crete imprisoned Daedalus and Icarus in the Labyrinth to punish Daedalus for helping the hero Theseus to kill the monster called the Minotaur and to escape with Minos' daughter, Ariadne. Daedalus knew that Minos controlled any escape routes by land or sea, but Minos could not prevent an escape by flight. So Daedalus used his skills to build wings for himself and Icarus. He used wax and string to fasten feathers to reeds of varying lengths to imitate the curves of birds' wings.

When their wings were ready, Daedalus warned Icarus to fly at medium altitude. If he flew too high, the sun could melt the wax of his wings, and the sea could dampen the feathers if he flew too low.

Once they had escaped Crete, Icarus became exhilarated by flight. Ignoring his father's warning, he flew higher and higher. The sun melted the wax holding his wings together, and the boy fell into the water and drowned. Daedalus looked down to see feathers floating in the waves, and realized what had happened. He buried his son on an island which would be called Icaria, and the sea into which Icarus had fallen would ever after be called the Icarian Sea (between the Cyclades and Asia Minor)." From TheEncyclopediaMythica http://www.pantheon.org/articles/i/icarus.html.
> *I understand the myth and get the point to moderate one's self, but at the same time some of us are meant to fly into the sun. And in a galaxy with over a billion burning stars, maybe it behooves a person to challenge the sun now and again and live with the burns from the effort.*

Resurrection | Chapter 7 p. 222
<u>Ephesians 5:13 NIV</u>: *A great quote for me to step from the darkness of my past to feel the sunlight on my wounds. To no longer hover on the "solar border" but to let the warmth of connection shine on a sinner begging for forgiveness.*

Resurrection | Chapter 8 p. 224
<u>"Song of Myself"</u>: "'Do I contradict myself? Very well then I contradict myself, (I am large, I

contain multitudes.) ...' From the poem 'Song of Myself' from the book of poems *Leaves of Grass*. There were nine editions starting with the first in 1855 to the deathbed version of 1891. This quote embodies the personal right to be many things ... everything and nothing but no longer one fixed, brutal and hateful thing." From The Walt Whitman Archive at University of Nebraska-Lincoln. http://www.whitmanarchive.org/.

Resurrection | Chapter 8 p. 225
Double consciousness: Du Bois, W.E.B. *The Souls of Black Folk*. New York: Penguin, 1995 (orig. 1903).

Resurrection | Chapter 10 p. 231
Cosmic religious feeling: Albert Einstein as quoted in the *New York Times Magazine* on November 9, 1930 pp 1-4. The quote has been reprinted in *Ideas and Opinions*, Crown Publishers, Inc. 1954, pp 36 - 40. It also appears in Einstein's book *The World as I See It*. New York: Philosophical Library, New York, 1949, 24 - 28.

Vedanta, Kmurt, Ramakrishna and Romian Rolland: Krishnamurti (1895-1986) - "Jiddu Krishnamurti is regarded as one of the greatest philosophical and spiritual figures of the twentieth century. Krishnamurti claimed no allegiance to any caste, nationality or religion and was bound by no tradition. His purpose was to set humankind unconditionally free from the destructive limitations of conditioned mind." From the Krishnamurti foundation of America (KFA) http://www.kfa.org/history-of-krishnamurti.php.
> Romain Rolland(1866-1944) - "French novelist, dramatist, essayist, mystic, pacifist, who was awarded the Nobel Prize for Literature in 1915. Romain Rolland saw that art must be a part of the struggle to bring enlightenment to people. In his work he attacked all forms of nazism and fascism, and struggled for social and political justice. Rolland never joined any party but he acquired a reputation as an ardent Communist ... 'A long meditative life is a great adventure. Sometimes it is even the culmination of the experience of a family or of a race; the answer given to the riddle of its age-long procession; the realization of its slow growth, bearing the mark of its errors, its success, its virtues and vices.'" From *Journey Within*, 1942. http://www.kirjasto.sci.fi/rolland.htm.
> Ramakrishna (1836-1886) - "Sri Ramakrishna, who was born in 1836 and passed away in 1886, represents the very core of the spiritual realizations of the seers and sages of India. His whole life was literally an uninterrupted contemplation of God. He reached a depth of God-consciousness that transcends all time and place and has a universal appeal. Seekers of God of all religions feel irresistibly drawn to his life and teachings. Sri Ramakrishna, as a silent force, influences the spiritual thought currents of our time." From Ramakrishna- Vivekananda Center of New York. http://www.ramakrishna.org/index.htm.
> *There is a great story to explain Vedanta as a spiritual practice: all major religions venture to this river with their holy cups in hand. The rabbis, imams, priests, bishops, lamas and nuns bend down with their vessels and fill them with the sacred flow to bring it back to their masses. Naming a multitude of things to describe the feel from this river's bounty. Vedanta is the study and practice of the river.*

Resurrection | Chapter 11 p. 235
"be a lamp unto yourself, be a light unto yourself": Kornfield, Jack. *Living Buddha Masters*. Somerville, MA: Wisdom Publishing, 1989, 31.

"We can never damage our soul....": Michael Berg, kabbalist. From Michael Berg, co-director of the Kabbalah Center and editor of the first-ever contemporary English translation of The Zohar. http://www.kabbalah.com/blogs/michael?page=6.

Resurrection | Chapter 12 p. 237

Sorrow songs:
"I walk through the churchyard,
    To lay this body down;
I know moonrise, I know star-rise;
I walk in the moonlight, I walk in the starlight;
I'll lie in the grave and stretch out my arms,
I'll go to judgment in the evening of the day,
And my soul and they soul shall meet that day,
    When I lay this body down.
NEGRO SONG.
They came out of the South unknown to me, one by one, and yet at once I knew them as of me and of mine."
Du Bois W.E.B. The Souls of Black Folk. New York: Penguin, 1995 (orig. 1903), 264.

Resurrection | Chapter 12 p. 238

"After the Egyptian ... keeps it from being torn asunder.": Du Bois W.E.B. The Souls of Black Folk. New York: Penguin, 1995 (orig. 1903), 45.

Resurrection | Chapter 12 p. 239

"Who taught you to hate yourself, from the top of your head to the soles of your feet?": Malcolm X, May 5, 1962, Los Angeles, CA. From http://www.youtube.com/watch?v=gRS-gUTWffMQ&feature=PlayList&p=6A5C5CBB021DFC7B&playnext=1&playnext_from=PL&index=5.

Resurrection | Chapter 13 p. 241

Kipling, Rudyard. Kim. New York: Barnes and Noble, 2003 (orig. 1901). "Kim is an orphan with too many fathers. As he develops deep bonds with both the lama and Mahbub Ali, these male characters symbolize Kim's struggle to choose between his Indian and English ancestry--for although both of Kim's parents were Caucasian, he was raised by a "half-caste" woman in a "native" setting and does not feel at home as a white "Sahib" at first. The reappearance of his biological father, symbolized by the appearance of his father's Irish regiment, in fact threatens to interfere with Kim's duty and desire to assist both the lama and Mahbub/Colonel Creighton in their apparently conflicting projects." From NYU School of Medicine: Literature, Arts and Medicine Database-http://litmed.med.nyu.edu/Annotation?action=view&annid=12065

Resurrection | Chapter 14 p. 243

Martin Buber: Buber, Martin, I and Thou. Trans. Walter Kaufman. New York: Touchstone, 1996. Originally Ich und Du, published 1923 and first trans. to English in 1937.
"Buber always insisted that the dialogic principle, i.e., the duality of primal relations that he called the I-Thou and the I-It, was not a philosophical conception but a reality beyond the reach of discursive language. In the initial exuberance of making this discovery Buber briefly

planned for I and Thou to serve as the prolegomenon to a five-volume work on philosophy, but he realized that, in Kaufmann's words, 'he could not build on that foundation' and hence abandoned the plan. It has been argued, however, that Buber nevertheless solved the inherent 'difficulty of dialogics that it reflects on, and speaks of, a human reality about which, in his own words, one cannot think and speak in an appropriate manner' (Bloch [1983] p. 62) by writing around it, inspired by one's conviction of its veracity." From Stanford Encyclopedia of Philosophy. - http://plato.stanford.edu/entries/buber/.

Resurrection | Chapter 14 p. 244

Calamus section of *Leaves of Grass*: "The 'Calamus' poems had their origin in a sequence entitled 'Live Oak with Moss,' which survived in manuscript (published, 1955, in Fredson Bowers's Whitman's Manuscripts). This sequence of twelve poems contained a sketchy account of "manly attachment" that ended in separation. Other poems were added to this core to comprise the 45 poems of the "Calamus" cluster in 1860. In subsequent editions of Leaves of Grass, Whitman dropped or shifted a few "Calamus" poems, ending with a total of 39 in 1881.

The poems of the 'Calamus' cluster, companion to the 'Children of Adam' cluster, celebrate friendship and 'manly attachment' (or 'adhesiveness,' a term that Whitman adopted from phrenology, as he did 'amativeness' for heterosexual love). In setting these clusters together in his book, he appears to be following a tradition of the personal essay, from Montaigne to Emerson: writing on love and friendship by drawing on personal experience as a basis for philosophical generalizations. Whitman explained his title 'Calamus' in the following way: "[I]t is the very large and aromatic grass, or root, spears three feet high—often called 'sweet flag'—grows all over the Northern and Middle States.... The recherché or ethereal sense, as used in my book, arises probably from it, Calamus presenting the biggest and hardiest kind of spears of grass, and from its fresh, aromatic, pungent bouquet" (Poetry and Prose 941). In his nude portrait of himself in section 24 of 'Song of Myself,' the phallic suggestiveness of Calamus (or sweet-flag) is made explicit: 'Root of wash'd sweet flag! timorous pond-snipe! nest of guarded duplicate eggs!'" From the Walt Whitman archive out of University of Nebraska-Lincoln. http://whitmanarchive.org/criticism/current/encyclopedia/entry_14.html

> *The Calamus poems always seemed very tender to me, more the soft underbelly of this great American Lion.*

Ralph Waldo Emerson, Harvard Divinity School Address: "Emerson offers the idea not that we are like God, but rather that we are divine, insofar as we act out of this inner, essentially moral or ethical law which is within us. Emerson also took aim at the preaching practices of the day, calling for all sermons to include personal experience. He had a 'trenchant critique' of relying on Scripture, doctrine, or tradition, said Lamberth, and argued that one has to 'speak out of solely that which you have experienced yourself.'" The Harvard Gazette June 23, 2012. http://news.harvard.edu/gazette/story/2012/02/when-religion-turned-inward/.

> *An amazing speech given by Ralph Waldo Emerson on June 15, 1838 at the Harvard Divinity School, the school from which he graduated years before. It was considered so heretical that he was not invited back for thirty years. In the speech he railed against the current practices of preaching and teaching that God was outside you.*

Nietzsche, Friedrich. *On the The Genealogy of Morals.* Trans: Douglas Smith. New York: Oxford University Press, 1996 (orig. 1887). The quote and the information come from the Third

Essay, "What is the meaning of the Ascetic ideal?" p. 77-136.
> *The quote that opens the essay is from Thus Spake Zarathusthra: "Unconcerned, contemptuous, violent—this is how wisdom would have us to be: she is a woman, she only ever loves a warrior."*

Resurrection | Chapter 18 p. 252
Reinhold Neibhur's "Serenity Prayer":
"God, give us grace to accept with serenity
the things that cannot be changed,
Courage to change the things
which should be changed,
and the Wisdom to distinguish
the one from the other.
Living one day at a time,
Enjoying one moment at a time,
Accepting hardship as a pathway to peace,
Taking, as Jesus did,
This sinful world as it is,
Not as I would have it,
Trusting that You will make all things right,
If I surrender to Your will,
So that I may be reasonably happy in this life,
And supremely happy with You forever in the next.
Amen."
"Reinhold Niebuhr, (born June 21, 1892, Wright City, Mo., U.S. - died June 1, 1971, Stockbridge, Mass.), American Protestant theologian who had extensive influence on political thought and whose criticism of the prevailing theological liberalism of the 1920s significantly affected the intellectual climate within American Protestantism. His exposure, as a pastor in Detroit, to the problems of American industrialism led him to join the Socialist Party for a time. A former pacifist, he actively persuaded Christians to support the war against Hitler and after World War II had considerable influence in the U.S. State Department. His most prominent theological work was *The Nature and Destiny of Man*, which was planned as a synthesis of the theology of the Reformation with the insights of the Renaissance." From Encyclopedia Britannica. http://www.britannica.com/EBchecked/topic/414557/Reinhold-Niebuhr.
> *This is the full prayer. The twelve-step program Alcoholics Anonymous has unofficially adopted the first paragraph of the prayer as a way many "groups" close or open their meeting.*

Resurrection | Chapter 20 p. 260
Each man had only one genuine vocation: Hesse, Hermann. *Demain*. New York: Harper, 1999 (orig. 1919), 111.

"heaven in a wild flower ... and eternity in an hour....": From William Blake's *Augeries of Innocence*, 1863.
"To see a world in a grain of sand,
And a heaven in a wild flower,
Hold infinity in the palm of your hand,

And eternity in an hour…"

> "Alongside his ecstatic visions, Blake was prone to fits of severe depression. In 1800, he recounted a descent into "a Deep pit of Melancholy, Melancholy without any real reason for it." These episodes were often followed by periods of "illumination" and intense creativity. This is highly suggestive of bipolar illness, albeit a mild form that did not disrupt his enormous creative achievement and may have been central to his transcendent artistic vision." From the American Journal of Psychiatry online (Am J Psychiatry 2005;162:866-866. 10.1176/appi.ajp.162.5.866). http://ajp.psychiatryonline.org/article.aspx?volume=162&page=866.

> *William Blake, 1757-1827, was a great poet and painter, and was considered by many accounts a person with the lived experience of a mental illness.*

Resurrection | Chapter 20 p. 261
Emerson, Ralph Waldo. *The Heart of Emerson's Journal.* Ed., Bliss Perry. Mineola, NY: Dover, 1995 (orig. 1926).

> *I like journals, letters and introductions to be introduced to the person behind these works. To see their faults and failings to make their works more accessible and brilliant.*

"A person should only give advice in matters where he will co-operate. If anybody asks me for good advice, I say I am ready to give it, but only on condition that he will promise me not to take it.": Eckermann, Johann Peter. *Conversations of Goethe with Johann Peter Eckermann.* Trans. John Exenford. New York: De Capo Press, 1998 (orig. London: 1930).

"If you meet the Buddha on the road, kill him." From *The Shambala Sun.* http://www.shambhalasun.com/index.php?option=content&task=view&id=2903Itemid=247.

Resurrection | Chapter 20 p. 262
"… throw these thunderheads overboard and float light and right.": Melville, Herman. *Moby Dick.* Norton Critical Edition, 2nd Edition. W.W. Norton & Company, 2002. Originally published October, 1851 by Richard Bentley (Britain) and November, 1851 by Harper & Bros. (US).

> *This quote was a perfect metaphor for me to drop the knowns and biases that had weighed on me for a lifetime. It also allowed a good visual of how best to "sail" this grand adventure and the tendency to burden ourselves with labels about ourself and others. Melville is my favorite American writer and his unabashed use of metaphor let me make my own journey with him every time we left port together.*

Resurrection | Chapter 22 p. 269
mind of Mushin: "Mushin is a Zen term, 'mu' meaning negation; 'Shin' meaning heart, mind or feeling, making the somewhat confusing translation as 'no mind'. The art of Mushin leads to a state of awareness that is void of distractive thoughts & emotions. This in turn produces a state of mental clarity and heightened awareness. Through Mushin the mind is not absent, but instead freed. Legend has it that the true Samurai were able to defeat their opponents easily because of their trained ability of enhanced perception, (sensory and intuitive), known as pure mind. Through the practice of meditation, the Samurai learnt to transcend the many distracting thoughts of the mind until a state of inner stillness and clear awareness, (Mushin) was reached." From Tai Shi Kai Wado-Ryu Karate-Do Academy, Australia. http://www.taishi-kai.com/medit2.htm.

Resurrection | Chapter 22 p. 270

The Grand Inquisitor from *The Brothers Karamazov:* Dostoevsky, Fyodor. *The Brothers Karamazov.* Trans. Constance Garnett. New York: Simon and Brown, 2011 (orig. 1880). "'The Grand Inquisitor' section is Chapter 5. It is a story within the story told by Alexei to his brothers. Christ returns to Spain during the Inquisition and is put on trial for his life. The Cardinal denounces Jesus and his Father for the freedom they bestowed on man and condemns him absolutely. Jesus listens silently and at the end kisses the Cardinal on the lips. 'When the Grand Inquisitor ends his denunciation, Jesus says nothing. Instead, he leans forward and kisses the old man on the lips. The Inquisitor does not have Jesus put to death after all. Instead, he sends him away, demanding he never return.'" From "Freedom by Necessity" in the *Lapham's Quarterly.* http://www.laphamsquarterly.org/reconsiderations/freedom-by-necessity.php?page=all.

Resurrection | Chapter 22 p. 271

"The wise are Children Who Know ... filled with the wisdom of the Great Nothing, the Way of the Universe.": Hoff, Benjamin. *The Tao of Pooh.* New York: Dutton, 1982, 151.
> *A gentle touch from the way, the flow, Vedanta, hidden in a book about a zen master and honey addict dressed like a bear.*

Resurrection | Chapter 26 p. 281

"Literature of the Spirit": Campbell, Joseph and Bill Moyers. *The Power of Myth.* New York: Anchor Books, 1991.
> *This book is an interview between Campbell and Moyers I saw on PBS. Amazing. Find it. Watch it. Live it.*

Resurrection | Chapter 26 p. 281

"absolute passivity": Herman, J., *Trauma and Recovery.* New York: Basic Books, 1997, 86.

Resurrection | Chapter 26 p. 282

Freedom from the Known: Krishnamurt, J. *The Awakening of Intelligence.* San Franscisco: Harper, 1987. "Can I know anything except the past? The moment I say 'I know' it is already the past. When I say 'I know my wife', I know her in terms of the past. In the past there is certainty and in the future there is uncertainty. So I want to draw the future into the past so that I will be completely safe. I see fear arises where thought is operating; if I did not think about tomorrow there would be no fear." - 426.
> *Freedom from the Known is a book of essays and talks by Krishnamurti in 1975, as well as, a general theme of many of his talks. It is an ability to see today without the fear and biases of yesterday. To be free of our psychological conditioning that freezes us in time.*

Resurrection | Chapter 26 p. 285

"... it was vanity.": Lawrence, T. E. *The Seven Pillars of Wisdom: A Triumph.* New York: Anchor, 1991. The full quote reads: "All men dream: but not equally. Those who dream by night in the dusty recesses of their minds wake up in the day to find it was vanity, but the dreamers of the day are dangerous men, for they may act their dreams with open eyes, to make it possible. This I did."
> *How great is the "This I did." Nice.*

Resurrection Day

"If I am only for myself, what am I? And if not now, when?": Collier, Peter. *Medal of Honor: Portraits of Valor Beyond the Call of Duty.* New York: Artisan, 2006, 138.

"Dont give up! ... Don't ever give up!": From a speech Jimmy Valvano gave when he was being honored at the very first ESPY awards on March 4, 1993. "…I just got one last thing, I urge all of you, all of you, to enjoy your life, the precious moments you have. To spend each day with some laughter and some thought, to get your emotions going. To be enthusiastic every day and as Ralph Waldo Emerson said, 'Nothing great could be accomplished without enthusiasm,' to keep your dreams alive in spite of problems whatever you have. The ability to be able to work hard for your dreams to come true, to become a reality." From http://www.jimmyv.org/about-us/remembering-jim/jimmy-v-espy-awards-speech/.

Resurrection | Chapter 27 p. 292
a man of light: Corbin, Henry. *Man of Light in Iranian Sufism.* Trans. Nancy Pearson. New Lebanon, NY: Omega, 1994, 23. From the Preface, "At the heart of Sohravardi's mystic science is the recognition that the 'I' of every self-aware entity is a pure, immaterial light … Thereupon, in the blazing light that awakens him, he departs in search of that Orient which is not the East of our maps but which lies in the cosmic North…"

> *I wanted to be all light. On that field, after a lifetime of darkness my senses seemed to break and I was allowed one second to believe I could connect to all that is and live the dream journey.*

Resurrection | Chapter 27 p. 293
Campbell, Joseph and Bill Moyers. *The Power of Myth.* New York: Anchor Books, 1991, 49.

Resurrection | Chapter 28 p. 294
"my poor": "Man is his own star; and the soul that can Render an honest and a perfect man, Commands all light, all influence, all fate…" From The Works of Ralph Waldo Emerson. http://www.rwe.org/?option=com_content&task=view&id=125&Itemid=42.

> *From the essay "Self-Reliance" first published in Emerson's 1841 collection, Essays: First Series. It espoused his core philosophy to follow your own ideas … heart … soul. He would donate to his poor and listen to his poor in spirit.*

"barbaric yawp":
"The spotted hawk swoops by and accuses me, he complains
        of my gab and my loitering.
I too am not a bit tamed, I too am untranslatable,
I sound my barbaric yawp over the roofs of the world."
> From the poem "Song of Myself" from the book of poems *Leaves of Grass* by Walt Whitman. From The Walt Whitman Archive at University of Nebraska-Lincoln. http://www.whitman-archive.org/.

> *I sound this call in my heart. I speak to my being to be free…to be free. Good luck "translating" me.*

Resurrection | Chapter 29 p. 295

"I have lived on the lip of insanity, wanting to know reasons, knocking on a door it opens. I have been knocking from the inside.": Barks, Coleman. *A Year with Rumi: Daily Readings.* New York: HarperOne, 2006, 352.

> *From a Poem called "A Door." Rumi is my Sufi Virgil, a guide for this life when I am scared and unsure of my path. But it is in the fear that I find salvation and in the struggle that I find my soul. Coleman Barks is a wonderful translator and conduit to the "mana." If I could speak with someone all day with a good cup of Egyptian coffee on a warm afternoon that birthed into a cold, naked night, it would be him.*

Acknowledgments

I am alive. I am free, and I am grateful. I have met the best and most dynamic people as I have fought to build a life, and while I cannot thank everyone by name, I wish I could. Here are a few who have helped me on my journey and who played a special role in helping me along the way and in making this book happen.

- To my editor, Kristy, and Treehouse Publishing. This book has been a mystical journey that we took together. We did something good here and I am proud to call you a friend. Thanks for having this 'baby' with me and not letting me get lost in Hell while I lived and re-lived it for over four years trying to create this sacred call back to the world.
- To all my Virgils … Thank you for never giving up on me. I felt alone my whole life, but have had the best group of friends a man could have holding on to his belt while he leaned over the abyss and stared straight into Hell.
- To my wife Cheryl, you believed in me when I couldn't believe in myself. You are noble, beautiful and the best person I have ever met. None of this happens without you. None of it. And we got a picture with Ice-T.
- To my daughter Olivia, I am proud of every breath you take. Nothing will ever compare to being your daddy. I have a secret for you…come here…can you hear me… ? *"I love you more than life."*
- I have to thank my parents, Bud and Nadine. They fought for me from day one and worked together to save me. I miss Bud everyday and use him as a model of fatherhood and manhood. Mom, you are the strongest person in the world. My sense of humor, power and intellect comes from you.
- Grandma Joanie, I miss you so much. It was always OK when I was talking to you "GG". I can't believe Olivia never got a chance to meet you. It breaks my heart, but she is part you.

- My sisters: Cecelia, you fought my fights when I was a young boy, and I always felt safe with big sis ready to kick some ass. Gabrielle, I am so proud of the path you chose for your life and the tireless work you put in to achieve your dreams. Watching your passion to help those with cancer has been a guide for me in my human rights advocacy.
- My brother-in-law Marc for always accepting me and standing with my family through all our ups and downs.
- My nephews Joe and Peter: You are the best 'big' cousins to Olivia and it's an honor to be your uncle.
- My in-laws, Chuck and Barb Reimer: You have accepted me as a son since we met. You are the most honest and dedicated people I have ever known and made me believe I could forgive and then love God again.
- Becky and Erik Matteo: My sister-in-law and the West Coast E, you guys are the best and I look forward to growing old with you both and bailing O and the cousins out of jail. Long live the Tolt River Farm!
- Samara and Jacoby: My Carnation-based niece and nephew. You two are miracles and I will give you neck kisses as long as you let me.
- Beth and Jay Reichgott: You have accepted me since day one and always made me feel like I could do anything. I hope Solomon can keep O out of jail on the East Coast.
- Nephew Larry: You are very special to me. I would do anything for you and look forward to seeing your art in museums and your beats on the radio.
- Aunt Pat and Uncle Herman: You always make me feel thought of and loved. Uncle Herman your conversations have helped me unlock the universe a bit at a time.
- Robbie Perez: You are a brother and a Virgil. You are the best of friends and you have stood shoulder to shoulder with me from the deepest pits of my life to today. I simply don't have this life without you. I DID NOT CALL YOU FROM FOODTOWN.
- Matt Beckman, my twin: You are a brother and a Virgil. I have loved spending my life walking with you and listening to Rush in the basement. How hard do we laugh together! You kept me alive in the VA hospital. You are awesome Becky…just awesome.
- Jerry Beckman: You were like a father to me. I loved 'reporting' to you while war movies played in the background and making sure I kept it regimental. Marsha Beckman, you let me live on the couch and eat your food for

years. You're the best, Mrs. B.

- Steve Duff, my best man: I love you my Taurian teammate. No one knows me like you. Thank you for the trips to talk with Bud while he was dying. I know it was brutal but you stood with me. You have always stood with me. Never forget Creek and the call about the handicapped pachyderm. Bold.
- Sean Hogan: You are a great friend and an absolute brother. You are an unbelievable father of daughters, and we will build the empire together. Love ya, Hoag.
- The Baron Rob Schwieger: You are the most true and authentic person I have ever met. A warrior, gentleman, intellectual and friend. Without you and your family this book literally doesn't happen. You are the measure of a man and brother. Our walks and talks rate as some of the best moments of my life.
- Frank Greenagel: We have walked the walk together. You are a true advocate and the most loyal of friends. We will help the nation's/world's college kids together.
- Elliot Berens: My Taurian brother, it has been a long journey together. I'm still not sure who's smarter, but I'll agree to call it a tie if you do.
- Dana Weiss, my first 'therapist': You are a great friend who has been with me for over twenty years. I could still talk to you on the phone for hours.
- The United States Navy: Serving in the Navy made me a man, and gave me the world. It was the best decision of my life. I am a forever sailor. God bless all that serve and have served.
- To all the veterans of the United States Armed Forces: Keep on Fighting. Like Neil Van Ess, a true hero, says, "It all comes later for vets … we start later but we finish strong!!!" Hell yeah, Neil.
- *To my Sailors:*

  ~ Jeff McManigal: You were the best guy to travel the world with on the USS Briscoe. Stop tearing sinks off walls when you go to Spain. We should go to Naples again and smash more cake off each other's heads. Thank you for the night in the Seminole Firehouse when I got to eat dinner with real heroes. I couldn't be prouder of you for being a paramedic/firefighter.

  ~ Paul Futrell: You kept me in A school in the Navy and out of jail and out of the scullery and let me be your little brother.

  ~ Jason Lorance: You're the funniest and fastest guy I ever met.

  ~ Shannon Hooper: I loved living with you, Hoop, and the wood couch from Indiana. Bubba's Beach Club.

- ~ Astra Lorance: You went from night to days in A school and are the coolest chick I know.
- Chris 'Whalen-san' Whalen: There is no place safer then under the Whalen umbrella. Thanks for not letting me be a jerk.
- Coach Bobby (Bobby J) Januska: I have needed your wisdom and faith many times in my journey. You are a great man Bobby and thousands of young children have succeeded and survived because of your care and compassion.
- Stephanie Mulfinger: My Trauma/Suicide and Faulkner advisor and the smartest MSW I have ever met. I can never thank you enough for your tireless efforts editing the book and my concepts.
- Dr. Jill Williams: You are a tremendous advocate and friend. You are the most dedicated and compassionate psychiatrist I know. That moment in your office asking for help was one of the greatest breakthroughs of my life. The basement in Buffalo was intense.
- Tim 'Sully' Sullivan: Diver and guitarist extraordinaire, you gave me the guidance to make this book real and national. We both know the second I step in the ocean, I get attacked by 200 sharks. Never gonna happen.
- Maryann Diaz: Thank you so much for pouring through the book and letting me see it was about forgiveness and Einar when I couldn't even see it.
- Debbie (Bertha) O'Connor: You are a great person and friend and the time you gave me with your Herd of O'Connor's will be forever appreciated. I promise coffee again soon in Frenchtown—you are a soulful and true person and I am lucky you gave me your insights and kindness while reading the book at a very early stage.
- Wayne Wirta: You pushed me to write the book. Your couches gave me the launch for my advocacy.
- Dr. Shanoy: For how you cared for my family while I was hospitalized in the VA.
- Mary Moller: My friend and mentor. You took a chance on me, Mary, and have helped me grow as a person and a professional. Your dedication is unmatched in improving the lives of people with mental illness. You are a rock for me.
- Kris McLoughlin and Jeanne Clement: I loved traveling the country with you both. You had no stigma dealing with me on the grant and have been

tremendous examples of care and professionalism. No matter how far you move away, Kris, you are still a Middlesex County Jersey girl!

- The American Psychiatric Nurses Association (APNA): How could a guy with 8,200 psychiatric nurses watching over him not recover?

- Pat Black: You are a true friend. Your care for me has made my dealing with the APNA a joy.

- Deborah Hobbs: You are a true friend. You have been a real blessing, and I have never felt more secure because I know you're in my corner.

- SAMHSA and Paolo and the gang: You do divine work and your support has skyrocketed my career.

- Dr. Steve Schroeder at UCSF: You have let me contact you for years since the SAMHSA presentation and you read my book in a week before it was even close to being done. Thank you so much for supporting me and giving me encouragement.

- Dr. Ken Duckworth: You have been a support since the radio show in NYC and then writing on the book. Your passion for people with mental illness shines through in all you do. Thanks, buddy.

- Pete Konczal: You are a Mystic, Seer and Virgil. The world is a more beautiful and soulful place with your 'eye' riveted on it. We will face the Infinity together and discuss it over espresso.

- St. Bartholomew's Class of 1984: I love you all. From 'rumble' on the pavement (the grass in fourth and eighth grades) and 10 cent pretzels to Friday Morning Mass and Eighth Grade Buddies, that place was magic. We were taught service, kindness and compassion, and it has been the guide of my life.

- John and Audrey Motusesky, "Nana" Fredericks and the entire Motusesky family: You were a safe place in the storm of my life. I always felt a member of the family and feel truly blessed to have had the opportunity to spend so much time in your home playing 'pitcher-catcher' in the backyard or watching WWF with Nana on Saturday mornings while eating spiced ham on a roll.

- Sister Michelle: My first grade teacher. You were so sweet and delicate with your young souls.

- The East Brunswick Police Department: Thank you for handling me with respect and not hurting me when you hospitalized me. And for how kind Joe Kowal was when he dealt with my Mom the morning Bud died.

- Wayne and Lita Guberman: The best neighbors in the world. I always knew my Mom was OK with Wayne next door taking care of her.

- Time to Share group: My life started in that sacred room with all the agricultural equipment lining the beginner meeting.
- Ed McGinty Esq., and Navy rescue swimmer: You guided and gave me strength during the beginning of my resurrection. Even though you tried to break both my legs every Monday playing basketball at Cook.
- Rutgers U Recovery house and Lisa Laitman: This powerful house and program has saved thousands of lives—of the people that lived there and those that could just stop by while in college to just feel safe. I never lived there but the program was a major part of my survival.
- Seamus McGuiness: The best trainer on earth and a great friend. I look forward to you dominating the world however you chose.
- Kevin Costello and the Costello brothers: The toughest group of Judo masters on the East Coast. I love ya, Kev, and we are exactly in tune, and no matter how long it goes between talking, you are my brother.
- Ann Cosgrove and Dr. Umberto Marin: The MSW and Psychiatrist that changed my life during early recovery. Ann you are small in stature but a giant in my recovery.
- Rutgers University: You gave me everything. I am honored to be a Scarlet Knight.
- American Studies Department at RU: The best major in the world. A place to discover the world while you discover yourself. Michael Rockland created a little academic nirvana in Ruth Adams.
- Leslie Fishbein: My friend and academic mother. Your support strengthened me in my early years at RU. Thanks for turning me to Orwell's Politics and the English Language and for saving my life.
- Jackson Lears: You gave me the confidence to trust my mind when that seemed impossible. And I still think the end of *The Heart of Darkness* has a few different ways to look at it. Power lunch soon. I don't know how to ask for help and yet you have offered it everyday I have known you.
- Angus Gillespie: You bought me into the major and share my birthday. Thanks my fellow Taurian scholar.
- Simply Yoga: While writing the book, I was starting to suffer and get lost in the flames. You are a safe harbor for me and a place to come home to myself.
- Rutgers Graduate School of Management and Labor Relations: I loved grad school here and found my intellectual voice in your halls off Ryders

Lane.

- Barbara Lee: You are the best Dean and supporter a student and person could have. Thank you for always guiding me as a student and for years after as your friend.
- Wanda Radowski: My friend, my friend, my friend ... you are the best and our conversations were fantastic. Glad you loved the Whitman book.
- David Feingold: You were Dean for a short time at SMLR, but you backed my advocacy award and celebrated my work for mental health advocacy.
- Eugene McElroy: The best librarian I know. I love how you travel the world and experience life. You are great, and I love our discussions and debates. Your Basque buddy, E.
- Mike Lakat: My first guide. Thanks for answering the phone so quickly when Bud got diagnosed.

To all of you, thanks and thanks again ... and remember it is your life ...set your own limits.

Live!

And if you are holding on by a thread, please don't give up. You are not alone ... you are never alone ... hold on ... I am coming ... I love you.

A Man on Fire,
Eric Arauz

About the Author

Eric Arauz is the president and owner of Arauz Inspirational Enterprises (AIE), an international keynote speaking and training company *(www.mylifemylimits. com)*. He is also an adjunct instructor at the Robert Wood Johnson Medical School, Department of Psychiatry; a contributor to *The New York Times*; Yale University lecturer; National Trauma Informed Recovery and Suicide Prevention lecturer, and special state officer on the New Jersey Governor's Council on Alcoholism and Drug Abuse. He was awarded a 2009 "Voice Award" for his national behavioral health advocacy from the Substance Abuse and Mental Health Services Administration (SAMHSA), he is a faculty member on SAMHSA's current five-year Recovery to Practice grant in association with the American Psychiatric Nurse Association, and he was named a 2012 SAMHSA "Voice Award" Fellow.

Eric served in the United States Navy from 1990-1994 as an Electronics Technician specializing in fleet-based satellite communications. He lives in Central New Jersey with his family.